T0331502

Convergence of Artificial Intelligence and Internet of Things for Industrial Automation

This book begins by discussing the fundamentals of Artificial Intelligence, the Internet of Things, and their convergence. It then covers techniques, algorithms, and methods of analysing and processing data over the Artificial Intelligence of Things. The text elaborates on important concepts such as body sensor networks for safety in smart factories, smart energy management, smart robotic assistive systems, and service-oriented smart manufacturing.

This book:

- Discusses the security and privacy aspect of Artificial Intelligence of Things (AIoT) for smart real-time applications.
- Explores challenges and issues of Artificial Intelligence and the Internet of Things in the field of industrial automation.
- Includes case studies in Artificial Intelligence of Things (AIoT) convergence for data processing.
- Showcases algorithms, techniques, and methods of analysing and processing data over the Artificial Intelligence of Things.
- Highlights operation management using human-robot, smart maintenance, and autonomous production.

It will serve as an ideal reference text for senior undergraduate, graduate students, and professionals in fields including industrial engineering, production engineering, manufacturing engineering, operations research, and computer engineering.

Convergence of Artificial Intelligence and Internet of Things for Industrial Automation

Edited by
Divya Mishra
Alok Kumar Verma
Shanu Sharma

CRC Press
Taylor & Francis Group
Boca Raton New York London

CRC Press is an imprint of the
Taylor & Francis Group, an **informa** business

Contents

Preface

In an era where technological innovation defines the pace of human progress, integrating Artificial Intelligence (AI) and the Internet of Things (IoT) is a beacon of transformative change. This book, *Convergence of Artificial Intelligence and Internet of Things for Industrial Automation*, is a testament to this evolving landscape, offering a panoramic view of the burgeoning field of AIoT – a symbiotic blend of AI and IoT. It presents a rich tapestry of research, insights, and forward-thinking perspectives, converging to illuminate the profound implications of AIoT in reshaping industries and daily life.

The chapters of this book are carefully curated to provide a comprehensive understanding of the multifaceted impact of AIoT. They delve into myriad applications, ranging from the nuts and bolts of industrial automation to the nuanced complexities of healthcare systems, painting a vivid picture of a future where intelligent machines and interconnected devices redefine efficiency and innovation.

Chapter 1: The Emerging Technologies of AIoT, embarks on an empirical exploration of AIoT, dissecting its current landscape while forecasting its future trajectory. This is aptly complemented by Chapter 2: Convergence of AI with IoT towards Industry 4.0. which narrows the focus to the industrial sector, elucidating how AIoT is a critical catalyst in ushering in the fourth industrial revolution.

The book does not shy away from the challenges and ethical considerations accompanying this technological dawn. Chapter 3: Issues and Challenges of AI for Industrial Automation and Colleagues, scrutinizes the ethical quandaries and hurdles inherent in the integration of AI in industrial settings. Similarly, Chapter 4: Deep Learning Algorithm and Approaches for Automation navigates the complexities of deep learning in industrial applications, offering a nuanced understanding of its role in big data analysis and automation.

Healthcare, a sector at the forefront of this technological revolution, is expertly covered in Chapter 5: The Role of IoT Devices and AI-based Health Care Monitoring Systems, and Chapter 6: Revolutionizing Healthcare: AIoT for Smart Wellness. These chapters unravel the significant strides AIoT is making in advancing healthcare diagnostics and patient monitoring, high-lighting its potential in early disease detection and management.

The scope of AIoT extends beyond these realms, as demonstrated in Chapter 7: Futuristic Wearable Technologies: A Fusion of ML and AI, which explores the exciting world of AI-enhanced wearable technologies. This is further expanded by Chapter 8 where AIoT has been explored in other advanced areas such as Image Processing and Data Analysis. Furthermore, Chapter 9 AIoT Empowerment in Agriculture, showcasing how AIoT is revolutionizing the agricultural sector through smart farming techniques and improved efficiency.

Addressing the pressing concerns of security in an interconnected world, Chapters 10: Security Concerns with IoT: Detecting DDoS Attacks in IoT Environments, provide an insightful analysis of the security threats posed to IoT networks, especially focusing on the prevalence and mitigation of DDoS attacks. Complementing this is Chapter 11: Data Privacy and Integrity in Complex Data and Others, proposing innovative solutions for safeguarding data privacy and integrity in complex AIoT systems.

Finally, the book culminates with Chapter 12: EEG-Based Online Finger Movement Identification, which presents a cutting-edge EEG-based inter-face for finger movement identification. This chapter not only underscores the potential of AIoT in assistive technologies but also serves as a beacon of hope for novel human–computer interaction paradigms.

In summary, *Convergence of Artificial Intelligence and the Internet of Things for Industrial Automation* is more than just a collection of scholarly articles. It is a narrative of a technological revolution, a guide for profession-als and enthusiasts alike, and a glimpse into a future where AIoT is not just an academic concept, but a lived reality transforming every facet of our existence.

About the editors

Dr. Divya Mishra has been working as a full-time academician for the past 16+ years. She has a PhD (Engineering) from Amity University Uttar Pradesh, and an MTech (Information Security) from Guru Gobind Singh Indraprastha University, New Delhi. She also holds a BTech (Computer Science & Engineering) from Sant Longowal Institute of Engineering & Technology, IKJPTU, Punjab. She has published 50+ papers in reputed international journals and conferences with Scopus & SCI indexing. She was also appreciated by the IEEE Sensors Council for the paper "Application of Non-Linear Gaussian Regression-Based Adaptive Clock Synchronization Technique for Wireless Sensor Network in Agriculture", *IEEE Sensors Journal*, Vol. 18, No. 10, May 2018, for the paper being one of the 25 most downloaded Sensors Journal papers in the month of February 2019. She is an active member of international societies such as IEEE, IAENG and an organizing committee for many international conferences, workshops, and seminars to enhance the teaching–learning process. She is also associated with a project on cloud computing security funded by the International Bilateral Cooperation Division, Department of Science and Technology, MS&T, Govt. of India. She has guided more than 30 students of MTech. Her research area includes networking, cloud computing, information security and the Internet of Things.

Dr. Alok Kumar Verma is working as a Senior Scientist I at Advanced Remanufacturing and Technology Centre (ARTC), Agency for Science Technology and Research (A*STAR), Singapore. Before joining A*STAR, he was a Research Scientist at the Rolls-Royce Electrical, Nanyang Technological University, Singapore from 2016 to 2020 and a Post-Doctoral Research Fellow at the National University of Singapore from 2015 to 2016. He received his PhD from the Indian Institute of Technology Patna in 2015. He has published several research papers in reputed journals and conferences and has also been granted three patents for his research. Dr. Verma is also a senior member of international professional bodies, namely IEEE. Presently, he is working as a Tech-lead and PI/Co-PI on several research projects. His research interests include condition & health monitoring, signal processing, data analysis, and machine learning.

Dr. Shanu Sharma is an Associate Professor in the Department of Computer Science & Engineering, ABES Engineering College, Ghaziabad (Affiliated to A.K.T University, Lucknow). She has a PhD from Amity University Uttar Pradesh and an MTech (Intelligent Systems) from IIIT Allahabad. She has 13+ years of teaching and research experience and has taught various courses at the graduate and undergraduate levels, such as image processing, data mining, machine learning, data science, data structures, the analysis and design of algorithms, and compiler design. Her research areas include cognitive computing, computer vision, pattern recognition, and machine learning. She has published 40+ research papers in renowned conferences and journals and is currently associated with various reputed international conferences and journals as a reviewer. She has edited various special issues in Scopus-indexed journals published by IGI Global and Bentham Science. She has edited five books with renowned publishers, including Springer, IGI, CRC Press, and River Publishers. She is a senior member of IEEE and also an active member of other professional societies such as ACM, the Soft Computing Research Society (SCRS), EUSFLAT, and IAENG.

Contributors

Ahmed M. Abdelmoniem
Queen Mary University of London
London, United Kingdom

Devendra Agarwal
Goel Institute of Technology &
  Management (GITM)
Lucknow, India

Salman Khursheed Ahmad
GL Bajaj Institute of Technology
  and Management
Greater Noida, India

Nikhat Akhtar
Goel Institute of Technology &
  Management (GITM)
Lucknow, India

Abdussalam Ahmed Alashhab
Alasmarya Islamic University Libya
Zliten, Libya

R. S. Anand
Indian Institute of Technology
  Roorkee
Roorkee, India

Monisha Awasthi
USCS, Uttaranchal University
Dehradun, India

Shiladitya Bhattacharjee
School of Computer Science, UPES
Dehradun, India

B. S. Bhavya
JAIN (Deemed-to-be University)
Bengaluru, India

Tanupriya Choudhury
School of Computer Science, UPES
Dehradun, India

Kamaluddeen Usman Danyaro
Universiti Teknologi PETRONAS
Perak, Malaysia

Ankur Goel
Meerut Institute of Technology
Meerut, India

Moniya Goel
Department of Computer
  Application CAEHS College
Meerut, India

J. Praveen Gujjar
JAIN (Deemed-to-be University)
Bengaluru, India

Km Ikra
Mangalmay Institute of Engineering
  and Technology
Greater Noida, India

Indu
ABES Engineering College
  Ghaziabad
Ghaziabad, India

J. S. Kale
MGM College of Engineering
Nanded Maharashtra, India

H. N. Naveen Kumar
Vidyavardhaka College of
   Engineering
Mysore, India

Rishi Kumar
Graphic Era (Deemed to be
   University)
Dehradun, India

M. S. Liew
Universiti Teknologi PETRONAS
Perak, Malaysia

Umar Danjuma Maiwada
Universiti Teknologi PETRONAS
Perak, Malaysia

Indu Malik
ABES Engineering College
Ghaziabad, India

Yusuf Perwej
Goel Institute of Technology &
   Management (GITM)
Lucknow, India

M. S. Guru Prasad
Graphic Era (Deemed to be
   University)
Dehradun, India

Sonia Rani
Lovely Professional University
Phagwara, India

Aastha Sharma
ABES Engineering College
Ghaziabad, India

Ambalika Sharma
Indian Institute of Technology
   Roorkee
Roorkee, India

Aliza Bt Sarlan
Universiti Teknologi PETRONAS
Perak, Malaysia

Divya Upadhyay
ABES Engineering College
Ghaziabad, India

Alok Kumar Verma
Advanced Remanufacturing and
   Technology Centre, Agency for
   Science, Technology and Research
   (A*STAR), Singapore

Chapter 1

The emerging technologies of Artificial Intelligence of Things (AIoT) current scenario, challenges, and opportunities

Yusuf Perwej, Nikhat Akhtar and Devendra Agarwal

Goel Institute of Technology & Management (GITM), Lucknow, India

1.1 INTRODUCTION

The Internet of Things (IoT), Artificial Intelligence (AI), blockchain, and cloud computing [1] have all just entered the big data age [2]. The Internet of Things (IoT) is a term used to describe the billions of physical objects that are all connected to the internet and collecting and sharing data to develop new applications and services [3]. The Internet of Things (IoT) is a network of connected objects that, depending on the data gathered from each object, can act individually [4] or collectively. IoT data is essentially a type of big data [5]. Sensors and other big data dimensions cross because of the broad usage of sensors for data collecting, the application of data obtained over extended periods of time, and the desire to grade data on a scale to aid in decision-making. The IoT sector would contribute $2.8 to $6.7 trillion to the global economy by 2025, according to a McKinsey prediction [6]. IoT devices frequently have CPUs, memory, internet connectivity, data-gathering sensors, and membership in a network with millions of other similar devices [7]. According to Business Insider Intelligence, by 2025 there will be more than 55 billion IoT devices, or more than four devices for every person on the planet. Although the IoT provides a framework for device-to-device connection and data collecting [8], AI gives the system a brain and enhances its ability to interpret the data at hand. AI refers to the capacity to replicate human intelligence via the use of computers that have been programmed to function and complete tasks in a manner that is comparable to that of people.

In this regard, both of these technologies may be mutually supportive and lead to the ultimate development of the Artificial Intelligence of Things (AIoT) [9]. As a result, when AI is included into the IoT, these devices will be able to analyse data on their own, make judgements, and execute actions based on those decisions. According to Gartner, more than 80% of commercial IoT programmers will employ AI by 2023. AIoT intelligence enables data analytics, which may be used to improve systems, and provide improved performance and business insights, as well as generating data that can be used to train systems and aid in their decision-making [10]. An AI-enabled

DOI: 10.1201/9781003509240-1

system is created to analyse and interpret data before correcting an issue or addressing a concern based on the interpretations. The more data an AI programme has, the more accurate its findings will be [11]. In the past, AI experienced difficulties because of slow processors and little datasets. Sensors didn't exist before the way they do now. Right now, we have everything we need, including fast CPUs, input devices, a network, and vast volumes of data. It makes sense that big data is required for Artificial Intelligence to exist [12]. A blockchain is a peer-to-peer distributed, open source, and unchangeable public digital record [13]. At its foundation, blockchain is a ledger made up of a number of blocks.

This ledger contains a permanent record of every contact and transaction that takes place between users of the dispersed and decentralized blockchain network [14]. The transaction and any asset exchanges between users (such those using Ether or Bitcoin) are detailed in each block header [15]. The creation of decentralized marketplaces and coordination platforms that can be used to trade computing resources, data, and other AI-related algorithms as well as other AI components can be facilitated by blockchain. These will pave the way for an onslaught of fresh ideas and the expanded usage of AI. After seeing security-related breaches impacting BitcoinGold, Etheru, ZCash, and a host of other cryptocurrencies, it is obvious that developing a safe and scalable blockchain for real-world applications would take some time. Blockchain, AI, and the IoT coming together will bring about a wide range of new technologies as well as transformations in society and the economy [16].

1.2 BACKGROUND

Many sensors and devices are gathering and processing environmental data, transferring it to data centers, and getting feedback online for connectedness and perception as a result of the IoT growth [18]. Complex environment perception employing these data [19], massive heterogeneous data transfer, and quick, informed decision-making are all difficult problems. Artificial Intelligence of Things (AIoT) technology combines IoT and AI [20] technologies. AIoT will enhance current IoT standards in order to create autonomous future communication architectures that enable intelligent data flow between billions of devices. This section examines current research and the AIoT. In response to the exponential increase in data volumes caused by the spread of Internet of Things devices, AIoT Edge Computing was created [21].

Venkatesh et al. offered advice and listed relevant works on AIoT in healthcare in order to develop the current healthcare system beyond version 4.0 [22]. A technique called AIoT, which [23] refers to convergence technology that produces, implements, and uses AI based on IoT's environment and attributes, was developed by Xu and colleagues. In particular, the AIoT (DNA, Data, Network, and AI) is a critical convergence technology that increases connectivity to virtual space while inadvertently expanding intelligence from form to super-convergence and fundamentally transforming the industry. Calo et al.'s [24] initial analysis of the need for AI in IoT applications was followed by an evaluation of potential IoT AI application methodologies.

A concept for an AI algorithm architecture that preserves the benefits of both edge processing and server-based/cloud [1] focused computing was also released by the group. Nikhat Akhtar et al.'s study from 2015 [25], which analyses recent contributions focusing on the Medical Internet of Things (MIoT) in-depth, provides this information. The medical Internet of Things-based healthcare services are expected to improve user experience while reducing expenses. In [26], authors investigate the effectiveness of recurrent neural network-based deep learning algorithms for detecting malware in cloud VMs. We focus on two important RNN architectures: LSTM (Long Short-Term Memory RNNs) and Bidirectional RNNs (Bidirectional RNNs) (BIDIs) [28].

In the opinion of Miller et al. [29], heterogeneous IoT information must be continuously produced and delivered over wired and wireless environments for AIoT edge computing. Debauche et al.'s [30] introduced a new architecture and altered AI models and algorithms to deliver micro services at the edge level. Yu and colleagues demonstrated that blockchain has a lot of potential for addressing a range of IoT difficulties in AIoT edge computing scenarios [31]. All that is needed to be resolved is the problem of distributed transmission, computation, and storage as blockchain users may transact with one another without the need for a central server and keep a consistent ledger. Blockchain is regarded as one of the disruptive technologies in a number of domains, including IT and the economy and community.

Applications for the Internet of Things require AI, as demonstrated by Calo et al. [32], who then covered a number of methods to incorporate AI into IoT. They also showed off an AI algorithm architecture that uses both edge processing and server-based cloud computing. Deep learning [34] for IoT was introduced into the edge computing environment by Li et al. [33]. To improve the performance of IoT deep learning applications, the authors also offered an edge computing offloading approach. According to Ermakova et al. [35], patients are still hesitant and less likely to prefer cloud platforms for storing their medical information because of privacy concerns. Currently, heart disease is identified by analysis of electrocardiogram (ECG) data.

With the use of two edge computing use cases, Xiong et al. [36] examined a variety of architectural challenges for creating a scalable and shared multi-tenant AIoT platform. The implementation of federated learning techniques by Chiu et al. [37] in an AIoT platform helped them to overcome network capacity problems and data privacy concerns. Deep learning for IoT was introduced to the edge computing environment by Li et al. [38]. In order to improve edge computing-based IoT deep learning applications, the authors additionally supplied flooding. Through the use of two edge computing use cases, Xiong et al. [39] examined a variety of architectural challenges for creating a scalable and shared multi-tenant AIoT platform. In an AIoT platform, Chiu et al. [40] used federated learning techniques to get over network bandwidth constraints and data privacy concerns.

1.3 ABOUT THE ARTIFICIAL INTELLIGENCE OF THINGS (AIoT)

IoT devices talk, collect, and exchange data on our online habits across the internet. They generate 1 billion GB of data each day. The Internet of Things (IoT) is a technical development that helps in our ability to rethink daily life [41], but AI will be the key to maximizing the IoT's potential. Artificial Intelligence (AI), also known as machine intelligence, is a branch of computer science that aims to equip software with the ability to analyses its environment using predetermined rule and search algorithms, pattern recognition, natural language processing, deep learning, voice recognition, image analysis, and machine learning models, and then make decisions based on those analyses [42]. In order to allow software developers or systems to respond with varied degrees of autonomy, AI tries to emulate biological intelligence [43]. This reduces the need for manual human intervention in a variety of operations. IoT and AI are both potent technologies in and of themselves. Figure 1.1 illustrates the effects of combining AI with IoT to produce AIoT.

In its simplest form, the AIoT is the nexus of Artificial Intelligence with the Internet of Things, bringing intelligence to the fore. While AI may be compared to a system's brain, IoT devices can be compared to the digital nervous system. A new phenomenon, IoT represents various essential digital connections between physical elements.

The AIoT, or Artificial Intelligence of Things, is the convergence of artificial intelligence and the Internet of Things. It enables the integration of intelligence at the edge of the network. While artificial intelligence may be compared to a system's brain, internet of things devices can be compared to the digital nervous system. The convergence of AI and IoT is depicted in Figure 1.1, where it can be seen that IoT technology enables the collection of important data through connected sensors which is further processed through AI algorithms to extract the intelligent information from it [44]. When discussing the expansion of capabilities on the Internet of Things (IoT) or how technology can utilize the IoT, businesses and other entities often mention the concept of Artificial Intelligence of Things (AIoT). Complexity and the need of real-time monitoring in various situations in these businesses necessitate the use of advanced technology and data analysis techniques.

A lot of incidents are significantly more sophisticated than simple event control. They require the use of analytical tools by applications to understand

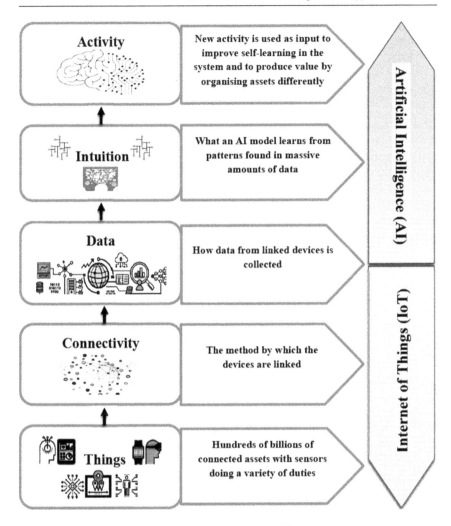

Figure 1.1 The Artificial Intelligence of Things (AIoT).

the event and start the appropriate actions. This is accurate despite the fact that certain IoT systems are built for straightforward event control, in which a sensor signal prompts a matching response [45], such as turning on and off lights depending on changes in ambient illumination.

A new IoT framework dubbed the Artificial Intelligence of Things (AIoT) is used to make this work. By pushing the boundaries of intelligence, it enables robots to interpret data, assess their surroundings, and make decisions on their own [46]. AIoT devices have become intelligent machines which are capable of undertaking self-driven analyses and responding autonomously thanks to the power of AI. They no longer serve as the control center's only information bearers. AIoT is now helping business leaders make choices regarding operations and strategy. It could enable businesses to succeed better than their rivals and dominate their sector.

The Internet of Things (IoT) is already a reality because of recent developments in both hardware (such as intelligent sensors, actuators, and low-power CPUs [47]) and software (such as embedded operating systems, virtualization technologies, and machine learning frameworks). IoT has a wide range of applications in next generation such as logistics & supply chain, smart factories [49], autonomous vehicles, machine-to-machine sensors to optimize operations, agriculture, security, and smart manufacturing devices that use real-time data analytics. Another significant use is the establishment of an AI decision as a service function for human resource experts utilizing the AIoT in conjunction with social media and platforms related to human resources.

1.4   WHY IS AIoT SO SIGNIFICANT?

The significance of AIoT technology comes because of the convergence of two powerful technologies i.e., AI and IoT. Due to the capability of collecting a wide range of data through connected devices and analyzing it through advanced AI algorithms, AIoT provides enhanced decision-making power along with efficient automation of existing operations. If artificial intelligence is used correctly, it may, if not all, enhance the end outcome of most tools or processes. Being an emerging technology, the Internet of Things (IoT) [46] may leverage machine learning and AI to progress quickly. Devices with AI capabilities will be able to adopt a proactive strategy instead of a reactive approach. Devices that may be used as sensors are frequently connected to cloud computing platforms.

The device's job will be to acquire all available data and send it to the cloud for processing, based on the settings. In such a case, it will be up to a cloud computing platform to assess the data and provide complete, helpful information. This platform will effectively serve as a network of passive sensors that can be utilized to collect, process, and analyse data. IoT devices might become more active than passive with the advent of AI processors. Instead of sending the complete audio recording to the cloud for analysis, an AI-enabled smart speaker can employ a natural language processing (NLP) model to analyses the trigger word locally. This simply means that an AI-powered IoT system will be more dependable, safe, and adaptable.

The ability of big data analytics and IoT systems to benefit each of these business areas is increased by AI. The selection of AI for IoT and data analytics will be crucial for effective and successful decision-making, particularly in the field of streaming data and real-time analytics connected with edge computing networks. For all AIoT use cases, market segments, and solutions, real-time data will be a major value proposition. By enabling it to receive streaming data, detect relevant traits, and make judgements in real-time, AIoT will elevate service logic to an entirely unique level. The service will frequently be the facts and valuable information. The majority of machine learning and AI models, however, [50] rely on data to carry out inference.

IoT-enabled devices may offer AI algorithms with enough data to produce forecasts, allowing the algorithms to operate effectively in a local setting. In the case of a self-driving car using an AI model, the model may rely on data from the vehicle's radar system if the camera input is obstructed for whatever reason. When a problem occurs, these AI-powered systems have the capacity to self-correct and choose whether or not to shut down a system. For instance, if the self-driving car model detects discrepancies in the data from several sensors, it may opt to disengage and demand that the human driver take control.

The moment has arrived to adapt your technology shift using AIoT and become nimbler. AIoT devices boost processing, security, and the danger of data manipulation during IO operations in alongside giving real-time information and being close to the user.

1.5 HOW DOES ARTIFICIAL INTELLIGENCE OF THINGS (AIoT) WORK?

While AI and IoT are complementary technologies, we believe that AIoT is the natural next step for both. While the IoT benefits from the AI's connectivity and data interchange, the AI benefits from the IoT's machine learning capabilities, which turn data into knowledge that is valuable. Edge computing, software, and chipsets are all parts of the device infrastructure that use AI and are interconnected via IoT networks [51]. Figure 1.2 depicts the important processes that are all integrated through Application Programming Interfaces (APIs). This will require compatibility at the platform level (components that may coexist in an ecosystem), the software level (operating systems and programmers), and the hardware level (such as chipsets). The APIs then focus on improving system and network efficiency while profiting from the generated data. AIoT technology, which has a big impact on all industries, enables the growth of a connected, imaginative, and knowledgeable civilization.

1.5.1 Phase 1: Data collection

The gadgets produce and collect data as the first stage. The data is gathered by the devices' sensors in order to capture different kinds of information. These sensors are found in Internet of Things (IoT)-connected devices [52]. There are ways to integrate many sensors into a single device to handle various types of data. It is feasible to connect many sensors to one device in order

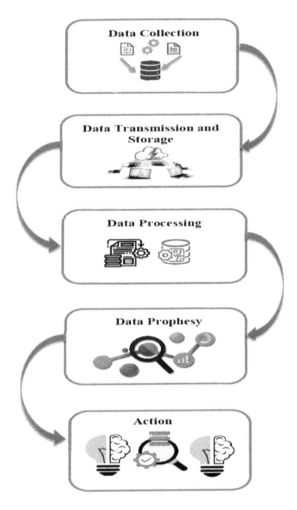

Figure 1.2 How does Artificial Intelligence of Things (AIoT) work?

to collect multiple types of data. For the purpose of gathering data, a gadget may have a number of sensors, such as a GPS, camera, and accelerometer.

1.5.2 Phase 2: Data transmission and storage

Subsequently, there is a process of collection. The collected data is organized into sets and kept in the cloud. The cloud makes it simpler and more affordable to store huge quantities of data than it is to put it on hardware. Since organizations don't have to invest a lot of money on hardware for data storage, cloud storage lowers total storage costs. Later, the stored data is examined and evaluated.

1.5.3 Phase 3: Data processing

For processing, the data is stored on cloud servers. The data is separated into phases based on the extraction and purification of pertinent information. The processes involved in data processing include data extraction from the cloud, data cleaning and anomaly removal, data translation to a standard format, and the use of algorithms to produce insights.

1.5.4 Phase 4: Data prophecy

Communication of the processed data occurs via a number of networks. Once compiled and reviewed, it gains value as knowledge. Machine learning algorithms aid in the prediction of future occurrences once the data has been studied. Making predictions based on the data at hand is easier after the relevant models have been created. For instance, anomaly detection models, text-based models, and clustering algorithms may recognize entities and classify texts while also predicting visual patterns.

1.5.5 Phase 5: Action

The useful information gathered will then be used more extensively. Machines make judgements based on the available information after generating forecasts. Business goals can be linked, procedures can be enhanced, and future plans can be created with the use of insights and enhanced dashboards. Tableau [53] and Microsoft Power BI are two data visualization solutions that can effectively present huge data with millions of data points. Real-time activities are aided by data points and predictions. In developing in-depth reports, graphic charting is advantageous.

1.5.6 The role of AI in IoT

It will be vital to invest in new technologies if IoT devices are to prosper in the future and realize all of their capabilities. Whole economic sectors might be transformed by the convergence of AI and IoT. IoT powered by AI develops smart devices that mimic intelligent behavior and helps in decision-making with little to no human participation. Internet of Things (IoT) is vital for Artificial Intelligence (AI). The main argument in favor of combining AI and IoT is that, while IoT devices collect data and send it to the cloud or a different location where data can be collected online, AI, which is known as the brain of AIoT, is what actually helps with decision-making and simulates how machines will act or respond [54]. The Internet of Things (IoT) just collects data from devices that are connected online. However, AI expands the technique and gives devices, software, and robotics autonomy. IoT and AI are two distinct technologies with a wide range of applications. It stands for the next stage in industrial automation and has the potential to drive the Industry 4.0 transformation [55]. In order to provide valuable information, a lot of these IoT devices create a lot of data, which must be collected and mined. Artificial Intelligence is used at this point. The Internet of Things is used to gather and handle the huge amounts of data that AI systems need. The data is subsequently transformed by these algorithms into useful, usable findings for IoT devices. IoT AI makes life easier for consumers by allowing them to control devices directly from their hands. The main objective of AI in the Internet of Things is to enhance and smarten enterprises in order to boost their efficiency and generate revenue. AI introduces the Machine-to-Machine (M2M) learning element of IoT. Connecting such clever gadgets brings complete automation one step toward reality. IoT provides AI with new possibilities. IoT connects AI to a variety of devices so that it may learn from them and advance for the coming generation. IoT devices and the network-wide data they generate would be meaningless without AI-powered analytics. Similar to this, absent the influx of IoT-generated data, AI systems would find it difficult to be useful in corporate settings. On the other hand, a potent fusion of AI and IoT has the potential to transform organizations and support them in making more intelligent choices in light of the daily deluge of data. The two might combine to create new value propositions, business models, income streams, and operations. If AI is the mind and IoT is the body.

1.6 HOW IS AIoT EVOLVING YOUR BUSINESS MODEL?

By enabling smart devices to complete exceedingly challenging tasks that are now unfeasible with existing IoT designs, AIoT pushes the boundaries of smart device intelligence. AIoT combines the computing power of AI with the widespread interoperability of the Internet of Things (IoT). The massive volumes of data that the IoT collects via internet connectivity and Artificial Intelligence are more easily absorbed and evaluated with the help of machine learning. IoT devices use machine learning [56] to find trends and detect problems with data collecting by utilizing better sensors. This method is used to determine inherent qualities, such as air stimulation, moisture, temperature, pollution, light, sound, vibrations, and so on [57]. Operational estimations are produced by IoT and machine learning 20 times more quickly and accurately than by previous technologies.

One of the main reasons why companies adopting AI technology see considerable revenue growth is due to this. Businesses and industries will ultimately embrace AIoT, leading to more advanced and useful cross-industry and inter-business solutions. These approaches' main focus will be on improving system and network performance as well as extracting value from industrial data utilizing greatly better analytics and decision-making approaches [58]. At the moment, whether it's a Fortune 500 company or a

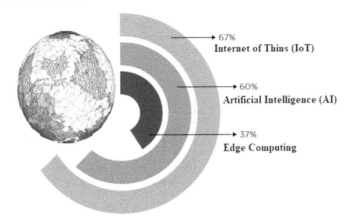

Figure 1.3 The most popular technologies currently using in real world.

small startup, IoT and AI are very in demand. Since they are both unlimited, businesses want to capitalize on both of these advantages and unleash their full capabilities. The combination of AI with commercial, industrial, and consumer product and service ecosystems will change a number of business verticals [59]. The provision of goods and services, supply chains, sales and marketing strategies, and support models are all anticipated to play important roles in corporate operations. According to a recent Tech Trend survey conducted by SADA System, IoT and AI are now the most extensively utilized technologies, as shown in Figure 1.3. It was also discovered that AI and IoT are the top technologies that businesses are putting money in to boost productivity and compete.

1.7 GAINS OF ARTIFICIAL INTELLIGENCE OF THINGS

With a beautifully tailored experience, proactive intervention, and intelligent automation, AIoT benefits both customers and enterprises. In this part, we'll go over some of the most well-known advantages of fusing these two cutting-edge technologies.

- **Increasing Operational Effectiveness:** Deployment of AIoT results in enhanced performance and accurate forecasts, which optimize company processes. AI and machine learning algorithms anticipate operating conditions and identify factors that need to be changed for improved results. AIoT offers reliable data streams, detects trends that aren't misleading on straightforward gauges, and offers practical insights to cut down on redundant processes and wasteful time utilization. By way of example, Google uses artificial intelligence and the Internet of Things to lower the cost of cooling its data centers.

- **Strengthening Cybersecurity:** In the global society we live in today, data is essential. Therefore, it is crucial to preserve such information. AIoT solutions may help companies of all sizes, across all sectors, and with all kinds of objectives. When IoT security solutions are based on artificial intelligence, IoT environments are more secure and reliable for organizations.

- **Comprehensive Risk Management:** The two innovations that aid in automated rapid reaction and risk prediction are Artificial Intelligence and the Internet of Things. They are therefore more able to deal with dangers to personnel safety, financial loss, and cyberspace. Fujitsu, for instance, uses AI to review data from connected wearable devices to ensure worker safety.

- **Creativity:** Partnerships between the IoT and AI provide enterprises a special potential. It raises the possibility of creating new services, goods, and approaches that use AI and IoT to make life easier for people.

- **Costly Unplanned Downtime is Eliminated:** Equipment failure may cause costly unplanned downtime in a variety of sectors, including offshore oil and gas and industrial production. Thanks to predictive maintenance using AI-enabled IoT, you can foresee issues and plan routine maintenance work in advance. You might therefore avoid the negative repercussions of an outage.

- **Increased Customer Satisfaction:** The supply of customized suggestions and the personalization of the shopping experience in the retail sector are made possible by Artificial Intelligence (AIoT) and are based on consumer intelligence, information about demographics, and habit.

- **Neural Processing Capacity Designed to Edge Devices:** To speed up neural network calculation, many edge devices use specialized processors (such GPUs in smartphones and intelligent cameras). Therefore, having neural processing abilities on edge devices is particularly beneficial for AIoT applications. It initially lowers network bandwidth use and processing latency. Only a minimal quantity of processed data has to be shared because the sensor data may be processed locally. The safekeeping and privacy of data can also be guaranteed. Enrolled user biometric data for biometric authentication, for example, may be held on local hardware with cryptography and just the built-in confirmation capacity on the edge devices accessible to the apps in order to decrease the risk of data leakage. Thirdly, it facilitates asymmetric and dispersed model training. On distributed edge devices with local sensor data, models may be trained using a federated learning architecture. Furthermore, depending on their usage scenarios, certain device groups may follow different model update protocols than others.

- **Product and Service Improvements:** Natural language processing (NLP) is being used to improve human–machine communication. Undoubtedly, combining IoT with AI may help businesses develop new products or better ones that already exist by enabling them to handle and analyze data quickly. A outstanding company using AI to identify perceptual trends and gather helpful data for IoT-enabled aviation engine maintenance is Rolls-Royce.

- **New Sources of Income:** For companies, the AIoT throws up a world of possibilities in terms of new goods and services that might increase profits and open up new markets. Natural language processing (NLP) to enhance human interactions, cutting-edge integrated systems to track the movements of vehicles in real time, drones to access locations that are difficult for people to reach, and other fields are just a few of the businesses that have begun to implement AIoT.
- **Excellent Scalability:** The Internet of Things includes sophisticated computers, sensors, and chipsets. The massive amount of data that is typical of IoT systems may be controlled thanks to sensors with batteries. For detecting, compressing, and analyzing the massive volume of data coming through cloud storage, AI is crucial. The IoT ecosystem as a whole becomes more scalable as the enormous volume of data is made controllable.
- **Intelligence in a Connected World:** Because of predictive analytics ("What will happen?"), prescriptive analytics ("What should be done?"), and adaptive analytics ("What are the necessary steps to consider?"), we may witness more "connected intelligence" with AI integrated in IoT. All of these inquiries, as well as how the system should respond to new developments, are handled by a single device.
- **Deep Learning with Privacy Protection:** In the framework of the AIoT, deep learning necessitates a large amount of data that has been collected by various devices from numerous users. If data is sent to the cloud and stored there, people can be concerned about the security and privacy of their data. To address these concerns, the deep learning and information security businesses have turned their focus to deep learning that protects privacy. Data can be preserved locally in dispersed devices using the conventional and promising federated learning architecture, which was newly proposed. In federated learning, homomorphic encryption is employed to stop data from leaking to the server.

1.8 AIoT WILL DRIVE TECHNOLOGY IN THE FUTURE

AIoT enables evaluation of a device's data-handling capacity as well as potential future developments. Consequently, processing and learning will be made feasible. The marriage of the Internet of Things (IoT) and Artificial Intelligence (AI) has led to the AIoT revolution. IoT uses a common interface to link AI-enabled devices to a network in order to gather data and derive insights and analytics from it. Simply said, by extending capabilities to the edge, AIoT enables formerly data-generating devices to become more self-sufficient and smarter.

It also enables us to develop new intelligence capabilities while at the same time requiring that we churn enormous amounts of data at the source in order to improve performance and decision-making. Despite the prospect that organizations may benefit from AIoT by getting insights from massive amounts of data, it is difficult to ignore the possible security risks. Every node in the network is at risk as cyber-threats and risks multiply. Organizations must learn from previous data in order to profit from AIoT, but it's also essential to protect that data. As a result, cybersecurity is becoming increasingly important in the ecosystem of the AIoT. Personal and professional data are stored on IoT devices.

As a result, using AI in some circumstances has become increasingly necessary. Based on past data, AI systems can anticipate an assault. AIoT will build up an early warning system and offer the customer the optimal security strategy. When AI and IoT work together, they could identify data abnormalities and alert the user. To effectively profit from AIoT, edge computing must be considered in the context of AI and IoT. The Internet of Things has issues with data latency and capacity limitations since there are so many connected devices and so much data generated at the edge. Both the computational and energy efficiency of nodes are growing.

As a result, AIoT emphasizes shifting some tasks to the edge in order to accelerate response times for crucial applications. When there is less communication traffic, network security is easier to manage. By looking for indications of manipulation in incoming communications, edge AI may be able to aid in enhancing device security. By utilizing edge computing, it is possible to process data locally on the system as opposed to sending it to a distant data center. The scope of current technology is smart appliances and thermostats; in the future, however, more complex devices like completely autonomous cars and house robots may be developed [17]. Another significant development is the spread of speech Artificial Intelligence in devices like speakers and phones. Today, it is possible to have a 1D intelligent speaker that follows the speaker's instructions. It can be replaced with speakers that make use of NLP technologies to comprehend the user more effectively. Voice-activated LCDs in two dimensions aid in information presentation. Through technology, an IoT development firm seeks to enhance enterprises. With the successful implementation of AIoT, the commencement of voice authentication for e-payments appears to be within reach in the coming decades. The application of Vision AI is well known. This gadget uses just Artificial Intelligence to distinguish huge objects in 4K resolution. Vision AI could be able to evaluate video on-the-go when combined with the Internet of Things. Additionally, it is projected that the display quality would go from 4K to 10K. In the upcoming years, AIoT will have an important impact, and we'll be interested by the fresh concepts that emerge.

1.9 USE CASES OF AIoT

Because of AI and IoT, communication in the globe has changed and developed over the past several decades. Thanks to a fresh, intriguing alliance known as Artificial Intelligence of Things (AIoT), this technology has now come a long way. Thus, when AI is included into the IoT, such devices will be able to independently evaluate data, make judgements, and take action on that data. These "smart" technologies help to increase productivity and efficiency. AIoT intelligence enables data analytics, which may then be utilized to improve systems, provide enhanced efficiency and business insights, and generate data that can aid the system in learning and making wiser decisions.

The benefits of these two technologies complement one another: AI improves IoT through machine learning capabilities whereas IoT improves AI through connectivity, data sharing, and signaling. Intelligent, linked systems may self-identify and correct themselves thanks to the AIoT. The AIoT is expected to be a significant change driver for all worldwide organizations in the future decade. It is already improving the capacities of a few key industries. Additionally, AIoT encourages human–machine interactions, enhancing the efficiency of analytics and data management. The Internet of Things and intelligent systems are integrated, making AIoT a powerful and useful tool for many use cases. The AIoT offers a variety of applications in practically every sector, each with its own set of challenges. Following is a list of some of them.

- **Robotics:** Manufacturing, which uses technologies like big data analytics, the Internet of Things, Artificial Intelligence, face recognition, deep learning, and robotics, is one sector that has already adopted cutting-edge advancements. Robotic vacuum cleaners utilize sensors to learn about their surroundings, and Artificial Intelligence is employed to decide how to move about. Robots employ Artificial Intelligence, as people do, to understand difficult (and even hostile) circumstances and modify their behaviors. This is carried out throughout production, package and food delivery, and search and rescue efforts during natural disasters. Due to their excellent efficiency, incredible work, and trustworthiness, robots in industries improve production. Factory robots are becoming more sophisticated as a result of implanted sensors that can transmit data. Robots with AIoT capabilities can streamline industrial processes, cut costs, and conform to new environments. The robots' artificial intelligence systems also allow them to potentially learn from new data [27].
- **Information Security:** New cyber-threats are found almost every day. Information security must be able to respond to different threats and defend itself. The advancement of information security must keep up with expectations and, on occasion, surpass challenges. With the help

of AIoT, which leverages data from various internet-connected devices to learn and act, this is made feasible. Block-based logic translation [60] has recently presented a straightforward technique that, while shrinking the size of the feature, also maintains the original feature, making it suitable for AIoT devices with constrained resources and defenseless against future assaults.

- **Medical Care:** Applications for AIoT in healthcare are numerous and include the detection and diagnosis of illnesses through the analysis of imaging data, remote monitoring of patient information via sensors and the raising of warns when oddities are discovered, forecasts of an individual's illness [61] risk via the analysis of EHRs, and the forecasting of drug interactions. The use of robotic surgical equipment also enables minimally invasive surgery by performing or assisting with extremely precise and difficult procedures.

- **Automation in Manufacturing:** To improve the detection of anomalies and quality control in the production line, AIoT and computer vision may be used. AIoT may also aid in preventative maintenance of machinery, resulting in reduced downtime, a longer machine's life, and lower production costs. Robots may be utilized on the manufacturing floor or in warehouses to transfer items, assist with the production process, inspect the product's quality, and do monotonous, extremely exact tasks.

- **Intelligent Retail:** AIoT may be advantageous to retailers in two ways. With the use of AIoT and predictive analytics, enormous volumes of data are gathered and evaluated, which is then used to assist merchants in forecasting and making data-driven business choices. As clients enter a smart retail environment, a camera system with computer vision capabilities can employ face recognition [62] to identify them. In order to effectively forecast customer behavior, the system collects information from customers on topics like gender, purchasing habits, traffic patterns, and other variables. It then processes the data to produce predictions about buyer behavior, using those predictions to make judgements regarding store operations like marketing and product placement. Cameras and sensors are used in retail analytics to monitor client movements and foretell when they are heading towards the checkout counter. The checkout procedure could move more quickly as a result of better-organized staff, and the output of the cashiers might rise. Future proactive management strategies might be made using the information acquired to determine peak periods. For instance, if the system identifies that Millennials are the majority of consumers [63] entering the shop, it may send out product adverts or in-store incentives that appeal to them, which would increase sales. As demonstrated at Alibaba's Hema store, customers may be spotted by smart cameras and offered the chance to bypass the checkout wait.

- **Production:** Production is one of the industries that has benefited from new discoveries and methods. The sector has expanded to its full potential thanks to advances in deep learning, IoT, and AI technology. Given the volume of normal processes in the industrial sector, AIoT is a suitable fit. This technology may make the entire manufacturing process more efficient, time-consuming, and expensive by improving data transfer and comprehension, identifying and fixing defects, predicting when equipment will wear out, and doing a lot more.
- **Traffic Control:** Google Maps is a fantastic illustration of AIoT in traffic control. In order to acquire data, the programme establishes connections with various devices. Artificial intelligence is then used to determine the kind of traffic. Traffic is also monitored by drones and other tools utilized by the police. It promotes safe driving practises and lowers traffic offences.

  Drone traffic control is one of the many practical uses of AIoT in a smart city. Congestion can be reduced if traffic [64] can be monitored in real time and the flow of traffic changed. Drones may send out traffic data while keeping an eye on a big region. After analysing this data, AI may decide, without the need for human involvement, how to alleviate traffic congestion by altering speed limits and traffic signal timing. ET City Brain from Alibaba Cloud uses AIoT to maximize the usage of urban resources. Through the use of this technology, ambulances might get to individuals in need of assistance more rapidly by seeing accidents, unlawful parking, and changing traffic signals. Another advantage of traffic management is the capability of tracking vehicles and routinely monitoring them. vehicles used to transport vulnerable individuals, government officials, or criminals.
- **Office Structures:** Smart office buildings are an additional field in which the Internet of Things and Artificial Intelligence are interacting. In their office tower, some companies seek to install a network of sophisticated environmental sensors. By altering lighting and climate management depending on building usage and user preferences, AIoT may assist businesses in reducing energy expenditures and improving the energy [65] efficiency of buildings. By controlling the lighting and temperature when people are present, these sensors may save energy. Another idea is that a smart building may regulate entry using facial recognition software. In the real world, AIoT refers to a system that combines networked cameras with Artificial Intelligence to assess real-time photos against a database to decide who should be permitted entry to an establishment. The requirement for employees to clock in and complete attendance forms for significant meetings would be handled by the AIoT system. They can also aid in optimizing system efficiency and offer early warnings of prospective system problems. Buildings may also be able to monitor people's physical mobility,

which is crucial for security management. Facial recognition technology may potentially be used to restrict access to intelligent building designs.

- **Farming:** Agriculture is another of the key sectors that AIoT can benefit. Artificial Intelligence (AI) is used to construct a smart system that changes settings according to the weather, water use, temperature, and crop/soil conditions [66]. Sensor data is processed to choose the best crops, apply fertilizer, apply irrigation, and select the best pest control strategies. AI aids farmers in increasing yields, maximizing resource utilization, and anticipating seasonal weather changes for agricultural planning. Artificial Intelligence and computer vision are used to monitor crops and extensive farmlands in order to identify regions of concern and issue notifications as required.

- **Administration of the Fleet:** AIoT is being used increasingly in fleet management to keep an eye on a fleet of cars, cut fuel costs, track vehicle maintenance, and spot risky driving behavior. Businesses can manage their fleets more efficiently thanks to AIoT, which integrates an AI system with IoT gadgets like GPS and other sensors.

- **Self-Driving Vehicles:** Self-driving cars are one of the principal uses of AIoT technology. IoT and AI are used in these smart gadgets to produce self-driving vehicles. The sensors and equipment in automobiles are linked to the internet through the Internet of Things (IoT). Using AI, the automobile is capable of making deliberative judgements that mimic those of a person. The market has been quite enthusiastic about autonomous vehicles, and for good reason [67]. To offer autonomous safety systems for automobiles, an incredible amount of sensors, connection, and analytical infrastructure are required. But that is not where the narrative ends. Another use of AIoT in today's world is in autonomous vehicles, such as Tesla's autopilot systems, which utilize radars, sonars, GPS [68], and cameras to collect data on road conditions before using an AI system to make judgements based on that data. Artificial Intelligence (AI) in the autonomous vehicle is programmed to react to its surroundings and conditions. The cars are made to respond to the weather, traffic information, and pedestrian behavior, among other things.

- **Wearable Technology:** The vast majority of people who are familiar with or have used wearable technology, including smart watches, smart glasses, and VR/AR headsets. Artificial Intelligence (AIoT) has expanded the usefulness of these devices, allowing us to measure our calorie burn, sleep length and quality, energy levels, and fitness levels in real time. These devices have a huge impact on the healthcare business, enabling remote patient care from medical experts who can digitally monitor patients' health. Wearables are currently continually monitoring your health and providing significant information. Someday, however, these wearables will be able to keep an eye on your health metrics and spot serious conditions such as cardiovascular problems. Google Glasses are revolutionizing the way we see the environment and interact with the people in it by providing instant access to linked gadgets and the ability to book a reservation for a meal while on the phone. Every day, our lives are becoming more effective and simpler thanks to advancements in wearable technology provided by the AIoT. Wearable technology is a great way to start utilizing bionics. Technology has already evolved to the point that it is now possible to build artificial body parts, even if they were originally designed for bettering human experiences.

- **Modes of Transportation:** The connected vehicle seems to be the largest disruptive factor to hit the transportation sector in more than a century. These days, travelling by car involves more than just travelling from point A to point B. According to McKinsey & Company, a sector that provides innovative services and apps and has a potential revenue of $5.6 trillion from transport services by 2030 is developing into an online platform for innovation. AIoT benefits fleet owners by lowering fuel costs, tracking repairs and maintenance, and spotting risky driving behaviors.
- **Self-Driving Service Robots:** Similar to the way in which it is utilized with unmanned vehicles, the AIoT is also employed in autonomous delivery robots. Robots have sensors that collect data about their environment, and they employ an in-built AI system to decide how to prioritize activities [61].
- **Intelligent Homes:** IoT was necessary for the creation of the concept of smart home systems. The term refers to household equipment and gadgets that are linked to a network. It was designed to make life easier for individuals and give them more control over technology. Machines will be able to learn commands and make decisions based on prior actions thanks to AI. As a result of AIoT, several appliances, such as refrigerators, microwaves, heating and cooling systems, faucets, and even window blinds, may now be managed by a single device. On the other side, AI takes things a step further by collecting and researching data to better understand user patterns and offer specialized services and assistance. This is a groundbreaking idea in which all [70] of the physical objects in the home are networked through IoT and utilize AI to make intelligent decisions about, among other things, whether to switch on/off the lights, the television, or when to lock the main gates. Smart technologies like AI may be able to improve the efficiency of domestic energy consumption in addition to the convenience that they provide. This saves money and dramatically lowers energy use [48].
- **Tesla's Autopilot:** Tesla's Autopilot technology utilizes AIoT in a split second to gather input from sensors, mix it into neural network designs, analyze the numerous connected qualities, and determine what the car should do next. The finest illustration of IoT and AI working together

comes from Tesla's self-driving vehicles. Such cars employ AI to predict how pedestrians and other road users would behave in hypothetical situations. We may recognize, for instance, the condition of the roads, the appropriate pace, the weather, and get smarter with each journey.

- **Intelligent Education:** Kids and teens can benefit from AIoT by learning to recognize new species, choose individualized learning materials, study their native or another language, and engage in social interaction while learning. Building a smart classroom on the Raspberry Pi through the use of word recognition and hand motion detection technology is described in [71]. With the help of this AIoT system, a user can instruct a Raspberry Pi to take notes on a whiteboard or blackboard using a static hand gesture, recognise the text in the image (such as numbers, characters, or symbols), and convert it into a format that can be edited and shared with students for additional editing or collaboration using a desktop application. Several smartphone translation apps that can translate tens of languages were on show at CES 2020. These programmes take benefit from deep learning and other developments in AI technology. Massive Open Online Course (MOOC) platforms like Coursera are increasingly being used to supplement traditional on-campus education.

- **ET City Brain:** AIoT and Alibaba Cloud underpin the urban planning tool ET City Brain. When the traffic is detected by this gadget, the traffic lights are changed to ease congestion. By adjusting the traffic signals as necessary, ambulances may get at their intended location faster. Through the use of this technology, traffic has been reduced by 15% while car accidents and illegal parking are detected with greater precision.

- **Intelligent Hospitals:** Healthcare delivery systems are being redesigned with the use of technologies like AI, ML, deep learning, and Robotic Process Automation (RPA). Robotics and IoT-connected technologies are being used by intelligent hospitals to provide a new generation of healthcare assistance and treatment. Sensors and software for telemedicine consultations and remote healthcare monitoring are just a few of the IoT devices and applications that are starting to develop for the healthcare industry. Utilizing AI and ML, several conventional medical devices are being created, such as intelligent asthma inhalers. This is how AIoT is advancing medical technology. Examples include real-time patient monitoring via wearable devices, enhanced diagnosis made possible by advanced image processing, and robotic surgical procedures.

- **Smart Enterprise:** For firms that operate on a "time is money" premise, which is the majority of them, the decrease of human error and automated procedures work well together. Real-time processing made possible by the AIoT allows effective data analytics to give instantaneous overviews of activities from a single central dashboard. A cost-effective method for avoiding mistakes and oversights has also been demonstrated to be the use of smart devices and supply-chain sensors. Automation intends to fundamentally transform a number of significant areas, in the same way in which it has transformed the work environment.

- **Smart Monitoring:** Analytics using real-time data are used in security smart monitoring to determine whether something strange is occurring in a certain region. Similar events are occurring, mostly in the retail industry, where consumer profiling enables surveillance cameras to assist in securing public shopping by detecting and catching repeat offenders who make a disturbance. Furthermore, Intel is setting standards for how quickly and cleverly monitoring equipment can digest vast volumes of data and react.
- **Devices for Security Access:** By using fob technologies for entry points, the business entry Control Technologies (ACT) combine AI and IoT. It uses data to recognise each employee's access habits, comprehend where they sit at work, and predict improved office layout for simpler entrance and leave. IoT is becoming sharper with the advent of AI, and enterprises will soon combine the two to find and draw important conclusions from data. The fundamental goal is to free robots and systems from the dependency on human contact, allowing them to make reliable judgements.
- **Face Detectors:** Face detectors are a significant application of AIoT. Face identification becomes crucial for crime scene investigation teams and even in businesses to identify employee faces for attendance purposes. Face detectors delivered good service throughout the COVID-19 timeframe. In many public settings, they are presently being used to assess whether individuals are wearing masks. Face scanners are frequently used in offices to take attendance and are helpful in criminal inquiries.
- **Intelligent Cities:** Thanks to AIoT technology, the idea of smart cities is rapidly moving from science fiction to reality. AIoT has the potential to create cities that are more efficient, maintain municipal infrastructure, and improve public services in nearby areas. Cities are benefitting fast from automated solutions and networked devices in areas, including public safety, energy efficiency, and integrated public transit systems [72]. To do this, data from various sensors and IoT devices may be collected and analyzed in order to gain insightful knowledge that can be used to make adjustments in real time. Waste management, public services including parking and traffic control, and smart lighting are just some of the examples of valuable AI uses. Drones can monitor traffic in real time without the need for human involvement, using the information to handle and clear traffic jams by modifying traffic lights or lane allocations. Similar to this, garbage can sensors are able to warn staff to only pick up trash when the cans are full, reducing costs.

- **Smart Grids:** AIoT is employed in smart grids to spot cyber-attacks, plan and monitor demand, and diagnose grid issues. Unmanned aerial vehicles (UAVs), for instance, are used to classify damage and analyze electricity distribution poles while connected to the control center through the cellular network [73]. The Convolution Neural Network is used to analyze the UAV-captured picture in the cloud to ascertain the extent of the fire and the amount of falling debris. Technologies based on AI have also increased the accuracy of detection. For instance, a convolutional sparse auto-encoder-based unsupervised learning technique based on voltage and current data has been proposed for identifying power transmission line defects [74]. A semi-supervised deep learning approach that uses auto-encoders and generative adversarial networks was recently proposed, and this has been successful in detecting attacks via false data injection in smart grids [80].
- **Recommender Mirrors for Shopping:** The act of shopping might be difficult for individuals who have to buy clothes. People usually have a hard time visualizing how an item would look on them while it is still hanging on the rack, only to put it on and find out. However, many people who shop alone can benefit from getting a friend's advice on whether to purchase a certain item of clothing. In an effort to address some of these issues, IBM provides mirrors that provide guidance on what products look best. The company collaborated with Vero Moda, and it eventually hopes to make the technology accessible to other companies. According to reports, the mirrors act as online fitting rooms and provide evaluations based on the products selected. These mirrors not only provide value to customers, but could also help businesses by letting them know which products do the best business. A continual drip of pertinent data might reduce the number of things that conventional physical shops have to provide at significant savings. Although it's uncertain whether or not these mirrors will become commonplace items.

1.10 CHALLENGES OF THE AIoT

AIoT is the term used to describe decision-making that is assisted by AI technology and connected IoT sensors, systems, or product data. The Internet of Things is a phenomenon that occurs when 'things' like wearable technology, mobile phones, coffee makers, refrigerators, air conditioners, sensors, and other equipment are linked to the internet, can be recognized by other devices, and can gather and analyse data. Artificial Intelligence (AI) is defined as a machine's ability to learn from data and perform a set of tasks thoughtfully. As a result, when AI and IoT are combined, such devices will be able to analyse data, draw conclusions, and take appropriate action without the need for human intervention. AIoT provides data analytics in order to enhance a system, offer enhanced efficiency and business insights, as well as data that aids in decision-making and from which the system may learn [75]. In this part, we'll look at some of the difficulties the AIoT faces.

- **AIoT Training:** We enter the training phase once we have gathered enough data to begin using machine learning. Each machine does this in a unique way, accounting for elements such as the model, data kinds, and likelihood of outcomes. After that, correlations between inputs and outcomes can be discovered using statistical techniques and the data. As a consequence of your training, you now know which algorithms are most effective for forecasting the behavior of your machine. Unfortunately, they will always be biased by this first set of seed data. So, if we want robots to genuinely learn, we must go above and beyond. We need more examples of machines functioning in actual environments, additional sensors to collect new inputs, and more classifications to achieve genuine machine learning. It is necessary to keep running this simulation model forever so that the AIoT frameworks can improve and develop with each new instance.

- **AIoT Asymmetric Data Processing:** In AIoT systems, several asymmetric sensors provide a large volume of data in a variety of formats, sizes, and timestamps, complicating further processing, transmission, and storage. It is possible to reduce network bandwidth and transmission latency by using the optimum coding strategy. For example, further research is needed to determine whether the machine-based video-coding approach can help with future computer vision jobs. In contrast, it is difficult to minimize bandwidth and latency when the structural representation, which is task-oriented, must be calculated at the network edge.

- **AIoT Technical Understanding:** A further obstacle is that clients fail to upgrade their equipment since they don't understand IoT and AI on a technical level. This happens because people don't understand how important software updates are. Technical problems can be resolved with software upgrades. When systems aren't kept up to date, problems arise, and gadgets cease working properly. The provision of adequate training is therefore necessary for handling financial transactions, and such human resources are still in limited availability.

- **AIoT Deep Learning on Edge Nodes:** AIoT systems' ability to handle data streams in real time and with minimal latency is dependent on Deep CNN models set up on edge hardware. On the other hand, edge devices' constrained processing and storage capacities. Therefore, learning how to create or automatically locate lightweight, computationally effective, and hardware-friendly DNN structures is useful yet complex. Network trimming, compression, and quantization require more study.

- **AIoT Data Understanding:** The obstacles of connecting objects to the internet have concealed the fact that many firms do not yet understand the data that their devices are sending. It is of little use to continuously feed data on voltage, temperature, battery, and friction if the machine's output cannot be understood. Additionally, data is meaningless unless it can be used to predict outcomes. This means that before we can map what is occurring, we need to know how machines really fail. After establishing connections between devices and collected data, we must wait and see what happens. We can help ourselves by getting more knowledge in this respect from subject matter specialists. For instance, a piece of equipment that vibrates a lot would eventually fail.
- **The Role of Government in AIoT Regulation:** Although some companies have adopted the Internet of Things quickly, others are hesitant. These companies usually wait for new norms and laws to be implemented by the government [76]. But considering that the Internet of Things, the cloud, and even the general internet are not restricted to a certain city, state, or area, who is in charge of enacting these regulations? The sheer number of IoT-connected devices increases the complexity of the situation. How can a local regulatory authority make sure that incoming shipments are of a high enough level given that these devices are sent from a variety of sources, including overseas partners and sellers? Despite the fact that the majority of experts agree that IoT regulation is necessary, there are currently no rules or recommendations available for the general public to follow.
- **AIoT Scheduling:** Cloud data centers, fog nodes, and edge devices are among the examples of the heterogeneous computing resources of the AIoT. Computational scheduling is an issue for real-world AIoT systems since they may need to move some intensive processing from edge devices to the fog node or cloud center. In each individual application situation, the following considerations should be made while allocating computation among different resources: data type and volume, network bandwidth, processing delay, efficiency precision, usage of energy, and data security and privacy.
- **Big Data in AIoT for Deep Learning:** Big data collected by several sensors is common in AIoT systems and has enormous potential for deep learning. However, labelling the majority of AIoT data would be costly and time-consuming. Despite the substantial gains in unsupervised learning, especially self-supervised learning [77], future projects are projected to employ AIoT data, especially multi-modal data. Furthermore, transfer learning, semi-supervised learning, and few-shot learning in the context of the AIoT may be able to handle issues caused by novel classes, exceptional circumstances, and device state drifting due to the small quantity of labelled data.
- **AIoT Security Breach:** AIoT devices must be cautious while engaging with potential hazards. If updates are not performed, the security of

financial data is compromised, making it vulnerable to hackers [78]. Therefore, devices need to be regularly inspected and updated to avoid security breaches from attackers who may ruin the company by disclosing financial data. There will be another security breach if certain products are delivered over the mail with a password and the passwords are not transformed.

- **AIoT Data Monopolies:** Data is a vital resource for developing new products and improving old ones in the age of AI. Massive amounts of data are collected and used by AIoT companies, opening up new prospects for slavery and slave labor. This positive feedback loop might lead to a data monopoly or a sizable collection of private data that is locked away by current interests. As an outcome, new competitors face a de facto barrier to entry, and a data monopoly threatens the free market's ability to compete.
- **AIoT and Confidentiality:** The whole private life of a person can be documented, utilized unfairly, or misused. Contractors have access to live recordings of the Google Assistant, Alexa from Amazon, and Cortana from Microsoft. When Apple's Siri covertly recorded conversations between doctors and patients about specific unlawful behaviors and sexual encounters, it raised serious ethical concerns in the past [78]. Delaying this is necessary. Apple has made a commitment to protecting consumer privacy. Privacy has become a severe issue as messages from various vendors continue to clutter message boxes on personal mobile phones and employees of banks and other organizations sell customers' private data for two pence with no recourse for the victim.
- **AIoT Data Protections:** Due to the widespread use of sensors in intelligent houses, hospitals, and cities, a significant quantity of biometric data, including voice, activity, pulse, and picture data, may be acquired from AIoT users or uninformed participants. This raises significant concerns about the safety of data. Whose property are these documents? How long will this information be kept? What purpose will this data serve?
- **AIoT Device Connectivity:** Currently, we must link every piece of technology and device in our environment to the internet. Basic devices, such lighting and temperature sensors, can connect over Bluetooth [78] or ZigBee, although these are offline protocols. These gadgets are still unable to access the internet, even if more advanced industrial equipment is likely to interact through OPC or proprietary socket connections.
- **AIoT Energy Usage:** The expansion of cloud computing facilities is corresponding with the expansion of AIoT applications. Therefore, additional efforts should be made to reduce data center energy use. Data centers will account for more than a third of that, or around 22% of communication technology's overall energy use. Optimizing data center energy efficiency [79] is therefore essential in the long run.

1.11 CONCLUSION

Artificial Intelligence of Things (AIoT), a brand-new technological environment, is created when the Internet of Things (IoT) and Artificial Intelligence (AI) are joined. The Internet of Things (IoT) is already transforming how people live. Consider IoT devices as the system's brain and AI as its digital nervous system. Artificial Intelligence in the things has given IoT operations and human–machine interactions a new lease on life. The difficulties posed by IoT development can now be solved because to recent developments in AI. As an outcome, the trend of combining AI with IoT technologies shows potential for promoting the healthy evolution of the IoT ecosystem. Artificial Intelligence (AIoT) will advance the Internet of Things (IoT), resulting in autonomous future communication architectures that will allow intelligent data exchange across millions of devices. Thanks to AIoT technology, users may get quick responses, which increase their happiness. AIoT fusion is becoming more and more popular since it is expected to push the boundaries of data processing and intelligent learning for years to come. In the end of this essay, we emphasize the open and promising future of AIoT systems.

1.12 AIoT IN THE FUTURE

It is now inevitable that AI and IoT will combine. AIoT as a framework is anticipated to benefit a variety of corporate use cases. With billions of smart gadgets on the market, Artificial Intelligence will be needed to develop solutions rather than a replacement for secure and reliable ones. This is groundbreaking and beneficial for both technologies since IoT adds value through better connection, signaling, and data sharing while Artificial Intelligence enhances data analytics and ability to make decisions via machine learning. Edge computing is expected to see more advanced AI processors that are affordable for practical use, guaranteeing that AIoT will lead the way in almost every industry, including hospitality, urban planning, self-driving and transportation, communications, VLSI, industrial automation, and almost every other one. The Internet of Things (IoT) cannot be ignored. Humanity is anticipated to gain from the Internet of Things (IoT) in a variety of fascinating and significant methods. We are only now starting to reap the benefits of this new technology, despite its promising potential.

REFERENCES

[1] N. Akhtar, Bedine Kerim, Y. Perwej, Anurag Tiwari, Sheeba Praveen, "A Comprehensive Overview of Privacy and Data Security for Cloud Storage", *International Journal of Scientific Research in Science, Engineering and Technology*, Volume 8, Issue 5, Pages 113–152, 2021, DOI: 10.32628/IJSRSET21852

[2] Y. Perwej, "An Experiential Study of the Big Data", *International Transaction of Electrical and Computer Engineers System, USA, Science and Education Publishing*, Volume 4, Issue 1, Pages 14–25, 2017, DOI: 10.12691/iteces-4-1-3

[3] S. Korade, V. Kotak, A. Durafe, "A review paper on internet of things (IoT) and its applications", *International Research Journal of Engineering and Technology*, Volume 6, Pages 1623–1630, 2019

[4] Y. Perwej, Firoj Parwej, Mumdouh Mirghani Mohamed Hassan, Nikhat Akhtar, "The Internet-of-Things (IoT) Security: A Technological Perspective and Review", *International Journal of Scientific Research in Computer Science Engineering and Information Technology*, Volume 5, Issue 1, Pages 462–482, 2019, DOI: 10.32628/CSEIT195193

[5] Nikhat Akhtar, Firoj Parwej, Yusuf Perwej, "A Perusal of Big Data Classification and Hadoop Technology", *International Transaction of Electrical and Computer Engineers System, USA*, Volume 4, Issue 1, Pages 26–38, 2017, DOI: 10.12691/iteces-4-1-4

[6] E. Lamarre, B. May, "Ten trends shaping the internet of things business landscape", *McKinsey Digital*, 2019.

[7] Y. Perwej, Mahmoud Ahmed AbouGhaly, Bedine Kerim and Hani Ali Mahmoud Harb. "An Extended Review on Internet of Things (IoT) and its Promising Applications", *Communications on Applied Electronics (CAE)*, New York, USA, Volume 9, Issue 26, Pages 8–22, 2019, DOI: 10.5120/cae2019652812

[8] L. Chettri, R. Bera "A comprehensive survey on Internet of Things (IoT) toward 5G wireless systems", *IEEE Internet Things*, Volume 7, Pages 16–32, 2019.

[9] Abdulhafis Abdulazeezosuwa et al., "Application of artificial intelligence in internet of things", *9th International, Conference on Computational Intelligence and Communication Networks (CICN)*, IEEE, Cyprus, 2018.

[10] G. Zhiwei, "Secure Artificial Intelligence of Things for Implicit Group Recommendations", IEEE, 2021, DOI: 10.1109/JIOT.2021.3079574

[11] A. Poniszewska-Maranda and D. Kaczmarek, "Selected methods of artificial intelligence for Internet of Things conception", *Federated Conference on Computer Science and Information Systems*, Volume 5, Pages 1343–1348, 2015

[12] Yusuf Perwej, Md Husamuddin, Fokrul Alom Mazarbhuiya, "An Extensive Investigate the MapReduce Technology", *International Journal of Computer Sciences and Engineering*, Volume 5, Issue 10, Pages 218–225, 2017, DOI: 10.26438/ijcse/v5i10.218225

[13] C. Christian, A. Elli, Angelo De Caro, K. Andreas, O. Mike, S. Simon, S. Alessandro, V. Marko et al., "Blockchain cryptography and consensus", *IBM Research Zurich*, June 2017.

[14] N. U. Hassan, C. Yuen, and D. Niyato, "Blockchain technologies for smart energy systems: Fundamentals, challenges, and solutions", *IEEE Industrial Electronics Magazine*, Volume 13, Issue 4, Pages 106–118, 2019.

[15] Y. Perwej, Nikhat Akhtar, Firoj Parwej, "A Technological Perspective of Blockchain Security", *International Journal of Recent Scientific Research (IJRSR)*, Volume 9, Issue 11, (A), Pages 29472–29493, 2018, DOI: 10.24327/ijrsr.2018.0911.2869

[16] Yusuf Perwej, Firoj Parwej, "A Neuroplasticity (Brain Plasticity) Approach to Use in Artificial Neural Network", *International Journal of Scientific & Engineering Research, France*, Volume 3, Issue 6, Pages 1–9, 2012, DOI: 10.13140/2.1.1693.2808

[17] Y. Perwej, Faiyaz Ahamad, Mohammad Zunnun Khan, Nikhat Akhtar, "An Empirical Study on the Current State of Internet of Multimedia Things (IoMT)", *International Journal of Engineering Research in Computer Science and Engineering (IJERCSE)*, Volume 8, Issue 3, Pages 25–42, 2021, DOI: 10.1617/vol8/iss3/pid85026

[18] Yusuf Perwej, Bedine Kerim, Mohmed Sirelkhtem Adrees, Osama E. Sheta, "An Empirical Exploration of the Yarn in Big Data", *International Journal of Applied Information Systems (IJAIS), Foundation of Computer Science FCS*, New York, USA, Volume 12, Issue 9, Pages 19–29, 2017, DOI: 10.5120/ijais2017451730

[19] Yusuf Perwej, "The Hadoop Security in Big Data: A Technological Viewpoint and Analysis", *International Journal of Scientific Research in Computer Science and Engineering (IJSRCSE)*, Volume 7, Issue 3, Pages 1–14, 2019, DOI: 10.26438/ijsrcse/v7i3.1014

[20] Yusuf Perwej, Nikhat Akhtar, Firoj Parwej, "The Kingdom of Saudi Arabia Vehicle License Plate Recognition using Learning Vector Quantization Artificial Neural Network", *International Journal of Computer Applications, USA*, Volume 98, Issue 11, Pages 32–38, 2014, DOI: 10.5120/17230-7556

[21] A. Ouaddah, A.A. Elkalam, A.A. Ouahman, "Towards a Novel Privacy-Preserving Access Control Model Based on Blockchain Technology in IoT", In *Europe and MENA Cooperation Advances in Information and Communication Technologies*, Springer: Cham, Switzerland, 2017; Volume 520, Pages 523–533.

[22] K. Venkatesh et al., "Role of Artificial Intelligence of Things (AIoT)inCovid-19Pandemic: A Brief Survey", *6th International Conference on Internet of Things, Big Data and Security*, Pages 229–236, ISBN: 978-989-758-504-3, 2021.

[23] L.D. Xu, W. He, S. Li, IoT in industries: A survey. *IEEE Transactions on Industrial Informatics*, Volume 10, Pages 2233–2243, 2014.

[24] S.B. Calo, M. Touna, D.C. Verma, A. Cullen, Edge computing architecture for applying AI to IoT. In: *2017 IEEE International Conference on Big Data*, Pages 3012–3016, 2017, DOI:10.1109/BigData.2017.8258272

[25] Nikhat Akhtar, Saima Rahman, Halima Sadia, Yusuf Perwej, "A Holistic Analysis of Medical Internet of Things (MIoT)", *Journal of Information and Computational Science (JOICS)*, Volume 11, Issue 4, Pages 209–222, 2021, DOI:10.12733/JICS.2021/V11I3.535569.31023

[26] Jeffrey C. Kimmell et al., "Recurrent Neural Networks Based Online Behavioural Malware Detection Techniques for Cloud Infrastructure", *IEEE Access*, Volume 9, Pages 68066–68080, 2021.

[27] Y. Perwej, "Recurrent Neural Network Method in Arabic Words Recognition System", *International Journal of Computer Science and Telecommunications*, Volume 3, Issue 11, Pages 43–48, 2012.

[28] Shobhit Kumar Ravi, Shivam Chaturvedi, Neeta Rastogi, Nikhat Akhtar, Yusuf Perwej, "A Framework for Voting Behavior Prediction Using Spatial Data", *International Journal of Innovative Research in Computer Science & Technology (IJIRCST)*, Volume 10, Issue 2, Pages 19–28, 2022, DOI: 10.55524/ijircst.2022.10.2.4

[29] D. Miller, "Blockchain and the Internet of Things in the industrial sector", *IT Professional*, Volume 20, Pages 15–18, 2018.

[30] O. Debauche, S. Mahmoudi, S.A. Mahmoudi, P. Manneback, F. Lebeau, "A new edge architecture for ai-iot services deployment", *Procedia Computer Science*, Volume 175, Pages 10–19, 2020. DOI: 10.1016/j.procs.2020.07.006

[31] F.R. Yu, J.M. Liu, Y. He, P.B. Si, Y.H. Zhang, "Virtualization for distributed ledger technology (VDLT)", *IEEE Access* 2018, 6, 25019–25028

[32] S.B. Calo, M. Touna, D.C. Verma, A. Cullen, "Edge computing architecture for applying AI to IoT". In: *IEEE International Conference on Big Data (Big Data)*. IEEE. Pages 3012–3016, 2017.

[33] Li, H., Ota, K., Dong, M.: Learning iot in edge: Deep learning for the internet of things with edge computing. *IEEE Network*, Volume 32, Issue 1, Pages 96–101, 2018.

[34] Yusuf Perwej, "An Evaluation of Deep Learning Miniature Concerning in Soft Computing", *The International Journal of Advanced Research in Computer and Communication Engineering*, Volume 4, Issue 2, Pages 10–16, 2015, DOI: 10.17148/IJARCCE.2015.4203

[35] T. Ermakova, B. Fabian, R. Zarnekow, "Security and privacy system requirements for adopting cloud computing in healthcare data sharing scenarios", 2013.

[36] J. Xiong, H. Chen, Challenges for building a cloud native scalable and trustable multi-tenant AIoT platform. In: *2020 IEEE/ACM International Conference on Computer Aided Design (ICCAD)*, Pages 1–8, 2020.

[37] T.-C. Chiu, Y.-Y. Shih, A.-C. Pang, C.-S. Wang, W. Weng, C.-T. Chou, Semi-supervised distributed learning with non-data for AIoT service platform. *IEEE Internet of Things Journal*, 2020. doi:10.1109/JIOT.2020.2995162

[38] H. Li, K. Ota, M. Dong, "Learning IoT in edge: Deep learning for the internet of things with edge computing", *IEEE Network* 32(1):96–101, 2018

[39] J. Xiong, H. Chen, "Challenges for building a cloud native scalable and trust-able multi-tenant AIoT platform", In *IEEE/ACM International Conference On Computer Aided Design (ICCAD)*, IEEE, pp 1–8, 2020.

[40] T.-C. Chiu, Y.-Y. Shih, A.-C. Pang, C.-S. Wang, W. Weng, C.-T. Chou, "Semi supervised distributed learning with non-iid data for AIoT service platform", *IEEE IT*, 2020.

[41] Y. Perwej, Kashiful Haq, Firoj Parwej, M. M. Mohamed Hassan, "The Internet of Things (IoT) and its Application Domains", *International Journal of Computer Applications (IJCA)*, USA, ISSN 0975–8887, Volume 182, Issue 49, Pages 36–49, 2019, DOI: 10.5120/ijca2019918763

[42] D. Lily, B. Chan, T. G. Wang, "A Simple Explanation of Neural Network in Artificial Intelligence", *IEEE Transactions on Control Systems Technology*, Volume 247, Pages 1529–5651, 2013.

[43] Y. Perwej, Asif Perwej, "Prediction of the Bombay Stock Exchange (BSE) Market Returns Using Artificial Neural Networks and Genetic Algorithms", *Journal of Intelligent Learning Systems and Applications (JILSA)*, Volume 4, Issue 2, Pages 108–119, 2012, DOI: 10.4236/jilsa.2012.42010

[44] A. Ghosh, D. Chakraborty, A. Law, "Artificial intelligence in internet of things", *CAAI Transactions on Intelligence Technology*, Volume 3, Issue 4, Pages 208–218, 2018.

[45] Yusuf Perwej, Majzoob K. Omer, Osama E. Sheta, Hani Ali M. Harb, Mohmed S. Adrees, "The Future of Internet of Things (IoT) and Its Empowering Technology", *International Journal of Engineering Science and Computing (IJESC)*, Volume 9, Issue No. 3, Pages 20192– 20203, 2019.

[46] Tsai, C.-C.; Cheng, Y.-M.; Tsai, Y.-S.; Lou, S.-J. "Impacts of AIOT Implementation Course on the Learning Outcomes of Senior High School Students", *Education Sciences*, 11, 82, 2021.

[47] P.P. Ray, D. Dash, D. De, "Edge computing for internet of things: A survey, e-healthcare case study and future direction", *Journal of Network and Computer Applications* 140:1–22, 2019.

[48] V. Ricquebourg, D. Menga, D. Durand, B. Marhic, L. Delahoche, C. Loge, The smart home concept: our immediate future. In: *1st IEEE International Conference on E-learning in Industrial Electronics*. pp 23–28, 2006.

[49] D. Lucke, C. Constantinescu, E. Westkämper, "Smart factory-a step towards the next generation of manufacturing. In: *Manufacturing Systems and Technologies for the New Frontier*", Springer, London. pp 115–118, 2008.

[50] Asif Perwej, K. P. Yadav, Vishal Sood, Yusuf Perwej, "An Evolutionary Approach to Bombay Stock Exchange Prediction with Deep Learning Technique", *IOSR Journal of Business and Management (IOSR-JBM)*, Volume 20, Issue 12, Ver. V, Pages 63–79, 2018, DOI: 10.9790/487X-2012056379

[51] M. Ge, X. Fu, N. Syed, Z. Baig, G. Teo and A Robles-Kelly, "Deep learning-based intrusion detection for IoT networks", *IEEE 24th Pacific Rim International Symposium on Dependable Computing (PRDC)*, Pages 256–25609, 2019.

[52] Tewari and B. B. Gupta, "A robust anonymity preserving authentication protocol for IoT devices", *Consumer Electronics (ICCE) 2018 IEEE International Conference on*, Pages 1–5, 2018.

[53] Nikhat Akhtar, Nazia Tabassum, Asif Perwej, Yusuf Perwej, "Data Analytics and Visualization Using Tableau Utilitarian for COVID-19 (Coronavirus)", *Global Journal of Engineering and Technology Advances*, Volume 3, Issue 2, Pages 28–50, 2020, DOI: 10.30574/gjeta.2020.3.2.0029

[54] A. H. Sodhro, S. Pirbhulal, V. H. C. de Albuquerque, "Artificial intelligence-driven mechanism for edge computing-based industrial applications", *IEEE Transactions on Industrial Informatics*, Volume 15, Issue 7, Pages 4235–4243, Jul. 2019.

[55] K. Zhou, Taigang Liu, Lifeng Zhou, "Industry 4.0: Towards future industrial opportunities and challenges", *Conference on Fuzzy Systems and Knowledge Discovery*, Pages 2147–2152, 2015.

[56] Y. Perwej, Ashish Chaturvedi, "Machine Recognition of Hand Written Characters using Neural Networks", *International Journal of Computer Applications (IJCA)*, USA, Volume 14, Issue 2, Pages 6–9, 2011, DOI: 10.5120/1819-2380

[57] González García. et al., "A review of artificial intelligence in the internet of things", *International Journal of Interactive Multimedia and Artificial Intelligence*, 2019.

[58] Przemek Lopaciuk, "These Three Industries are About to be Hit by AIoT", readwrite, 7 June 2020.

[59] M. Poniszewska et al., "Selected methods of artificial intelligence for internet of things conception", *Federated Conference on Computer Science and Information Systems (FedCSIS)*, pages 1343–1348, IEEE, 2015.

[60] W. Yang, S. Wang, G. Zheng, J. Yang, and C. Valli, "A privacy-preserving lightweight biometric system for internet of things security", *IEEE Communications Magazine*, Volume 57, Issue 3, Pages 84–89, 2019.

[61] F.-C. Ghesu, B. Georgescu, Y. Zheng, S. Grbic, A. Maier, J. Hornegger, and D. Comaniciu, "Multi-scale deep reinforcement learning for realtime 3d-landmark detection in CT scans", *IEEE Transactions on Pattern Analysis and Machine Intelligence*, Volume 41, Issue 1, Pages 176–189, 2017

[62] Aparna Trivedi, Chandan Mani Tripathi, Yusuf Perwej, Ashish Kumar Srivastava, Neha Kulshrestha, "Face Recognition Based Automated Attendance Management System", *International Journal of Scientific Research in Science and Technology (IJSRST)*, Volume 9, Issue 1, Pages 261–268, 2022, DOI: 10.32628/IJSRST229147

[63] Kameswara Rao Poranki, Yusuf Perwej, Nikhat Akhtar, "Integration of SCM and ERP for Competitive Advantage", *International Journal's-Research Journal of Science & IT Management of Singapore, Singapore*, Volume 4, Number 5, Pages 17–24, 2015.

[64] Z. Zhu, D. Liang, S. Zhang, X. Huang, B. Li, and S. Hu, "Traffic-sign detection and classification in the wild", in *Proceedings of the IEEE Conference on Computer Vision and Pattern Recognition*, 2016, Pages 2110–2118.

[65] E. Mocanu, D. C. Mocanu, P. H. Nguyen, A. Liotta, M. E. Webber, M. Gibescu, and J. G. Slootweg, "On-line building energy optimization using deep reinforcement learning", *IEEE Transactions on Smart Grid*, Volume 10, Issue 4, Pages 3698–3708, 2018.

[66] B. H. Y. Alsalam, K. Morton, D. Campbell, and F. Gonzalez, "Autonomous UAV with vision based on-board decision making for remote sensing and precision agriculture", in *Proceedings of the IEEE Aerospace Conference*, Pages 1–12, 2017.

[67] Shubham Mishra, Versha Verma, Nikhat Akhtar, Shivam Chaturvedi, Yusuf Perwej, "An Intelligent Motion Detection Using OpenCV", *International Journal of Scientific Research in Science, Engineering and Technology (IJSRSET)*, Volume 9, Issue 2, Pages 51–63, 2022, DOI: 10.32628/IJSRSET22925

[68] Kameswara Rao Poranki, Yusuf Perwej, Asif Perwej, "The Level of Customer Satisfaction related to GSM in India", *International Journal's-Research Journal of Science & IT Management*, Volume 04, Number: 03, Pages 29–36, 2015.

[69] Shubham Mishra, Versha Verma, Nikhat Akhtar, Shivam Chaturvedi, Yusuf Perwej, "An Intelligent Motion Detection Using OpenCV", *International Journal of Scientific Research in Science, Engineering and Technology (IJSRSET)*, Volume 9, Issue 2, Pages 51–63, March-April 2022, DOI: 10.32628/IJSRSET22925

[70] J. Pan, R. Jain, S. Paul, T. Vu, A. Sai., and M. Sha, "An internet of things framework for smart energy in buildings: designs, prototype, and experiments", *IEEE Internet of Things Jou.*, Volume 2, Issue 6, Pages 527–537, 2015.

[71] S. He, M. Han, N. Patel, and Z. Li, "Converting handwritten text to editable format via gesture recognition for education", in *Proceedings of the 51st ACM Technical Symposium on Computer Science Education*, 2020, Pages 1369–1369

[72] Z. Xiaoyi, W. Dongling, Z. Yuming, K. B. Manokaran and A. Benny Antony, "IoT driven framework based efficient green energy management in smart cities using multi-objective distributed dispatching algorithm", *Environmental Impact Assessment Review*, Volume 88, Pages 106567, 2021.

[73] M. M. Hosseini, A. Umunnakwe, M. Parvania, and T. Tasdizen, "Intelligent damage classification and estimation in power distribution poles using unmanned aerial vehicles and convolutional neural networks", *IEEE Transactions on Smart Grid*, 2020.

[74] K. Chen, J. Hu, and J. He, "Detection and classification of transmission line faults based on unsupervised feature learning and convolutional sparse autoencoder", *IEEE Transactions on Smart Grid*, Volume 9, Issue 3, Pages 1748–1758, 2016.

[75] R. Al-Ali, I. A. Zualkernan, M. Rashid, R. Gupta and M. Alikarar, "A smart home energy management system using IoT and big data analytics approach", *IEEE Trans. Consum. Electron.*, Volume 63, Issue 4, Pages 426–434, 2017.

[76] Al-Mushayt O., Haq Kashiful, Yusuf Perwej, "Electronic-Government in Saudi Arabia; a Positive Revolution in the Peninsula", *International Transactions in Applied Sciences*, Volume 1, Number 1, Pages 87–98, 2009.

[77] Y. Perwej, "The Bidirectional Long-Short-Term Memory Neural Network based Word Retrieval for Arabic Documents", *Transactions on Machine Learning and Artificial Intelligence (TMLAI)*, Volume 3, Issue 1, Pages 16–27, 2015, DOI: 10.14738/tmlai.31.863

[78] Dixit, Nikhat Akhtar, Anurag Kumar Jaiswal, "A Systematic Literature Review on the Cyber Security", *International Journal of Scientific Research and Management (IJSRM)*, Volume 9, Issue 12, Pages 669–710, 2021, DOI: 10.18535/ijsrm/v9i12.ec04

[79] Y. Perwej, Kashiful Haq, Uruj Jaleel, Sharad Saxena, "Some Drastic Improvements Found in the Analysis of Routing Protocol for the Bluetooth Technology Using Scatternet", *Special Issue on The International Conference on Computing, Communications and Information Technology Applications (CCITA-2010)*, which is published by Ubiquitous Computing and Communication Journal (UBICC), Seoul, South Korea, ISSN Online: 1992-8424, ISSN Print: 1994-4608, Volume CCITA-2010, Number 5, Pages 86–95, 2010.

[80] E. Oró, V. Depoorter, A. Garcia and J. Salom, "Energy efficiency and renewable energy integration in datacenters. Strategies and modelling review", *Renewable and Sustainable Energy Reviews*, Volume 42, Issue C, Pages 429–445, 2015.

Chapter 2

Convergence of Artificial Intelligence with the Internet of Things towards Industry 4.0

J.S. Kale

MGM College of Engineering, Nanded Maharashtra, India

2.1 INTRODUCTION

In an era marked by the relentless pursuit of innovation and efficiency, the amalgamation of cutting-edge technologies has paved the way for the fourth industrial revolution, commonly referred to as Industry 4.0. This transformative paradigm shift represents a convergence of digitalization, automation, and data-driven decision-making that has revolutionized modern manufacturing processes. At its core, Industry 4.0 embodies a fundamental reconfiguration of industrial operations, fostering a new era of intelligent and interconnected production systems.

2.1.1 Industry 4.0: A modern manufacturing renaissance

In the annals of industrial history, each epoch has witnessed a profound transformation in manufacturing techniques. From mechanization during the first industrial revolution to mass production in the second and automation in the third, each phase brought about substantial advances [5]. However, it is Industry 4.0 that is set to redefine manufacturing in ways previously unimaginable.

Industry 4.0 is characterized by the pervasive use of digital technologies to create "smart factories" where physical systems seamlessly interconnect with cyber-physical systems. These smart factories employ real-time data analytics, machine learning, and AI to optimize production processes, resulting in increased efficiency, reduced waste, and enhanced product quality. This paradigm shift is not limited to a single industry but has far-reaching implications across sectors, from automotive and aerospace to healthcare and agriculture.

2.1.2 The pillars of Industry 4.0: Artificial Intelligence and the Internet of Things

At the heart of Industry 4.0 lie two foundational technologies: Artificial Intelligence (AI) and the Internet of Things (IoT). These transformative

DOI: 10.1201/9781003509240-2

forces have enabled machines to transcend their traditional roles as mere tools and evolve into intelligent entities capable of autonomous decision-making [3].

Artificial Intelligence, often described as the simulation of human intelligence by machines, encompasses a wide spectrum of capabilities, including machine learning, deep learning, and natural language processing. These AI techniques empower machines to learn from data, adapt to changing circumstances, and make predictions or decisions based on patterns and insights extracted from vast datasets. In the context of Industry 4.0, AI is the driving force behind predictive maintenance, quality control, and the optimization of production schedules.

The Internet of Things, on the other hand, represents a network of interconnected physical devices and objects embedded with sensors, software, and connectivity features that enable them to collect and exchange data. IoT enables the real-time monitoring and control of devices and systems across vast manufacturing environments. In Industry 4.0, IoT sensors and devices serve as the eyes and ears of the smart factory, providing a continuous stream of data for AI algorithms to analyze and act upon.

This chapter aims to provide a comprehensive exploration of the convergence of Artificial Intelligence with the Internet of Things towards Industry 4.0. The following objectives guide our exploration:

1. To elucidate the evolution and significance of Industry 4.0 in modern manufacturing.
2. To define the core concepts of Artificial Intelligence and the Internet of Things in the context of Industry 4.0.
3. To examine how the convergence of AI and IoT is shaping the future of manufacturing.
4. To analyze real-world applications and case studies highlighting the synergistic benefits of AI and IoT in Industry 4.0.
5. To address the challenges, considerations, and future prospects associated with this convergence.

In this chapter we delve into the historical evolution of Industry 4.0 and its impact on diverse industries.

Section 2.2 defines and explains the fundamental concepts of Artificial Intelligence and the Internet of Things. Section 2.3 explores the convergence of AI and IoT in the context of Industry 4.0, accompanied by illustrative examples. Section 2.4 navigates through the practical applications and benefits of this convergence. Furthermore, Section 2.5 is devoted to addressing the challenges and ethical considerations, while offers a glimpse into future trends and possibilities. Various future trends and outlooks are discussed in Section 2.6. Finally, Section 2.7 concludes the chapter, summarizing key takeaways and providing insights for researchers and practitioners alike.

2.2 BACKGROUND

The evolution of Industry 4.0, often dubbed the fourth industrial revolution, has ushered in a transformative era of manufacturing and production. Rooted in technological advancements and the growing interconnectivity of the digital world, Industry 4.0 represents a profound shift in how industries operate, optimize processes, and deliver value to customers. In this section, we consider the historical development of Industry 4.0, its far-reaching impact across diverse sectors, and the fundamental concepts of Artificial Intelligence (AI) and the Internet of Things (IoT) that underpin this revolution.

2.2.1 Evolution of Industry 4.0 and its impact

The journey towards Industry 4.0 can be traced back to the early 2010s when digitalization, automation, and data-driven decision-making converged to redefine manufacturing. [1] The previous industrial revolutions laid the foundation for this transformation. The first introduced mechanization, while the second brought mass production, and the third ushered in computerization and automation. Industry 4.0 builds upon these foundations, emphasizing the fusion of the physical and digital worlds.

One of the defining characteristics of Industry 4.0 is the integration of cyber-physical systems (CPS) into industrial processes. These CPS are the nexus between the physical components of production, such as machines and robots, and the digital components, including sensors, data analytics, and AI algorithms. This integration has enabled the emergence of "smart factories" capable of real-time monitoring, decision-making, and optimization.

The impact of Industry 4.0 extends across various industries, ranging from manufacturing to healthcare, agriculture, logistics, and beyond. In manufacturing, it has paved the way for intelligent, self-optimizing production lines that reduce downtime, enhance product quality, and streamline supply chains. In healthcare, it has enabled remote patient monitoring and personalized treatment plans. In agriculture, it has led to precision farming techniques that maximize crop yields while conserving resources. The common thread among these industries is the relentless pursuit of efficiency and innovation that Industry 4.0 facilitates.

2.2.2 Core concepts of AI and IoT

To understand the essence of Industry 4.0, it is imperative to grasp the core concepts of Artificial Intelligence (AI) and the Internet of Things (IoT), the two technological pillars that empower this revolution.

Artificial Intelligence (AI): AI encompasses a broad spectrum of technologies that enable machines to mimic human intelligence and reasoning. Machine learning, a subset of AI, equips machines with the ability to learn from data, recognize patterns, and make predictions or decisions based on insights gleaned from vast datasets. Deep learning, a subset of machine learning, is inspired by neural networks and excels in tasks like image recognition and natural language processing [12]. AI systems can perceive their environment, reason about it, and act autonomously to achieve specific goals. In Industry 4.0, AI is the engine that drives predictive maintenance, quality control, and intelligent decision-making, optimizing manufacturing processes.

Internet of Things (IoT): IoT refers to the network of interconnected physical devices embedded with sensors, software, and communication capabilities. These devices, which range from sensors on factory equipment to wearable health monitors and smart home appliances, collect and transmit data to central hubs or the cloud. IoT enables the real-time monitoring, control, and coordination of devices and systems across vast, geographically dispersed environments. In Industry 4.0, IoT sensors serve as the eyes and ears of smart factories, continuously generating data that fuels AI-driven analytics and decision-making.

2.2.3 Role of AI and IoT in the context of Industry 4.0

In the context of Industry 4.0, AI and IoT are not mere technologies but the linchpins that bridge the physical and digital realms. Their roles are as follows:

AI's Role: AI empowers machines to analyze massive datasets in real time, enabling the identification of patterns, anomalies, and trends that human operators might miss. It facilitates predictive maintenance by analyzing equipment data to foresee breakdowns, minimizing downtime [11]. Additionally, AI enhances quality control by inspecting products with greater precision than human inspectors. It optimizes production schedules by adjusting them dynamically in response to changing conditions, leading to improved efficiency and resource utilization.

IoT's Role: IoT sensors and devices form the foundation of Industry 4.0 by collecting and transmitting data from machines, products, and the factory environment. This real-time data stream provides insights into equipment health, production status, and environmental conditions. [14] IoT facilitates remote monitoring, enabling operators to supervise multiple sites simultaneously. Furthermore, it enables the automation of routine tasks and the orchestration of complex workflows, contributing to increased productivity and operational agility.

The synergy between AI and IoT is at the heart of Industry 4.0, allowing industries to achieve unprecedented levels of efficiency, agility, and competitiveness. This convergence is the driving force behind the modern manufacturing renaissance that is reshaping industries across the globe. In the subsequent sections of this chapter, which delve deeper into the practical applications, benefits, challenges, and future prospects of this powerful synergy.

2.3 CONVERGENCE OF AI AND IoT

The convergence of Artificial Intelligence (AI) and the Internet of Things (IoT) is the cornerstone of the Industry 4.0 revolution. These two transformative technologies are converging and complementing each other in unprecedented ways, reshaping industries and opening new avenues for innovation. This section will explore how AI and IoT technologies are merging, the advantages of this convergence, and present real-world examples and case studies that illustrate their powerful synergy across diverse sectors.

2.3.1 Applicability of AIoT

The convergence of AI and IoT signifies the amalgamation of data generation, data analysis, and decision-making within a unified framework. Here's how these technologies are coming together:

- **Data Fusion and Analysis:** IoT devices, equipped with sensors and communication capabilities, generate vast amounts of data. AI, especially machine learning and deep learning algorithms, can process and analyze this data in real-time. By applying AI to IoT-generated data, it becomes possible to extract meaningful insights, identify patterns, and make informed decisions.
- **Edge Computing:** Edge computing is a crucial component of the AI and IoT convergence. It involves processing data locally on IoT devices or at the edge of the network, rather than sending all data to centralized cloud servers [5]. AI models can be deployed on IoT devices or edge servers, allowing for faster response times and reduced latency. This edge intelligence is vital for applications that require real-time decision-making, such as autonomous vehicles and industrial automation.
- **Predictive Analytics:** AI can be used to create predictive models based on IoT data. For instance, predictive maintenance systems can use AI algorithms to analyze data from sensors on machinery to predict when maintenance is needed, reducing downtime and maintenance costs.

2.3.2 Benefits of combining AI and IoT

The convergence of AI and IoT brings forth a multitude of benefits, significantly enhancing data analysis and decision-making capabilities:

- **Improved Data Analysis:** AI can process and analyze vast datasets generated by IoT devices much faster and more accurately than humans. This leads to better insights and more informed decisions.
- **Real-time Decision-Making:** The combination of AI and IoT at the edge enables real-time decision-making, critical in scenarios like autonomous vehicles, healthcare monitoring, and industrial automation.
- **Cost Reduction:** Predictive maintenance powered by AI and IoT can reduce equipment downtime and maintenance costs by addressing issues before they lead to failures.
- **Enhanced Product Quality:** AI-driven quality control systems in manufacturing can identify defects with high precision, improving product quality and reducing waste.

2.3.3 Real-world examples and case studies

Let's explore some real-world examples and case studies that showcase the power of AI and IoT convergence:

- **Healthcare:** In healthcare, wearable IoT devices, such as fitness trackers and health monitors, collect data on patients' vital signs [3]. AI algorithms analyze this data in real time, enabling early detection of health issues and providing personalized recommendations for patients.
- **Manufacturing:** Smart factories utilize IoT sensors to monitor equipment performance and product quality. AI algorithms analyze this data to optimize production processes, detect anomalies, and predict maintenance needs. For instance, a car manufacturer may use AI and IoT to ensure the quality of every component in real-time, reducing defects and enhancing efficiency [13].
- **Agriculture:** IoT sensors installed on farms collect data on soil conditions, weather, and crop health. AI analyzes this data to optimize irrigation, fertilization, and pest control, resulting in higher crop yields and resource conservation.
- **Energy Management:** Smart grids in the energy sector employ IoT devices to monitor electricity consumption in real-time. AI algorithms analyze this data to optimize energy distribution, reduce wastage, and enhance the reliability of the grid [9].
- **Retail:** AI-powered IoT sensors in retail stores track customer behavior and inventory levels. This data is used to personalize marketing, improve stock management, and enhance the overall shopping experience.

The real-world examples and case studies presented here underscore the transformative potential of the convergence of AI and IoT. In each industry, this synergy enhances efficiency, accuracy, and innovation, making Industry 4.0 a reality that is reshaping our world. The following sections, will delve into specific applications and the profound impact of AI and IoT convergence on manufacturing and other sectors.

2.4 APPLICATIONS OF AI AND IoT IN INDUSTRY 4.0

The convergence of Artificial Intelligence (AI) with the Internet of Things (IoT) has unleashed a wave of innovation in manufacturing and Industry 4.0 [10]. This section will delve into specific applications where AI and IoT are making a profound impact, including predictive maintenance, quality control, and supply chain optimization. Now will also discuss how AI-driven analytics are revolutionizing production processes and the advantages and challenges associated with these applications.

2.4.1 Predictive maintenance

Predictive maintenance represents a paradigm shift from traditional scheduled maintenance to a data-driven approach that aims to detect and address equipment issues before they lead to costly breakdowns [9]. AI and IoT play a pivotal role in this transformation:

- **Sensor-Driven Data Collection:** IoT sensors continuously collect data from industrial machinery, capturing parameters such as temperature, vibration, and wear and tear.
- **Real-time Analytics:** AI algorithms analyze this sensor data in real-time, looking for anomalies and patterns indicative of impending equipment failure.
- **Proactive Maintenance:** Predictive maintenance systems provide early warnings to maintenance teams, allowing them to schedule maintenance activities precisely when needed. This minimizes downtime and reduces maintenance costs.

2.4.2 Quality control

Ensuring product quality is paramount in manufacturing. AI and IoT synergize to enhance *quality control* processes:

- **Automated Inspection:** AI-powered cameras and sensors inspect products with precision, identifying defects that might escape human inspectors.

- **Real-time Feedback:** IoT sensors provide real-time data on production processes. AI algorithms analyze this data to make adjustments on the fly, preventing defects and improving product consistency.
- **Reduced Waste:** By catching defects early in the production process, manufacturers can reduce waste and optimize resource utilization.

2.4.3 Supply chain optimization

AI and IoT bring unprecedented visibility and efficiency to supply chain management:

- **Real-time Tracking:** IoT sensors attached to products and shipments enable real-time tracking and monitoring of goods in transit.
- **Demand Forecasting:** AI analyzes historical data and current market conditions to make accurate demand forecasts, enabling just-in-time inventory management.
- **Route Optimization:** AI algorithms optimize logistics by selecting the most efficient routes and modes of transportation, reducing costs and delivery times.

2.4.4 Impact of AI-driven analytics on production processes

Beyond specific applications, AI-driven analytics have a profound impact on overall production processes:

- **Efficiency:** AI optimizes production schedules, resource allocation, and energy consumption, leading to greater efficiency.
- **Customization:** AI allows for mass customization by adapting production processes on the fly to meet customer demands for personalized products.
- **Data-Driven Decision-Making:** AI provides actionable insights and data-driven decision support, enabling manufacturers to respond quickly to changing market conditions.

2.4.5 Advantages and challenges

- While the advantages of AI and IoT in Industry 4.0 are clear, there are also challenges that need to be addressed:
- Advantages:
  - Improved Efficiency: AI and IoT applications result in more efficient processes and resource utilization.
  - Cost Reduction: Predictive maintenance and quality control lead to reduced downtime and waste.

- Enhanced Product Quality: Quality control ensures consistent and high-quality products.
- Real-time Decision-Making: AI-driven analytics enable rapid responses to changing conditions.
- Competitive Advantage: Firms that adopt AI and IoT gain a competitive edge in the market.
- Challenges:
  - Data Security: The influx of data raises concerns about data security and privacy.
  - Integration Complexity: Integrating AI and IoT into existing systems can be complex and costly.
  - Skill Gaps: There is a shortage of skilled personnel who can develop and manage AI and IoT systems.
  - Ethical Concerns: The use of AI and IoT raises ethical issues, such as bias in algorithms and job displacement.
  - Initial Investment: Implementing AI and IoT solutions often requires a significant initial investment.

In conclusion, the applications of AI and IoT in Industry 4.0 are redefining manufacturing processes and supply chains. These technologies offer a multitude of advantages, from cost reduction to enhanced product quality and real-time decision-making [11]. However, they also come with challenges that must be carefully addressed to fully realize their potential in the industrial landscape. In the subsequent sections, we will delve into specific use cases and real-world examples that showcase the transformative power of AI and IoT in Industry 4.0.

2.5 CHALLENGES AND CONSIDERATIONS

The convergence of Artificial Intelligence (AI) with the Internet of Things (IoT) brings with it a multitude of transformative possibilities for Industry 4.0. However, its widespread adoption is not without its share of challenges and considerations that must be carefully addressed to ensure a successful and responsible integration.

2.5.1 Barriers to adoption

While the potential benefits of AI and IoT in Industry 4.0 are substantial, several barriers hinder their widespread adoption:

- **Cost of Implementation:** Deploying AI and IoT infrastructure can be capital-intensive, which may deter smaller enterprises from adopting these technologies.

- **Skills Gap:** The shortage of skilled professionals who can design, deploy, and manage AI and IoT systems remains a significant barrier.
- **Legacy Systems:** Many manufacturing facilities still rely on legacy systems that are not easily compatible with modern AI and IoT technologies.
- **Data Integration:** Integrating data from various sources and legacy systems can be complex, requiring careful planning and investment.
- **Resistance to Change:** Employees may resist adopting new technologies, requiring change management efforts.

2.5.2 Security and privacy concerns

The interconnected nature of AI and IoT systems presents unique security and privacy challenges:

- **Data Breaches:** The vast amount of data collected by IoT devices can be a target for cyber- attacks, leading to data breaches and the exposure of sensitive information.
- **Device Vulnerabilities:** IoT devices are often resource-constrained, making them susceptible to security vulnerabilities that can be exploited by attackers.
- **Data Privacy:** Concerns about the collection, storage, and use of personal data by IoT devices raise privacy issues that need to be addressed.
- **Regulatory Compliance:** Adhering to data protection regulations, such as GDPR, HIPAA, and industry-specific standards, is critical but can be complex in global supply chains.

2.5.3 Regulatory and ethical considerations

The integration of AI and IoT technologies into Industry 4.0 prompts regulatory and ethical considerations:

- **Regulatory Frameworks:** Governments and regulatory bodies are still developing comprehensive frameworks to govern the use of AI and IoT, creating uncertainty for businesses.
- **Ethical AI:** The design and use of AI algorithms must address ethical concerns, including bias, fairness, and transparency.
- **Job Displacement:** The automation enabled by AI and IoT may lead to job displacement, necessitating policies to support the workforce through retraining and up skilling.
- **Environmental Impact:** The energy consumption of AI and IoT infrastructure, if not managed efficiently, can have adverse environmental effects.
- **Data Sovereignty:** Issues related to data ownership and data sovereignty may arise when data is transmitted and stored across borders.

2.5.4 Addressing challenges and considerations

To overcome these challenges and ensure responsible adoption, organizations and policymakers must take several steps:

- **Invest in Education and Training:** Address the skills gap by investing in education and training programs to develop a skilled workforce capable of managing AI and IoT systems [7].
- **Prioritize Security:** Implement robust security measures, including encryption, authentication, and regular security assessments, to protect IoT devices and data.
- **Privacy by Design:** Build privacy considerations into the design and deployment of AI and IoT systems, ensuring compliance with data protection regulations.
- **Collaboration:** Collaborate with industry peers, regulators, and technology providers to establish best practices, standards, and guidelines for AI and IoT in Industry 4.0 [17].
- **Transparency and Accountability:** Maintain transparency in AI decision-making processes and establish mechanisms for accountability in case of unintended consequences.
- **Sustainability:** Implement energy-efficient practices and consider the environmental impact of AI and IoT deployments.

Addressing these challenges and considerations is paramount to unlocking the full potential of AI and IoT in Industry 4.0. By doing so, businesses can drive innovation, improve operational efficiency, and meet ethical and regulatory responsibilities, ensuring a responsible and sustainable future for Industry 4.0[1]. In the subsequent sections of this chapter, we will explore emerging trends and future prospects in the convergence of AI and IoT.

2.6 FUTURE TRENDS AND OUTLOOK

The convergence of Artificial Intelligence (AI) with the Internet of Things (IoT) has already made significant strides in reshaping Industry 4.0. Looking ahead, we can anticipate several emerging trends and innovations that promise to further accelerate this transformation and amplify its impact on various industries.

2.6.1 Emerging trends

- **Edge AI:** The deployment of AI algorithms at the edge, closer to where data is generated, will become more prevalent. This trend will enable faster decision-making, reduced latency, and enhanced privacy, particularly in applications such as autonomous vehicles and industrial automation.

- **5G Connectivity:** The rollout of 5G networks will provide high-speed, low-latency connectivity, enabling more IoT devices and applications to thrive [6]. This will be crucial for real-time data transmission and edge computing.
- **AIoT:** The integration of AI and IoT, often referred to as AIoT, will deepen. AIoT solutions will leverage advanced AI techniques, including reinforcement learning and natural language processing, to create smarter, more autonomous systems.
- **Interoperability Standards:** To facilitate the seamless integration of diverse IoT devices and systems, interoperability standards will continue to evolve, reducing complexity and promoting collaboration among technology providers.
- **AI-Powered Robotics:** In manufacturing and logistics, AI-driven robots will become more versatile and collaborative [5]. They will work alongside human operators, taking on complex tasks and improving productivity.

2.6.2 Potential advancements and innovations

- **Autonomous Factories:** AI and IoT will enable factories to operate autonomously, with machines and systems making real-time decisions about production schedules, maintenance, and quality control.
- **Digital Twins:** Digital twins, virtual replicas of physical assets or processes, will become more sophisticated. These twins will facilitate predictive modeling, optimization, and troubleshooting.
- **Personalized Production:** AI and IoT will enable mass customization, allowing consumers to order products tailored to their preferences. Factories will adapt production lines dynamically to accommodate these custom orders.
- **AI-Enhanced Healthcare:** Healthcare will see the rise of AI-powered medical devices and diagnostics, enabling earlier disease detection and personalized treatment plans.
- **Sustainable Manufacturing:** AI and IoT will be instrumental in achieving sustainability goals. They will optimize energy consumption, reduce waste, and promote eco-friendly practices in manufacturing [16].

2.6.3 Future impact on Industry 4.0

- The future impact of AI and IoT on Industry 4.0 is poised to be transformative:
- **Hyper-Efficiency:** As AI-driven analytics and IoT continue to evolve, manufacturing processes will become hyper-efficient, reducing waste, energy consumption, and production costs.
- **Mass Customization:** Consumers will enjoy a wider range of personalized products, and businesses will be able to respond rapidly to shifting market demands.

- **Smart Supply Chains:** IoT and AI will enable the creation of smart supply chains that are responsive, transparent, and resilient to disruptions.
- **Healthcare Revolution:** In healthcare, AI and IoT will revolutionize patient care with remote monitoring, early disease detection, and AI-assisted diagnostics.
- **Innovation Acceleration:** AI and IoT will foster innovation across industries by enabling data-driven insights, automation, and the development of new AI-driven products and services.
- **Global Competitiveness:** Countries and businesses that invest in AI and IoT capabilities will enhance their global competitiveness by staying at the forefront of Industry 4.0.

Looking to the future, it is evident that the convergence of AI and IoT will continue to drive Industry 4.0 forward, ushering in an era of unprecedented innovation, efficiency, and connectivity. To capitalize on these trends and innovations, organizations will need to adapt, invest in technology, and embrace the opportunities presented by AI and IoT, paving the way for a more dynamic and intelligent future in Industry 4.0.

2.7 CONCLUSION

This chapter embarked on a journey through the transformative landscape of Industry 4.0, where the convergence of Artificial Intelligence (AI) with the Internet of Things (IoT) is shaping the future of manufacturing and beyond. To conclude, let us reflect on the key points discussed and reiterate the profound significance of AI and IoT convergence in the context of Industry 4.0.

2.7.1 Key points summarized

Throughout this chapter, the following critical facets are explored:

- Introducing the concept of Industry 4.0, a modern manufacturing renaissance driven by digitalization, automation, and data-driven decision-making.
- Defined and explained the core concepts of AI and IoT, recognizing them as foundational pillars underpinning Industry 4.0's evolution.
- Examined the convergence of AI and IoT, highlighting how these technologies complement each other, share data, and together bring intelligence to the industrial ecosystem.
- Ventured into specific applications, such as predictive maintenance, quality control, and supply chain optimization, showcasing how AI and IoT are reshaping manufacturing processes, enhancing efficiency, and elevating product quality.

- Acknowledged the advantages and challenges associated with these applications, from cost reduction to data security and the need for workforce upskilling.
- Delved into the ethical and regulatory considerations surrounding AI and IoT deployments, recognizing the importance of responsible and accountable technology use.
- Glimpsed into the future, envisioning trends, innovations, and the far-reaching impact of AI and IoT on Industry 4.0, including hyper-efficiency, mass customization, and smart supply chains.

2.7.2 The profound significance of convergence

The convergence of AI and IoT represents the keystone of Industry 4.0, a force reshaping industries and economies worldwide. It holds the promise of elevating manufacturing and industrial processes to levels of efficiency, precision, and adaptability previously thought unattainable [2]. This synergy empowers us to unlock the full potential of data, translating it into actionable insights that drive innovation and competitiveness.

2.7.3 Recommendations for researchers and practitioners

As look forward to a future in which AI and IoT continue to converge and redefine Industry 4.0 offer the following recommendations:

- **Continuous Learning:** Researchers and practitioners should invest in ongoing education and training to stay abreast of the evolving landscape of AI and IoT technologies.
- **Security and Privacy:** Prioritize robust security measures and data privacy protocols to protect against emerging threats in an interconnected world.
- **Ethical AI:** Embrace ethical AI practices, ensuring transparency, fairness, and accountability in AI algorithms and decision-making.
- **Collaboration:** Foster collaboration among industry stakeholders, regulators, and technology providers to establish standards and best practices for AI and IoT integration.
- **Innovation:** Encourage a culture of innovation within organizations, promoting the development of AI-driven products, services, and solutions that align with Industry 4.0 goals.
- **Reskilling:** Recognize the importance of reskilling and upskilling the workforce to adapt to AI and IoT technologies, ensuring a smooth transition in the workplace.

In closing, the convergence of AI and IoT has ushered in a new era of intelligence and connectivity. It is reshaping industries, enhancing competitiveness, and revolutionizing the way to manufacture, produce, and deliver goods and services. As we embrace this transformative journey, we stand at the cusp of Industry 4.0's full realization, empowered by the synergy of AI and IoT, and poised to embrace a future marked by innovation, efficiency, and sustainable progress.

REFERENCES

[1] K. Schwab, "The Fourth Industrial Revolution," *World Economic Forum*, 2016. DOI: 10.1038/s41597-019-0212-1

[2] M. F. S. Othman, R. A. Othman, and N. F. Hani, "Internet of Things (IoT) in Industrial Applications: A Review," in *IEEE Region 10 Symposium (TENSYMP)*, 2016. DOI: 10.1109/TENCONSpring.2017.8070074

[3] T. M. Mitchell, *Machine Learning*, McGraw-Hill, 1997. DOI: 10.5555/207369.207371

[4] A. Madakam, R. N. Sheth, and S. B. Gohil, "Internet of Things (IoT): A Literature Review," in *IEEE Internet of Things Journal*, 2016. DOI: 10.1109/JIOT.2015.2498472

[5] V. N. Sundararajan, *Predictive Maintenance: Concepts and Methodologies*, CRC Press, 1993. DOI: 10.1201/9780367803321

[6] T. O. Boucher and N. J. Taylor, "AI in Quality Control: An Overview," in *Proceedings of the IEEE*, 1985. DOI: 10.1109/PROC.1985.13268

[7] W. D. Nordhaus, "The Health of Nations: The Contribution of Improved Health to Living Standards," NBER Working Paper No. 8818, 2002. DOI: 10.3386/w8818

[8] A. Agarwal and B. Mittal, "IoT in Agriculture: A Comprehensive Survey," in *IEEE Access*, 2017. DOI: 10.1109/ACCESS.2017.2734319

[9] M. Christopher, *Logistics & Supply Chain Management*, Pearson, 2016. DOI: 10.15358/9783800656733

[10] R. John, *AI for Everyone: Master the Basics*, Packt Publishing, 2021. DOI: 10.1002/9781119712336

[11] European Commission, "Ethics Guidelines for Trustworthy AI," 2019. DOI: 10.2777/053222

[12] J. L. Fingas, "AI and IoT Will Make New Demands on Chip Architectures," *Engadget*, 2017. DOI: 10.1109/MCE.2017.2714638.

[13] R. K. Gupta, R. P. Gupta, and M. Jain, "Challenges and Issues of IoT in 5G," in *IEEE International Conference on Advanced Networks and Telecommunications Systems (ANTS)*, 2016. DOI: 10.1109/ANTS.2016.7947821

[14] J. Gubbi et al., "Internet of Things (IoT): A Vision, Architectural Elements, and Future Directions," *Future Generation Computer Systems*, 2013. DOI: 10.1016/j.future.2012.07.001

[15] D. W. B. Skellern, "The Use of Artificial Intelligence and Expert Systems in Predictive Maintenance," *IEEE Transactions on Industry Applications*, 1991. DOI: 10.1109/28.81038

[16] B. C. Paul and K. P. R. Menon, "Internet of Things (IoT): A Vision, Architectural Elements, and Future Directions," *Procedia Computer Science*, 2016. DOI: 10.1016/j.procs.2016.04.036

[17] E. Brynjolfsson and A. McAfee, *The Second Machine Age: Work, Progress, and Prosperity in a Time of Brilliant Technologies*, W. W. Norton & Company, 2014. DOI: 10.1016/j.techfore.2013.10.120

[18] A. Luong et al., "A Survey of Internet of Things (IoT) Architecture, Protocols, Application, Security, Privacy, Real-Time Issues, and Future Directions," *Journal of King Saud University - Computer and Information Sciences*, 2019. DOI: 10.1016/j.jksuci.2018.05.020

[19] J. M. Mendel, "Fuzzy Logic Systems for Engineering: A Tutorial," *Proceedings of the IEEE*, 1995. DOI: 10.1109/5.364485

Chapter 3

Issues and challenges of Artificial Intelligence for industrial automation

J. Praveen Gujjar
JAIN (Deemed-to-be University), Bengaluru, India

M. S. Guru Prasad
Graphic Era (Deemed to be University) Dehradun, India

B. S. Bhavya
JAIN (Deemed-to-be University), Bengaluru, India

Rishi Kumar
Graphic Era (Deemed to be University) Dehradun, India

H. N. Naveen Kumar
Vidyavardhaka College of Engineering, Mysore, India

3.1 INTRODUCTION

In recent years, the field of Artificial Intelligence (AI) has witnessed remark-able advancements that have permeated various aspects of our lives. One domain where AI has shown tremendous promise and transformative potential is industrial automation. As industries strive to enhance efficiency, productivity, and safety, the integration of AI technologies into industrial processes has become increasingly prevalent. This integration, however, comes with a set of complex issues and challenges that demand careful con-sideration and innovative solutions. This book chapter delves into the multi-faceted landscape of AI in industrial automation, aiming to shed light on the pivotal issues and hurdles that confront practitioners, researchers, and poli-cymakers in this evolving field. From the factory floor to supply chain man-agement, AI is reshaping how industries operate, but this transformation is not without its share of dilemmas and obstacles. In the pages that follow, we will explore the nuanced interplay between AI and industrial automation, unraveling topics such as data privacy and security, ethical considerations,

DOI: 10.1201/9781003509240-3

technical challenges, and the evolving role of the human workforce in this automated ecosystem. Through an in-depth analysis of these issues, we will seek to provide valuable insights, strategies, and recommendations for navigating the intricate landscape of AI-driven industrial automation. As we embark on this journey, it is essential to recognize that the fusion of AI and industrial automation has the potential to redefine the very fabric of our manufacturing processes and supply chains. Yet, by addressing the issues and challenges head-on, we can unlock the full potential of AI while ensuring that it aligns with our values, safeguards our data, and empowers individuals in this new era of industrial excellence.

3.2 EVOLUTION OF AI FOR INDUSTRIAL AUTOMATION

Artificial Intelligence (AI) is impacting local communities and global society, transforming the way we live, work, and interact with each other. It has the potential to impact various economic sectors, including medicine, pharmaceuticals, entertainment, banking, retailing, and commerce (Ajami and Karimi 2023). There is a need for an integrated platform for Industrial Automation (IA) and Artificial Intelligence (AI) in order to ensure real-time performance in the factory. This will involve the development of a cloud-edge computing-based Industrial Cyber Intelligent Control Operating System (ICICOS) to replace the outdated Programmable Logic Controller (PLC) and support AI, especially deep learning algorithms. The ICICOS framework is built based on the IEC61499 programming method and focuses on virtualization for IA and AI (Su et al. 2023). Automating processes with intelligence can be a key factor in revolutionizing contemporary manufacturing. AI gives humans the right knowledge to make decisions and warns them of potential problems. Based on their desire to incorporate them into their equipment, industries will utilize AI to process data supplied through linked machines and Internet of Things (IoT) devices. It gives businesses the capacity to completely monitor all of their end-to-end operations and procedures. (Javaid et al. 2021). AI has gained more popularity along the diffusion of the fourth industrial revolution and has become a perfect ingredient for every sector to flourish. As a result of the industrial revolution, businesses are now looking for low-cost methods to increase production output and product quality. Rapid technology advancements are driving the fourth industrial revolution, or Industry 4.0, which is changing people's lives via the use of AI, blockchain, AR, robots, and IoT (Pellicer, Tungekar, and Carpitella 2023). The creation of a predictive study of the equipment's features and the eventual simplification of production lines, Artificial Intelligence, and computer training improve quality management and standardization. The application of AI has allowed enterprises to improve customer service, streamline manufacturing procedures, reduce operational costs, and make quick, data-driven choices. (Dal Mas et al. 2019). Anticipating delivery dates, and producing the highest-quality products, industries may prevent downtimes. Computer vision may be used to monitor the manufacturing process and find errors like small cracks in production facilities. AI may notify businesses of issues with production lines that might result in poor quality. When Industry 4.0 is still in its early phases of growth, the more significant ones can be avoided (Javaid and Haleem 2019). Vehicle AI systems are able to predict the driver's behavior, categorize the passengers, and evaluate road conditions and traffic jams in order to monitor vehicle operation. Autonomous vehicles are undoubtedly the next big thing in the automobile industry. Although AI self-driving technology is still in its research and testing phases in many nations, it has the potential to replace human driving and make traffic safer (Ruiz-Sarmiento et al. 2020). AI techniques are predicted to emerge as the next digital frontier, quickly converting vast amounts of data into insightful information and resulting in a high level of automation and intelligence in business and industry as AI talent continues to develop. Even while building projects generate unprecedented amounts of technical data, the application of AI technology is still lagging behind other industries (Pan and Zhang 2021). The industry's excessively manual processes make project management more complicated and time-consuming than it needs to be. Artificial Intelligence (AI) is a leading digital technology that has significantly improved industrial efficiency, company operations, and service procedures in recent years. Black-box machine learning systems don't provide an explanation for their results; instead, they operate in this manner. Construction professionals must comprehend the system's decision-making process in order to foster trust in such systems. In order to create explainable models and make it possible for people to comprehend, trust, and operate the systems, this necessitates the use of explainable AI (XAI) (Abioye et al. 2021). One key issue—for which the 5G-enabled environment is crucial—is high-speed data transport. However, these IoT devices communicate data utilizing protocols that are based on centralized design, which might lead to a number of security problems for the data. AI and 5G wireless technologies combine to tackle a number of challenges, including virtual reality, self-driving cars, autonomous robotics, and security difficulties. The system's main goal is to foster confidence among network users without relying on outside authority (Dwivedi et al. 2021). Digitalization and Artificial Intelligence are related to the UN 2030 Agenda. The report goes on to identify the primary obstacles to developing robust and sustainable supply chain management (SCM) business models. Based on the findings, the authors create a conceptual framework for digitalization and artificial intelligence in SCM to improve sustainability and accountability, particularly during unexpected crises when corporate resilience is crucial (Di Vaio et al. 2023).

3.3 COMPARE AI AND WITHOUT AI FOR INDUSTRIAL AUTOMATION

Comparing Industrial Automation with and without AI reveals several key differences in terms of capabilities, efficiency, adaptability, and decision-making.

3.3.1 Automation without AI

Rule-Based Automation: Traditional industrial automation relies on rule-based systems and programmable logic controllers (PLCs) to perform predefined tasks. These systems follow strict instructions and are often inflexible.

Limited Adaptability: Non-AI automation systems are less adaptable to changing conditions and unexpected events. They typically require manual reprogramming to handle new tasks or scenarios.

Reactive: Automation without AI primarily responds to predefined triggers or conditions, making it reactive rather than proactive. It lacks the ability to predict issues or optimize processes autonomously.

Fixed Decision-Making: Decision-making in non-AI automation is fixed and based on preprogrammed rules. It cannot analyze complex data or adapt its decisions based on real-time information.

Limited Learning Capability: These systems do not have learning capabilities. They cannot improve their performance over time or optimize processes independently.

Maintenance Scheduling: Maintenance in non-AI automation is often scheduled based on time intervals or usage hours rather than actual equipment condition. This can lead to unnecessary downtime or premature maintenance.

Cost-Effective for Simple Tasks: Non-AI automation is cost-effective for repetitive, simple tasks where processes remain stable and unchanging.

3.3.2 Automation with AI

Adaptive and Learning: AI-driven industrial automation systems can adapt to changing conditions and learn from data. They continuously improve their performance and decision-making.

Predictive and Proactive: AI systems can predict equipment failures, quality issues, and process inefficiencies before they occur, enabling proactive maintenance and optimization.

Real-Time Data Analysis: AI can analyze vast amounts of real-time data from sensors, cameras, and other sources to make informed decisions. It can detect anomalies and respond quickly to deviations.

Optimization: AI can optimize processes in real time, adjusting parameters to maximize efficiency, quality, or resource utilization.

Customization: AI-driven automation can be customized for specific tasks or products, making it versatile across a wide range of applications.

Enhanced Quality Control: AI can perform advanced quality control, detecting defects or variations that may be difficult for human operators or rule-based systems to identify.

Energy Efficiency: AI can optimize energy usage, reducing operational costs and environmental impact.

Human–Machine Collaboration: AI can work alongside human operators, complementing their skills and handling repetitive or dangerous tasks.

Cost-Effective for Complex Tasks: While the initial investment in AI-driven automation can be higher, it often provides a significant return on investment for industries with complex, dynamic processes or a need for high-quality control.

AI-driven industrial automation offers greater adaptability, intelligence, and efficiency compared to traditional automation without AI. It can predict issues, optimize processes, and make informed decisions in real time, leading to improved productivity, reduced downtime, and better resource utilization. However, the choice between AI and non-AI automation depends on the specific needs and complexities of an industrial operation, as well as factors like budget and existing infrastructure.

3.4 KEY CONCERNS THAT ACCOMPANY THE INTEGRATION OF ARTIFICIAL INTELLIGENCE (AI)

As industries increasingly turn to AI to enhance their operations, it is crucial to understand and address these concerns to ensure the responsible and effective deployment of AI technologies. The below paragraph outlines the key concerns that accompany the integration of AI. Key concerns are illustrated in the Figure 3.1

- Safety and Reliability: Safety and reliability are paramount concerns when implementing AI in industrial automation. AI systems, particularly in critical applications such as manufacturing and energy production, must operate with a high degree of dependability.
- Job Displacement: One of the most significant concerns surrounding AI in industrial settings is the potential for job displacement. As automation technologies advance, there is a fear that AI-driven systems may replace human workers, raising questions about the future of employment in these industries. We will discuss the complexities of this issue, including the need for upskilling and workforce adaptation.

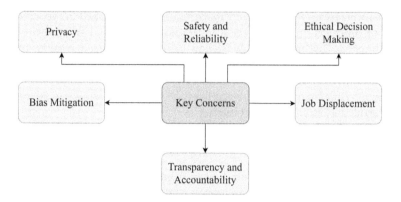

Figure 3.1 Key concerns that accompany the integration of AI.

- Transparency and Accountability: The transparency of AI decision-making processes is essential for building trust in AI systems. We will explore the challenges of making AI algorithms and their decision-making processes understandable to humans. Additionally, we will discuss the role of accountability in ensuring that AI system creators are held responsible for their technology's actions.
- Bias Mitigation: Bias in AI systems, which can result in unfair or discriminatory outcomes, is a critical concern in industrial applications. We will investigate the methods and techniques for identifying and mitigating bias in AI algorithms to ensure that automated processes do not reinforce existing prejudices or inequalities.
- Privacy: Privacy concerns arise when AI systems collect and process data in industrial settings. This section will examine the challenges of balancing data collection for optimization with the need to protect sensitive information, trade secrets, and individual privacy rights. We will also discuss regulations and best practices related to data privacy in AI-driven industries.
- Ethical Decision-Making: AI systems often make decisions that have ethical implications. This part of the chapter will explore the ethical considerations in industrial AI, including the use of AI in decision-making that affects the environment, product quality, and societal well-being. We will also discuss frameworks for ethical AI design and deployment. By addressing these key concerns in the integration of AI into industrial settings, we aim to provide a foundation for responsible and ethical AI adoption. Recognizing and mitigating these challenges is essential for reaping the benefits of AI-driven industrial automation while minimizing potential pitfalls and negative consequences. In the following sections we will delve deeper into each of these concerns, providing practical insights and recommendations for navigating this transformative landscape.

3.5 LANDSCAPE OF AI-DRIVEN INDUSTRIAL AUTOMATION

AI-driven industrial automation is transforming the landscape of manufacturing and industrial processes across various sectors. It combines Artificial Intelligence (AI) technologies with robotics, data analytics, and Internet of Things (IoT) to optimize production, improve efficiency, and enhance decision-making. AI-driven automation enables smart manufacturing, where machines and systems can communicate with each other, self-optimize, and make real-time decisions. This results in increased efficiency, reduced downtime, and better resource utilization.

AI algorithms analyze data from sensors and machinery to predict when equipment is likely to fail. This allows for proactive maintenance, reducing unplanned downtime and minimizing maintenance costs. AI-powered computer vision systems can inspect products for defects with high precision and speed. This ensures that only high-quality products reach consumers, reducing waste and recalls. AI helps optimize supply chain logistics by predicting demand, improving inventory management, and finding the most cost-effective shipping routes. This results in reduced lead times and lower operating costs. Robots equipped with AI are being used for tasks ranging from pick-and-place operations to complex assembly tasks. These robots can adapt to changing conditions and work alongside human workers in collaborative settings. AI-driven algorithms continuously analyze and optimize industrial processes, such as chemical reactions or refining processes, to maximize efficiency and reduce resource consumption. AI systems help in monitoring and optimizing energy usage in industrial facilities. This not only reduces operational costs but also contributes to sustainability efforts. AI-driven automation is designed to work alongside human workers, enhancing their capabilities rather than replacing them. This human–machine collaboration is essential for certain tasks that require human judgment and dexterity. The vast amount of data generated by industrial processes is analyzed by AI systems to uncover insights and patterns. This data-driven decision-making improves efficiency and productivity. AI-driven automation can enhance workplace safety by monitoring and responding to safety-critical situations in real time, reducing accidents and improving overall safety. AI systems can help industrial organizations comply with regulations and standards by ensuring that processes and products meet required specifications. AI-driven automation allows for more personalized and customized manufacturing processes, enabling the production of unique products on a large scale. The AI-driven industrial automation landscape includes a growing ecosystem of AI software providers, hardware manufacturers, system integrators, and consulting firms specializing in AI implementation. While the benefits are significant, there are challenges to consider, such as data security, privacy concerns, the need for skilled personnel, and the potential for job displacement. AI-driven industrial automation can contribute to sustainability goals by optimizing resource usage, reducing waste, and minimizing environmental impact. AI-driven industrial automation is reshaping the manufacturing and industrial landscape by offering increased efficiency, improved quality, enhanced safety, and a path towards greater sustainability. As technology continues to advance, it is expected that AI will play an increasingly central role in shaping the future of industrial processes and manufacturing.

3.6 ISSUES AND CHALLENGES OF ARTIFICIAL INTELLIGENCE FOR INDUSTRIAL AUTOMATION

Artificial Intelligence (AI) has the potential to revolutionize industrial automation; it also comes with several issues and challenges that need to be addressed for its successful implementation. Figure 3.2 illustrate the issues and challenges of Artificial Intelligence for industrial automation

Data Quality and Availability: AI systems heavily depend on data for training and decision-making. Poor data quality or the unavailability of relevant data can hinder AI's effectiveness. In many industrial settings, historical data may be incomplete or inaccurate. While AI can optimize processes and reduce waste, it also consumes significant

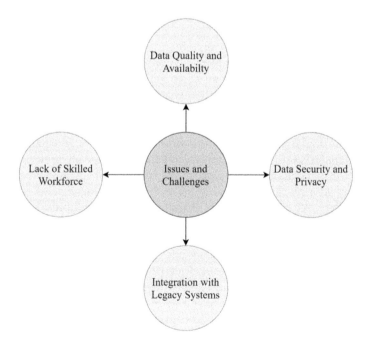

Figure 3.2 Issues and Challenges of AI for industrial automation.

computational resources, which can have environmental implications. Determining the right balance between human workers and AI-driven automation can be challenging, especially in industries where human judgment and decision-making are critical.

Data Security and Privacy: Industrial data often includes sensitive information about processes, equipment, and products. Protecting this data from cyber-threats and ensuring compliance with privacy regulations is a significant challenge. When AI systems control critical processes or interact with humans, safety is paramount. Ensuring that AI-driven automation does not compromise safety is a complex task. Industries often operate under strict regulatory frameworks.

Integration with Legacy Systems: Many industrial facilities have older equipment and systems that were not designed with AI integration in mind. Retrofitting these systems to work with AI can be costly and complex. AI models and algorithms require continuous monitoring, maintenance, and updates. Ensuring that AI systems remain effective and secure over time is an ongoing challenge.

Lack of Skilled Workforce: There is a shortage of skilled personnel who can develop, deploy, and maintain AI systems in industrial settings. Training and upskilling the workforce is essential.

Different AI solutions and devices may not always work seamlessly together. Ensuring interoperability among various AI-driven components is crucial for a cohesive automation ecosystem. AI systems must operate reliably in industrial environments, which can be harsh and unpredictable. Ensuring the robustness and reliability of AI systems is a significant challenge.

Ethical and Bias Concerns: AI algorithms can inherit biases present in the data they are trained on. Ensuring that AI systems are fair and unbiased, especially in contexts like hiring or quality control, is an ongoing concern. Employees may resist the introduction of AI-driven automation due to fears of job displacement or changes in job roles. Managing this cultural resistance is important for successful implementation. Addressing these issues and challenges requires a holistic approach that combines technology, organizational changes, and a commitment to ongoing improvement. Industrial automation with AI has the potential to bring significant benefits, but it must be implemented thoughtfully and responsibly to mitigate risks and maximize its potential.

3.7 ETHICAL CONCERNS FOR AI IN INDUSTRIAL AUTOMATION

Ethical concerns surrounding AI in industrial automation are important to address to ensure the responsible and safe use of this technology. One of the most significant concerns is the potential for AI and automation to lead to job displacement. As machines become more capable of performing tasks traditionally done by humans, there is a risk of job loss in various industries. Ethical considerations include retraining and reskilling programs for affected workers and finding ways to ensure a just transition for those impacted. AI-powered automation systems must prioritize safety to prevent accidents and harm to workers. There is a need to ensure that AI systems are reliable, robust, and tested thoroughly to minimize the risk of failures and accidents. Transparency in AI decision-making processes is also essential for identifying and mitigating safety risks. The use of AI in industrial settings often involves the collection and analysis of large amounts of data, including employee data. Ethical concerns include protecting the privacy of workers and ensuring that data is used responsibly and in compliance with data protection regulations. AI systems can inherit biases from their training data, which can result in unfair treatment or discrimination. In industrial automation, biases can affect hiring, promotion, and performance evaluation processes. It is crucial to address bias in AI algorithms and ensure fairness in decision-making. Determining accountability and liability in cases of AI-related accidents or failures can be challenging. Ethical considerations include establishing clear lines of responsibility and liability, as well as defining who is accountable when AI systems make critical decisions. AI systems in industrial automation often operate as "black boxes," making it difficult to understand their decision-making processes. Ethical concerns revolve around the need for transparency and explainability to ensure that decisions made by AI systems can be understood, audited, and justified. Designing AI systems to make ethical decisions in complex situations is a challenge. There is a need to develop ethical frameworks and guidelines for AI in industrial automation to ensure that the technology aligns with societal values and ethical standards. As industries rely more on AI and automation, there is a concern about the potential for over-reliance on technology, which could lead to reduced human oversight and control. Maintaining a balance between human and AI decision-making is essential. The use of AI in industrial automation can have environmental implications, such as increased energy consumption and electronic waste. Ethical considerations include minimizing the environmental footprint of AI systems and adopting sustainable practices. Ethical concerns extend beyond immediate impacts and should consider the long-term consequences of widespread automation, including economic, social, and cultural changes. Ethical decision-making should account for these broader impacts.

REFERENCES

Abioye, Sofiat, Lukumon O. Oyedele, Lukman Akanbi, Anuoluwapo O. Ajayi, Muhammad Bilal, Olúgbénga O. Akinadé, and Ashraf Ahmed. 2021. "Artificial Intelligence in the Construction Industry: A Review of Present Status, Opportunities and Future Challenges." *Journal of Building Engineering* 44 (December): 103299. doi:10.1016/j.jobe.2021.103299

Ajami, Riad A., and Homa A. Karimi. 2023. "Artificial Intelligence: Opportunities and Challenges." *Journal of Asia-Pacific Business*, 1–3. doi:10.1080/10599231.2 023.2210239

Dal Mas, F., Piccolo, D., Cobianchi, L., Edvinsson, L., Presch, G., Massaro, M., ... Bagnoli, C. (2019, October). The effects of artificial intelligence, robotics, and industry 4.0 technologies. Insights from the Healthcare sector. In *Proceedings of the first European Conference on the impact of Artificial Intelligence and Robotics* (pp. 88–95). Reading, UK: Academic Conferences and Publishing International Limited.

Di Vaio, Assunta, Badar Latif, Nuwan Gunarathne, Michèle Gupta, and Idiano D'Adamo. 2023. "Digitalization and Artificial Knowledge for Accountability in SCM: A Systematic Literature Review." *Journal of Enterprise Information Management.* doi:10.1108/jeim-08-2022-0275

Dwivedi, Ashutosh Dhar, Rajani Singh, Keshav Kaushik, Raghava Rao Mukkamala, and Waleed S. Alnumay. 2021. "Blockchain and Artificial Intelligence for 5G-enabled Internet of Things: Challenges, Opportunities, and Solutions." *Transactions on Emerging Telecommunications Technologies.* doi:10.1002/ett.4329

Javaid, Mohd, and Abid Haleem. 2019. "Industry 4.0 Applications in Medical Field: A Brief Review." *Current Medicine Research and Practice* 9 (3): 102–109. doi:10.1016/j. cmrp.2019.04.001

Javaid, Mohd, Abid Haleem, Ravi Pratap Singh, and Rajiv Suman. 2021. "Artificial Intelligence Applications for Industry 4.0: A Literature-Based Study." *Journal of Industrial Integration and Management* 7 (1): 83–111. doi:10.1142/ s2424862221300040

Pan, Y., and Limao Zhang. 2021. "Roles of Artificial Intelligence in Construction Engineering and Management: A Critical Review and Future Trends." *Automation in Construction* 122 (February): 103517. doi:10.1016/j.autcon.2020.103517

Pellicer, Miguel Rivas, Mohamed Yoosha Tungekar, and Silvia Carpitella. 2023. "Where to Place Monitoring Sensors for Improving Complex Manufacturing Systems? Discussing a Real Case in the Food Industry." *Sensors*, 23(7), 3768. https://doi.org/10.3390/s23073768

Ruiz-Sarmiento, José-Raúl, Javier Monroy, Francisco-Ángel Moreno, Cipriano Galindo, J.M. Bonelo, and Javier González-Jiménez. 2020. "A Predictive Model for the Maintenance of Industrial Machinery in the Context of Industry 4.0." *Engineering Applications of Artificial Intelligence* 87: 103289. doi:10.1016/j. engappai.2019.103289

Su, Weibin, Gang Xu, Zhengfang He, Ivy Kim D. Machica, Val Quimno, Yi Du, and Yanchun Kong. 2023. "Cloud-Edge Computing-Based ICICOS Framework for Industrial Automation and Artificial Intelligence: A Survey." *Journal of Circuits, Systems, and Computers* 32(10). https://doi.org/10.1142/s0218126623501682

Chapter 4

Deep learning algorithm and approaches for automation

Aastha Sharma

ABES Engineering College, Ghaziabad, India

4.1 INTRODUCTION

Deep learning is the method of learning via the numerous layers involved in computing the task and requires going through deep analysis in addressing the problem and forecasting the process in execution. The word "deep" stands for going beyond the deep discussion statement, and "learning" means learning layer by layer and calculating and eliminating errors for computer optimization. Alexy Grigoryevich Ivakhnedo and Valentina Grigoryevich Lapa pioneered deep learning principles and methods in 1965 [1, 2]. It is a subset of machine learning and Artificial Intelligence in which the computer learns via the dataset and generates predictions based on the prior pattern analysis in the computation. Deep learning is a method that allows it to solve complicated problems and eliminate errors caused while completing tasks over time [2, 3]. It involves the use of period generation in computing mathematical analysis or hidden pattern generation in executing the work that needs to be done through deep analysis and the transmission of the input layer to the hidden layer to the output layer creation in the computing process. In future optimization, the organization will move to quantum learning, where the machine may learn through some complex problem and mathematical computation to solve the problem quickly while maintaining its scalability, flexibility, reliability, transparency, and optimization [3]. The system divides the deep learning working area into three phases, where the activation function calculates and computes the learning model approach. Within layer creation, the input layer, hidden layer, and output layer pick and extract feature details to generate and promote pattern analysis while calculating or computing the hidden layer analysis.

Neuroscience mostly uses deep learning to learn layer by layer and perform effective analysis on neural networks [4]. The Artificial Neural Network (ANN) is a common method for learning through hidden parameters and patterns and reducing errors in computer tasks.

As depicted in Figure 4.1, AI represents a technique utilized to teach a computer to predict, analyze, and emulate the functioning of the human brain. On the other hand, machine learning (ML) represents a learning

DOI: 10.1201/9781003509240-4

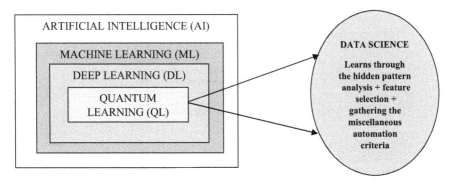

Figure 4.1 Deep learning intelligence.

pattern that utilizes prior patterns in the dataset to forecast and manipulate various patterns in computation. Deep learning entails examining a dataset's hidden layers in order to optimize it or minimize errors. On the other hand, quantum learning is the most rapid and adaptable method for forecasting outcomes through in-depth pattern analysis [3, 4].

4.2 LEARNING APPROACHES

The ways to learn and identify parameters in deep learning are based on the problem or the dataset that can be implanted to code and execute the system's strategies to get better results in sequence. By passing data from the hidden layer (comprising multiple layers) to the output layer, as illustrated in Figures 4.2 and 4.3, the learning models can be acquired. The algorithmic approach, code optimization, and thorough error identification are all part of the process that the system uses to formulate and sow the seed of

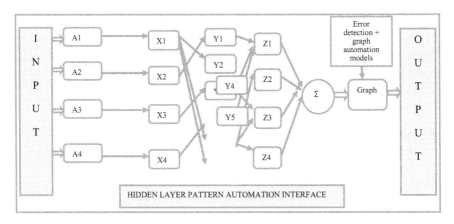

Figure 4.2 Deep learning approaches.

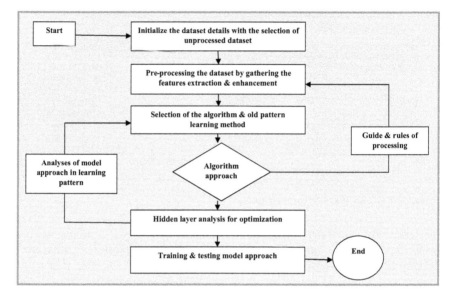

Figure 4.3 Learning pattern flowchart.

the problem statement [1, 2]. The interconnected learning strategy in deep networks can be identified and analyzed in the following steps:

1. Identify the problem domain.
2. Perform a survey and collect the data related to identified problem.
3. Analyze the collected data and find the issue.
4. Select an appropriate problem to solve the identified problem.
5. Generate a hypothesis for required output and initiate the learning process through random values.
6. Optimize the learning process through error calculation repeatedly.
7. Repeat the process to get a trained network for the defined problem.

Essentially, the process of computing and developing techniques to lower hidden layer error rates is difficult to execute, code, and compute layer by layer [3, 4]. It also analyzes hidden patterns and roughly chooses features for feature selection and extraction in calculating the issues.

4.3 UNDERSTANDING OF THE ISSUES IN A DEEP LEARNING ALGORITHM

Deep or neural networks have a vast learning pattern, and disciplined strategies are required to execute and compute the tasks of the deep learning method in automation due to the high risk and the system requirements for authentication and automation, which require network space to compute and make analytical predictions. Similarly, challenges arise when utilizing

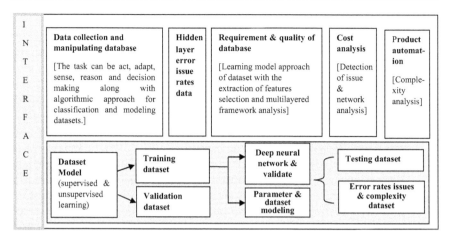

Figure 4.4 Issues in deep learning pattern.

analytical and predictive methods, pattern recognition, and previous datasets to instruct the computer to make predictions based on past requirements [4, 5]. Figure 4.4 illustrates the effectiveness of the approach in decision-making, communication, and normalization. The approach's implications are significant in both supervised and unsupervised learning patterns, affecting data features. Furthermore, the analysis incorporates reinforcement learning via the environment setup approach. The concerns are [6]:

1. Over-fitting & under-fitting problem
2. Computational issues
3. Selection of the correct algorithmic approach
4. Black box problem
5. Abstraction of data features & extraction
6. Labeled & unlabelled dataset
7. Increment of the error rates
8. Flexibility of prediction in analysis
9. Previous pattern are inadequate approach
10. Lack of transparency
11. Lack of reliability & approximation
12. Lack of optimization states
13. Complexity issue
14. Space & time complexity and running time for large space taken in calling task.
15. Training model-biased decision etc.

4.4 ALGORITHMS

The algorithm is a phenomenon process that can illustrate the analysis of maintaining the set of rules and the set of calculative strategies used in the processing to execute and learn the task in deep learning analysis [5, 6].

A few more deep learning algorithms have been implanted to retrieve and analyze dataset patterns and make decisions based on past patterns of learning strategies in the learning model approach. The ML and deep learning algorithms are:

1. **SOM (Self-Organizing Maps):** The SOM is a powerful learning model that utilizes an unsupervised neural network approach to construct a dimensional map of data. It effectively reduces the dimensionality of the data, allowing for efficient learning and analysis. It employs the hidden layer strategy to input and output the data for self-mapping, dimensional grouping, and clustering using the same data inputs [6]. Figure 4.5 shows a few SOM processes that work, such as executing and exaggerating the task and performing fast computing. Examples include geographical land mapping, text mining, kernel databases, 3-D weighted datasets, oceanography modeling approaches, and so on.

2. **Deep reinforcement learning (DRL):** The DRL is a strategy that is commonly used in robotics analysis to make the robot act like a human being, naturally maximizing the environment by engaging in action and repeating approaches while learning the system (Figure 4.6). It makes decisions at every stage by understanding the context of the action [6].

3. **Recurrent neural network (RNN):** This is the name of the process by which the system is called to grasp information using an artificial neural network analysis approach to learn the hidden layer information step by step. Each segment of learning the task through time remembers and makes decisions accordingly. The LSTM is a task execution process that remembers each area as it moves from input to output over time. For example, consider speech recognition, language

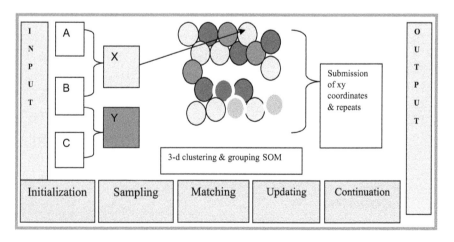

Figure 4.5 SOM formation learning.

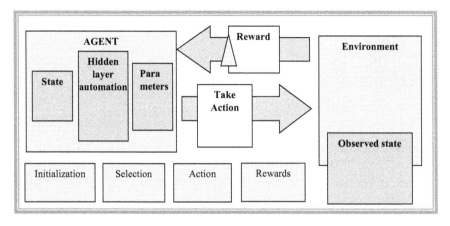

Figure 4.6 Reinforcement learning.

processing, and the MNIST dataset [7, 8]. Each stage of executing one-time data is subjected to multiple hidden layer analyses for task creation and execution, resulting in methods that reduce error rates during task execution in the system depicted in Figure 4.7.

4. **Capsule network (Caps-Net):** The capsule network is a layered technique that generates a nested loop layer network within the capsule layer analysis. It is the system that splits the task into some form of capsule or the cell form of capsule constructed to analyze deep learning in hidden layer analysis and for the rapid computing method. It also eliminates the network of segmentation and recognition of the deep learning approach. Figure 4.8 depicts the aggregate of tasks split into layered analyses step by step, resulting in the output within the hidden layer method structure [9]. Caps-Net also gathers the same amount of information at once and processes it into a hidden layer approach for quick analysis and processing, such as the MNIST dataset.

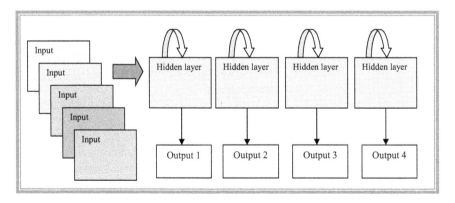

Figure 4.7 Recurrent calling neural network.

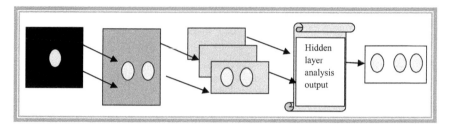

Figure 4.8 Caps-Net learning.

5. **Transformer Neural Network:** The transformer neural network is a technique that deals with problem solving by continually calling the task throughout problem execution and fetching and analyzing the dataset's detailed features. It is a revolutionary strategy that utilizes the architecture of the synchronous calling method to tackle the huge number of dependencies in the execution problem. Following steps are performed to implement the network:
   - Initialize the input dataset
   - Embedding or sampling the dataset as per the requirement
   - Encoding the data
   - Multilayer analysis approach
   - Initiate the layered structure Feed-forward the analysis
   - Update the network
   - Output

6. **Long short-term memory network (LSTM):** This utilizes the recurrent neural network approach to solve the problem by synchronously executing the task and is capable of acquiring knowledge of long-term dependencies to predict and resolve future outcomes. In essence, it is utilized for training and testing, concealed layered analysis, implementation, processing, modeling, classification, inputting the detailed structure of the dataset, and generating the result [1]. For instance, problems involving time series, text mining, and managing massive amounts of data and speech, etc.

7. **Restricted Boltzmann machine (RBM):** The RBM, which is a type of deep learning technique model, generates and predicts the outcome of a futuristic analysis through unsupervised learning [2, 3]. This is achieved by utilizing the learning capabilities and probability of task complexity during task execution, as well as optimizing the system's running state. Primarily, pattern recognition based on previous analysis and noise removal from the dataset via data sampling, a radar system for detection, and text determination techniques are implemented.

8. **Perceptron learning:** Perceptron learning, a deep learning approach, learns from linear classifiers and weights to compute and make

decisions at each stage of the calculation process. This method allows neural networks to silently discover information as it progresses through the hidden layer formation, compute error rates on formation, or predict outcomes from the dataset [3, 4]. Additionally, it is capable of operating on both single-layered and multilayered perceptron. It computes the weights and determines the data output.

9. **Radial basic function network:** Neural network learning operates on the principle of the cover theorem and handles complex structures with multiple layers of hidden layers. In the case of feed-forward neural networks, these structures consist of three distinct phases: the input layer, the hidden layer, and the output layer. It is responsible for determining the center and radius of the nucleus during the formation of the hidden layered computation, as well as making decisions at each stage of task distribution. As illustrated in Figure 4.2 [6], the radial basis function is computed to generate the linear weights and output, which are utilized to forecast future analyses.

10. **Artificial neural network (ANN):** ANN is a method that analyzes human behavior and the formation of the human brain to predict future outcomes. For instance, ANN utilizes the structure of neuron cells, which are interconnected and regulate the entire body's functions. Decisions are made based on a specific situation or previous pattern analysis, as illustrated in Figure 4.2. It is an interconnected formation in which all data associated with a particular aspect of the output prediction is displayed in the parallel processing capabilities to compute and accelerate the dataset correspondingly. They perform the limited phases [8].

    • Initialize the input
    • Input layer sampling
    • Hidden layer approach
    • Feed-forward details
    • Output layer
    • Prediction result.

11. **Auto-encoder:** The auto-encoder is a deep learning method that deals with unlearned datasets and uses learned data to predict future outcomes, known as unsupervised learning, with the help of clustering or sampling the datasets [8]. The auto-encoder also eliminates noisy data from the dataset prior to training and testing, employing pre-processing techniques to decode and analyze the output results. Additionally, it computes the hidden layer agenda approach for expedited computation.

Nowadays, the market is using more algorithms for dataset selection, modeling, extraction, and data processing based on task requirements. This chapter delves into the current development of a few hidden or multilayered automation strategies in deep learning. Deep learning commonly employs several techniques to extract additional features and manipulate the dataset [10].

- Random forest algorithm
- Stochastic gradient decent optimization algorithm
- CNN
- Naïve Bayes classification algorithm
- Back propagation algorithm
- PCA
- Image segmentation
- Vectors algorithm
- Generative adversarial network
- Multilayer perceptron

4.5 DEEP LEARNING CLOUD SERVICES

Cloud services provide an imaginary platform for doing or executing tasks, as well as tools for automating the deep learning method in practical analysis.

1. **AWS (Amazon Web Services):** AWS has a few libraries that allow it to function and deploy resources in the cloud over the internet. It also improves speed, transparency, flexibility, reliability, and the capacity to operate with several processors at once. In Figure 4.9, there are a few architectural frameworks that work in the cloud to provide resources for users, such as Apache, TensorFlow, Microsoft Tools, Caffe, Caffe2, Theano, Torch, and others, such as Netflix, Pinterest, the education portal, Ucal, Claire, and Edmuds. It also makes use of the Amazon Alexa virtual assistant. There are a few steps to begin deep learning in the Amazon interface [11].
   - Open the EC2 console and sign up.
   - Configure your resources.
   - Choose deep learning (AMI).
   - Select the language type.
   - Connect to the system tools or toolkit.
   - Access your notebook.
   - Installed the entire library package.
   - Terminate your console.
2. **AZURE:** This is the platform for extending and improving the features of the learning model framework approach in machine learning or the deep neural network model approach in cloud services. It is mostly based on Platform as a Service (PaaS) architecture and provides users with Infrastructure as a Service (IaaS) and Software as a Service (SaaS)

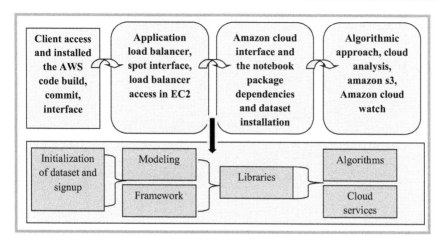

Figure 4.9 AWS Deep learning.

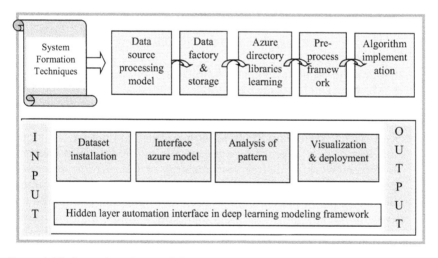

Figure 4.10 Azure learning model.

solutions on a cloud platform. Figure 4.10 focuses primarily on analytical techniques, pattern recognition, algorithmic approaches, virtual computing, and the networking architecture for deep learning. It has the potential to increase speed, flexibility, and transparency [12].

3. **GOOGLE CLOUD:** This is a phenomenon-based strategy that interacts and communicates digitally with users, datasets, and deep learning model services. The Virtual Machine(VM) is a collection of cloud libraries used to speed up the interface and execute tasks in the most artificial working architecture possible to evaluate and calculate hidden

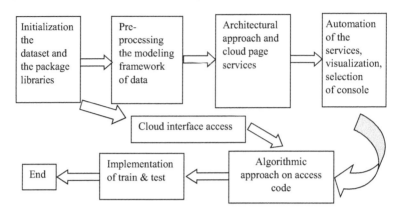

Figure 4.11 Google Cloud analysis.

layers in services and deploy them. Figure 4.11 shows a few actions that can be conducted in the Google cloud to make services available to users: [13].

- The VM cloud page caters to the cloud learning space.
- Click on launch.
- Enter the deployment class on the page.
- Machine and language libraries
- Selection of the algorithm and the code of the dataset services, and repeat.

4. **GPU:** This service model deals with parallel computing techniques, accelerates job execution, and models a hidden layer automation framework to deliver vast amounts of information and results promptly. The difficulty of completing the work or the vast amount of data required to create the requirements package to call and execute the task. Figure 4.12 [14] demonstrates how an optimization model strategy can improve the deep learning method's flexibility and scalability.

There are a few more cloud services offered by some companies and agencies for automation and modeling the framework of the deep learning method and analysis. Some of the other cloud based services for deep learning frameworks which work as a PaaS are:

- IBM
- Robotics
- Google TPU
- Tensor flow
- Data bricks
- Ribbon etc.

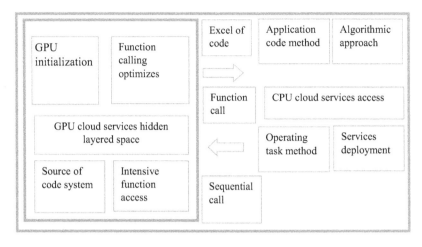

Figure 4.12 GPU pattern learning.

4.6 CONCLUSION AND FUTURE OPPORTUNITIES

In deep neural network learning, the industry is still focusing on the hidden layer technique to demonstrate modeling and architectural framework analysis for computing. The deep learning model is an extension and deep function of the artificial and machine learning framework, focusing primarily on the 3-dimensional layered structure to calculate and optimize the computing technique and model approach. Here are a few industries in which it can apply pattern learning, feature selection enhancement, processing, scalability, and fast computing in deep learning networks. These industries include [3, 5, 7]:

- Manufacturing
- Pharmaceuticals
- Textiles
- Financial databases
- Automotive car
- Voice assistants
- NLP etc.

There are a few approaches to automation in industry, education, and research, and people are still working on the hidden layer-dimensional approach to demonstrate and make the best planted approach for the computational complexity, error rates, and issues in the operating system and the naturally executing the tasks. Some prominent terminologies have the potential to create a hierarchy of tasks within a given formation.

- Pruning system
- Knowledge base

- Task performer
- Environment habitat
- Operating system
- Shell operating algorithm
- Controlling execution performer etc.

REFERENCES

1. Y. Li, "Research and Application of Deep Learning in Image Recognition," *2022 IEEE 2nd International Conference on Power, Electronics and Computer Applications (ICPECA)*, Shenyang, China, 2022, pp. 994–999. https://doi.org/10.1109/ICPECA53709.2022.9718847
2. Alzubaidi, L., Zhang, J., Humaidi, A.J. *et al.* Review of deep learning: concepts, CNN architectures, challenges, applications, future directions. *J Big Data* 8, 53 (2021). https://doi.org/10.1186/s40537-021-00444-8
3. Wang, Weiyu & Siau, Keng. (2019). Artificial Intelligence, Machine Learning, Automation, Robotics, Future of Work and Future of Humanity: A Review and Research Agenda. *Journal of Database Management.* 30. 61–79. https://doi.org/10.4018/JDM.2019010104
4. Sathio, Anwar & Lakhan, Abdullah. (2024). Deep Learning Algorithms and Architectures for Multimodal Data Analysis. https://doi.org/10.1007/978-3-030-77746-3_001
5. V. Khomenko, O. Shyshkov, O. Radyvonenko and K. Bokhan, "Accelerating recurrent neural network training using sequence bucketing and multi-GPU data parallelization," *2016 IEEE First International Conference on Data Stream Mining & Processing (DSMP)*, Lviv, Ukraine, 2016, pp. 100–103, https://doi.org/10.1109/DSMP.2016.7583516
6. Zhao, Linya, Tan, Kun, Wang, Xue, Ding, Jianwei, Liu, Zhaoxian, Ma, Huilin & Han, Bo. (2022). Hyperspectral Feature Selection for SOM Prediction Using Deep Reinforcement Learning and Multiple Subset Evaluation Strategies. *Remote Sensing.* 15. 127. https://doi.org/10.3390/rs15010127
7. Ma, Zhifeng, Zhang, Hao & Liu, Jie. (2023). MM-RNN: A Multimodal RNN for Precipitation Nowcasting. *IEEE Transactions on Geoscience and Remote Sensing.* 1–1. https://doi.org/10.1109/TGRS.2023.3264545
8. Yin, Qiyue, Yu, Tongtong, Shen, Shengqi, Meijing, Zhao, Ni, Wancheng, Huang, Kaiqi, Wang, Liang, Yang, Jun & Liang, Bin. (2024). Distributed Deep Reinforcement Learning: A Survey and a Multi-player Multi-agent Learning Toolbox. *Machine Intelligence Research.* 1–20. https://doi.org/10.1007/s11633-023-1454-4
9. Jacob, I. Jeena. (2020). Performance Evaluation of Caps-Net Based Multitask Learning Architecture for Text Classification. *Journal of Artificial Intelligence and Capsule Networks.* 2. 1–10. https://doi.org/10.36548/jaicn.2020.1.001
10. Chen, Shuangshuang & Guo, Wei. (2023). Auto-Encoders in Deep Learning—A Review with New Perspectives. *Mathematics.* 11. 1777. https://doi.org/10.3390/math11081777

11. Balajee, M. & Jayanthi Kannan, M. K. (2023). Intrusion Detection on AWS Cloud through Hybrid Deep Learning Algorithm. *Electronics*. 12. 1–21. https://doi.org/10.3390/electronics12061423

12. Mittal, Krish. (2023). *Early stage detection of Alzheimer's disease with Microsoft Azure based deep learning.* https://doi.org/10.13140/RG.2.2.17747.76322

13. Bisong, Ekaba. (2019). Building Machine Learning and Deep Learning Models on Google Cloud Platform: A Comprehensive Guide for Beginners. https://doi.org/10.1007/978-1-4842-4470-8

14. Ye, Zhisheng, Gao, Wei, Hu, Qinghao, Sun, Peng, Wang, Xiaolin, Luo, Yingwei, Zhang, Tianwei, Wen, Yonggang. (2023). Deep Learning Workload Scheduling in GPU Datacenters: A Survey. *ACM Computing Surveys*. 56. https://doi.org/10.1145/3638757

Chapter 5

The role of IoT devices and Artificial Intelligence-based health care monitoring systems

Sonia Rani

Lovely Professional University, Phagwara, India

5.1 INTRODUCTION

Nowadays due to different environmental conditions such as water pollution, air pollution and urban lifestyle, human beings are suffering from many health-related issues. Different environmental conditions like water pollution, air pollution, and life habits of human beings suffering from many health issues. Issues related to health should be of the utmost concern to human beings. The main challenge is the accurate diagnosis of a wide range of diseases such as diabetes, thyroid, cancer, depression, stress, autism spectrum disorder, etc. With the emerging trends in using technology, the medical field is also a progressive area. In medical science, Internet of Things (IoT) devices and expert systems are used to diagnose diseases with high accuracy and in their earliest stages. IoT devices are non-computing devices that transmit data by connecting to a wireless network. These standard devices, such as laptops, desktops, tablets, and smartphones, are connected through the internet and communicate data. IoT devices and some wearable devices enabled with sensors are useful for remotely monitoring patients' diseases. These devices are capable of capturing the patient's vitals, which can also be used to maintain the patient's medical history. This study describes the REST API and Raspberry Pi systems, Nano smart health care technologies like pill cameras and wearable water-resistant sensor devices, and IBM Watson's electronic devices which can be used to diagnose several mental and physical health issues. The structure of this study is as follows: Section 5.1 is the introduction to the chapter. Section 5.2 gives a literature review of IoT devices and their use cases in disease diagnosis, along with the role of cloud computing, artificial neural networks, and machine learning methods to develop health monitoring systems. Section 5.3 gives a diagrammatic presentation of the distribution of studies, and the summary of the review studies is defined in table form. Finally, in Section 5.4 there is a discussion of these healthcare monitoring systems' current trends and future perspectives.

DOI: 10.1201/9781003509240-5

5.2 THE ROLE OF IoT IN HEALTHCARE

5.2.1 IoT devices, technologies, and wearable devices

REST API is a lightweight open-source interface for exchanging data over a solid HTTP system connection in an IP-enabled system [1]. The task uses the MSSQL DB module to link a Raspberry Pi, a GSM module, and an interface. Raspberry Pi is a small single-board microcontroller. It is a cheap and absolute method, and the main target of using this system is to update the data once and then send an alert to the doctor [2]. Raspberry Pi may be regarded as built-in software that enables users to program and design animation, games, or video. For client–server communication, Python language has been used in this work to write the script [3]. Clinical Significance HRV, heart failure, diabetic neurology, depression, and body temperature are measured by the DS18B20 sensor. The results are given in degrees F and C [4]. Many hospitals use IoT devices, through, for example, the use of Wi-Fi sensors with RFID, NFC tags, sensor nodes, and E-healthcare systems to get patient information [5]. IBM Watson is one of the company's initiatives; it provides support through its existing services and can be integrated with any application to create Internet of Things (IoT)-based health apps [6]. An early warning system predicts mental disorder disease by matching some specific symptoms. The categories of psychiatric biomarkers include genetics, proteins, or 'neuroimaging' findings [7]. To detect relative skin temperature variations, a thermopile infrared-based sensor was applied. The Arduino microcontroller displays the temperature value with this sensor which could detect the thermal coefficient. In the second step, another sensor measured the pulse rate for detecting the thyroid by placing the finger on the sensor. This model gave an accuracy rating of 83.33% [8].

A pill camera is an example of Nano smart healthcare. This is a simple device with an image sensor to grasp the footage and wirelessly send this data to a recorder. It is powered by a small battery and charged with the help of a data recorder. It takes a high-resolution image of internal organs once a pill has been swallowed [9]. Similarly, Cooey is a health monitoring system to measure blood pressure and diagnose any condition. It stores and organises the health history and gives it to your doctor [10]. An ontology-based healthcare system diagnoses several health issues, such as hypertension and diabetes management, to make adequate therapeutic and diagnosis for patients [11]. PHQ-9 Mind at Ease makes the process less persistent by implementing medical imaging (brain scans) and depression detection [12].

Some wearable devices are specially designed so that a human can bear it, and the device can collect data and perform some processing. The devices comprise several sensors. They are useful because they can be wearable or transported to interior places where healthcare services are required or in the event of a medical emergency [13]. The smart healthcare device with an IoT framework can monitor patients' basic health with the room condition in the real-time presence of patients. A total of five sensors, measuring heartbeat, room temperature, body temperature, and CO and CO_2 levels, were used to represent the hospital data. The percentage of error was less than 5% for each case. The patients' conditions are fetched by a medical staff portal; through that, they can determine the present situations of the patients. The system's effectiveness proved that the developed system was well suited to monitor the patient's health conditions [14]. Wrist-worn water-resistant devices are used to determine a person's physical activities without discomfort and during activities of daily living, including while sleeping [15]. Artificial Intelligence is widely applied to enhance intelligent systems to maintain the records of patients' history. However, the records here must be entered manually, which can prove a big limitation [16]. The IoT-enabled healthcare monitoring systems diagnose the high blood pressure and diabetes of patients. The rural areas have no instant access available to healthcare monitoring devices in emergency clinics for testing. Buying these devices is not possible due to the high costs involved. The systems were developed for measuring heartbeat, body temperature and oxygen saturation in blood and transferring the data to mobile apps using Bluetooth. The MIT invertor app was developed to receive data using Bluetooth, and the study aims to increase the usage, making it affordable for people to use at home. To measure and determine patients' health parameters, a 95% confidence interval with a relative error of 5% was considered. These tools and devices can greatly impact people's lives [17]. The IoT's potential smart applications in healthcare are used to improve life quality. The future discussions and challenges are mainly concerned with security reasons, important forensics, and the identity of IoT devices for wider social acceptance. Future research must address meaningful interactions in healthcare services, such as advances in smart home technologies. It involved the data identification, collection, organisation, and presentation level to record the activities of IoT devices [18].

5.2.2 Cloud computing, GPS, Bluetooth, Wi-Fi technology, and MATLAB

Cloud computing, combined with IoT, can be a useful tool for a short duration to increase performance and provide a reliable result [19]. MANETS (Mobile Adhoc Networks) communication infrastructure is a wireless network. In this networking, sensor nodes gather the patient's data from the deployed environment and spread the data to devices in the base station [20]. The architecture of large-scale IoT-enabled healthcare was proposed. Internet coverage tools with a clustering approach were used to communicate with the healthcare devices and tools of communications high-altitude platforms, internet, satellite, wireless sensor networks, MNNET, RFID, and cellular. The classifications of IoT-enabled healthcare environments into active and passive things network simulation packages measured the performance of healthcare architecture that is IoT-enabled [21].

Mobile health (MHealth) is a medical health infrastructure supported by mobile devices and IoT, and this consists of GPS, Bluetooth technology, and 4G systems to examines human activities [22]. The protocol for the internet gives any microcontroller access to the Wi-Fi network that supports a common standard of Wi-Fi, meaning that the microcontroller must be Wi-Fi- or network-enabled [23]. A computerized system was developed with a bottom-up approach considering the basal body temperature module to monitor the thyroid [24].

A comprehensive, detailed review and bibliometric analysis was performed on IoT in healthcare. Articles were analysed based on journal publication year, authors, institutions, countries, and bibliometric analysis. The important topics related to IoT healthcare applications are blockchain applications, 5g telecommunication, AI techniques, computing technologies, fog computing, data analytics, cloud–IoT integration, and smart cognitive healthcare. Their review also offers a detailed understanding of the current status of IoT research in healthcare, and it also found the knowledge gap for further research in future. This review also described healthcare professionals the latest trends in IoT applications and developments in the healthcare sector [25]. A study was reviewed to find out and compare systematically and classify the investigations in healthcare systems, and some 146 articles published between 2015 and 2020 were analysed and classified into five separate categories based on resource, sensor, application, communication, and security. The limitations and benefits of selected methods were evaluated with the comparison evaluation tools, techniques and evaluation metrics. The study explained that the latest future trends in fog computing, blockchain, big data analysis, trust and privacy, power management, the nano devices' internet, interoperability and challenges and mobility-based implementation are required to research IoT systems in future [26]. The advances in healthcare applications and technology services have helped to address issues in this area. IoT technology has helped healthcare doctors diagnose and monitor several diseases or health issues by measuring the health parameters and providing diagnostic facilities remotely, transforming healthcare from a hospital-centric to a patient-centric system [27, 28].

An exploratory study was performed about the latest trends in the system using the IoT and compared the efficiency, effectiveness, privacy security, data protection, and monitoring of various systems. The healthcare monitoring sensor systems were classified by exploring the wearable and wireless sensor-based IoT monitoring systems. They also elaborated on the open issues and challenges regarding the privacy and security of systems. The recent trends also describe technology and future directions [29]. A study of IoT enhancements and solutions in medicine was presented, i.e., record keeping, integrated devices, sampling, and disease causes and diagnosis. Their study aims to perform the COVID-19 case treatment by detecting the parameters using IoT-based technology, and it helps surgeons to minimize risk and increase performance. IoT can also help with medical challenges such as price, speed, complexity, and price. It can also monitor the treatments of diabetes, asthma, and arthritis of patients with COVID-19. This digital technology controls the health management systems, increasing the overall performance of healthcare systems during COVID-19 [30].

In [31] an analysis is performed by authors on IoT in healthcare-related relevant themes from year 2015 to2020. The study provided the researchers with a better understanding of IoT in healthcare opportunities and further directions in research [31]. Due to sensitive medical data transfer through IoT-enabled healthcare, privacy data leakage can be caused by unauthorized users. So, to maintain the privacy of medical data, an attribute-based secure access control mechanism is proposed. A graph convolutional network is applied to a social graph with a loss function. Experimentation results show that their proposed method achieves accuracy with low privacy leakage of medical data and high data integrity [32]. The study of IoT devices in the medical domain has greatly affected and improved the effectiveness and quality of medical services. Smart services like mobile devices and wireless networks are used in more than 80% of healthcare hospitals, meaning more health institutions and centres have activated smart healthcare devices. The growth of digital devices and IoT technologies connected to the internet has dispensed manual records with pen and paper. Now, doctors and patients depend on the internet, and devices such as tablets, computers, and mobiles are always connected. A case study of 9 patients and variations in their results are also reviewed [33]. The literature survey explores and examines that IoT can play an important role in cancer diagnosis and assessment procedures about patient-driven and drug delivery and monitoring mental health [34].

In literature it has been found that IoT has the highest priority in health-care sector for achieving sustainable development. The top opportunities to apply IoT applications in healthcare are in the areas of dental health, ultra-violet radiation, and fall detection [35]. A study was done on IoT applications and some characteristics and parameters. The role of IoT in healthcare and its technologies was examined and opportunities were identified. The cloud-based conceptual framework can help the healthcare industry implement solutions with regard to healthcare IoT devices [36].

IoT based systems have also been explored in rural areas. In [17], authors have developed systems for measuring heartbeat, body temperature, and blood oxygen saturation and transferring data to mobile applications using Bluetooth. The MIT invertor app has been developed to receive data using Bluetooth. The aim is to increase the usage with affordability to people at home at normal cost. A 95% confidence interval with a 5% relative error is applied to measure and determine patients' health parameters. The usage of these tools and devices can have a big impact on people's lives [17]. In the current scenario, people prefer remote healthcare solutions for personal activity trackers and wearable healthcare monitoring devices. The patient data is recorded and can be monitored remotely by professionals to guide patients and save records for future health issues. The healthcare scenario needs to change from reactive to proactive and preventive. They have also highlighted the IoT devices in healthcare problems. IoT and IoHT are discussed in terms of three layers: device, fog, and cloud. The challenges can also be resolved by pervasive patient monitoring supported by IoT [37].

5.3 ARTIFICIAL NEURAL NETWORK METHODS

Artificial Neural Networks (ANN) were used to develop Artificial Intelligence-based systems. Clinical trials and randomized controlled trials involving ANN in diagnosis have increased. There are two recurring concerns about ANNs. The first is the use of principal statistical methods to control model complexity, with the use of cross-validation. The second key is transparency for network predictions [38]. A convolution neural network, computer-aided SPECT images, and other machine learning techniques such as support vector machine (SVM), K Nearest Neighbor (KNN), and decision tree predicted the risk of developing a thyroid disease [39]. Elderly care presents the greatest opportunity for utilising robots in healthcare. It reminded them about regular activities and guided them through unfamiliar environments [40]. Convolution neural networks (CNNs) explore connectivity patterns efficiently with shared weights, such as those utilized in ImageNet competition. It focuses on applying machine learning techniques to medical imaging data. This covers topics such as traditional machine learning techniques including principal component analysis and SVM. Transfer learning addressed insufficient medical image data for training [41]. An overview of IoT and wearable devices using technologies included collected data and devices for elderly healthcare. It presents the existing area of wearable devices with IoT technology and offers research opportunities in healthcare applications. They analysed the healthcare designer solutions and developers in technology-supported older people to increase their quality of life.

5.3.1 Distribution of IoT healthcare studies

Figure 5.1 demonstrates the distribution of studies in IoT healthcare between 2006 and 2023. Summary of some research studies.

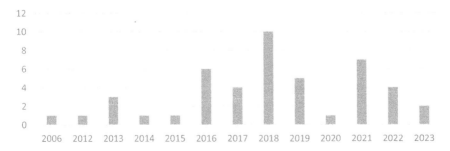

Figure 5.1 Distribution of Studies in IoT Healthcare from 2006 to 2023.

Table 5.1 A brief summary of some research studies of IoT in healthcare

Ref	Authors, Year	Technology	Summary
[20]	(Alamelu & Mythili, 2017)	MANETS (Mobile Adhoc Wireless Networks)	Spread the data to devices in the base station.
[2]	(Banka et al., 2018)	MSSQL DB, Raspberry Pi, GSM module, and interface	To update the data once and send an alert to the doctor.
[11]	(Chen et al., 2019)	Ontology-based system	Diagnoses several health issues, such as hypertension and diabetes.
[10]	(Gupta et al., 2016)	Cooey health monitoring system	To diagnose BP and stores and organise the health history.
[23]	(Gupta & Johari, 2019)	Microcontrollers enable access to the Wi-Fi network	Supports a common standard of Wi-Fi.
[1]	(Jabbar et al., 2017)	REST API lightweight open-source interface	For exchanging data over a solid HTTP system connection.
[5]	(Khan, 2017)	Wi-Fi sensors with RFID, NFC tags, and sensor nodes	E-healthcare systems to get patient information.
[15]	(Mannini et al., 2013)	Wrist-worn water-resistant devices	To determine a person's physical activities.
[21]	(Said & Tolba, 2021)	High-altitude platforms, Satellites, Wireless sensor networks, MNNET, RFID and Cellular with Internet	The clustering approach was used to communicate with the healthcare devices and tools.
[13]	(Park & Subramaniyam, 2017)	Wearable devices and interior places	Healthcare services for medical emergency
[12]	(Poonkodi et al., 2016)	PHQ-9 Mind	To implement brain scans and depression detection
[4]	(Rajput et al., 2016)	DS18B20 sensor	To diagnose HRV, heart failure, diabetic neurology, depression, and body temperature.
[6]	(Rath & Pattanayak, 2018)	IBM Watson's electronic devices	To plan the best treatment for the patient by checking vital medicinal examinations.
[22]	(Subasi et al., 2018)	Mobile devices, IoT, GPRS, GPS, Bluetooth, 4G systems	Medical health infrastructure supported by Mobile to examine human activities.

[19]	(Yattinahalli & Savithramma, 2018)	Cloud Computing with IoT	To increase performance and give a reliable result for a short duration
[3]	(Zhao et al., 2015)	Raspberry Pi, client-server, Python	Enable users to program and design animation, games, or video.
[24]	(Mohanty et al., 2016)	basal body temperature module	The bottom-up approach used to monitor the Thyroid.
[8]	(Malathi et al., 2019)	Thermopile infrared-based sensor, Arduino microcontroller	Thyroid diagnosis by placing the finger on the sensor using detect skin temperature and pulse rate.
[32]	(Lin et al., 2023)	A graph convolutional network	To achieve accuracy with low privacy leakage of medical data and high data integrity
[40]	(Reddy et al., 2018)	Robots in smart healthcare systems	To care for elderly patients using reminding them about regular activities and guiding them through unfamiliar environments.
[17]	(Khan, 2022)	Bluetooth technology and MIT invertor app	To measure heartbeat, body temperature, oxygen saturation in blood and transferring data to mobile.
[38]	(Lisboa et al., 2006)	ANN, Principal statistical methods	To develop AI-based systems and measure model complexity using cross-validation and transparency for network predictions.
[39]	(Wang et al., 2019)	SPECT images, SVM, KNN, and Decision Tree, CNN	Computer-aided systems to predict the risk of a chance of obtaining thyroid disease.
[41]	(Zhang et al., 2019)	CNN, ImageNet, Machine learning methods PCA, SVM and Transfer learning	To explore connectivity patterns, train the medical imaging data, and address insufficient medical image data for training.
[14]	(Islam et al., 2020)	CO and CO_2 Sensors	To detect heartbeat, room temperature, body temperature.

5.4 CURRENT TRENDS AND FUTURE PERSPECTIVES

With the advancement of technology and IoT devices, the development of smart healthcare monitoring devices has been more beneficial in the medical field and can be a great revolution in healthcare. These IoT devices not only help doctors maintain patients' records history and perform their duties wisely and with less effort but are also useful for patients to be alert about the prediction of diseases. With the recent development of deep neural networks, computer vision, and robotics, AI offers the promise of less expensive diagnostic and treatment services. The most important application of IoT is to predict diseases and make fast decisions in critical conditions.

Four main areas of AI have received the greatest attention: patient monitoring, clinical decision support, patient administration, and healthcare interventions. Computer vision can also assess a patient's condition through facial expressions. Smart healthcare monitoring systems are certainly particularly beneficial for society. Because of these systems, we can easily diagnose many health problems at a lower cost and time anywhere and at any time. On October 16, 2019, Jessica Kent, of UC San Francisco, launched Intelligent Imaging, advancing the applications of Artificial Intelligence tools in medical imaging. Thyroid hormonal problems, heart failure, brain tumours, skin diseases, breast cancer and many more diseases can also be predicted with AI-based IoT devices and thermal sensors. IoT data is a valuable addition to other clinical data sources. Artificial Intelligence and the vital associated technologies are considered as provided to multiple benefits to patients and doctors. Artificial Intelligence combines machine learning and other emerging technologies to create IoT-based smart hospitals which can easily diagnose health problems and cost-effective healthcare solutions, which will prove very beneficial for society.

REFERENCES

[1] S. Jabbar, F. Ullah, S. Khalid, & M. Khan, "Semantic Interoperability in Heterogeneous IoT Infrastructure for Healthcare", *Wireless Communication and Mobile Computing*, vol. 9731806, pp. 1–10, 2017. doi: 10.1155/2017/9731806

[2] S. Banka, I. Madan, & S. S. Saranya, "Smart Healthcare monitoring using IoT", *International Journal of Applied Engineering Research*, vol. 13, pp. 11984–11989, 2018.

[3] C.W. Zhao, J. Jegatheesan & S.C. Loon, "Exploring IoT using Raspberry Pi", *Intentional Journal of Computer Networks and Applications*, vol. 2, 2015.

[4] D.S. Rajput & R.R. Gour, "An IoT Framework for Healthcare Monitoring Systems", *International Journal of Computer Science and Information Security*, vol. 14, no. 5, 2016.

[5] S.F. Khan, "Health Care Monitoring System in Internet of Things by using RFID", *International Conference on Industrial Technology and Management*, vol. 978, pp. 5090–5330, 2017.

[6] M. Rath & B. Pattanayak, "Technological improvement in modern health care applications using IoT and novel health care approach proposal", *International Journal of Human Rights in Healthcare*, vol. 12, pp. 148–162, 2018.

[7] I.D. La, T. Diez, M.A. Franco & S.G. Alonso, "IoT-Based Services and Applications for Mental Health in the Literature". *Journal of Medical System*, vol. 36, pp. 93–101, 2018.

[8] M. Malathi, P. Keerthigasri, & S. Balambigai, "A Non-Invasive Technique to Detect Thyroid Using Infrared Sensor", *International Journal of Computer Applications*, vol. 182, pp. 0975–8887, 2019.

[9] P. Sundaravadivel, E. Kougianos & S.P. Mohanty, "Everything You Know About Smart Health Care", *IEEE Consumer Electronics Magazine*, vol. 7, no. 1, 2018.

[10] P. Gupta, D. Aggarwal, J. Chhabra & PK Dhir, "IoT-based Smart HealthCare Kit", *International Conference on Computational Techniques in Information and Communication Technologies*, 2016.

[11] L. Chen, D. Lu, & M. Zhu, "An ontology-based model for diagnosis and treatment of diabetes patients in remote healthcare system", *International Journal of Distributed Sensor Networks*, vol. 15, pp. 1–5. 2019.

[12] M. Poonkodi, A. Srinivasan, B. Tumma & S. Ramaswamy, "A Comprehensive Healthcare System to Detect Depression", *Indian Journal of Science and Technology*, vol. 9, no. 47, 2016.

[13] S.J. Park & M. Subramaniyam, "Development of the Elderly Healthcare Monitoring System with IoT", *Advances in Intelligent Systems and Computing*, vol. 482, pp. 309–315, 2017.

[14] Md. M. Islam and A. Rahaman, "Development of smart healthcare monitoring system in IoT environment," *SN Computer Science*, vol. 1, no. 3, May 2020, doi: 10.1007/s42279-020-00195-y.

[15] A. Mannini, S.S. Intille, & W. Haskell, "Activity Recognition Using a Single Accelerometer Placed at the Wrist or Ankle", *Journal of the American College of Sports Medicine*, vol. 45, no. 11, 2013.

[16] K. Ullah, M.A. Shah & S. Zhang, "Effective Ways to Use Internet of Things in the Field of Medical and Smart Health Care", *International Conference on Intelligent Systems Engineering*, 2016.

[17] M.M. Khan, T. M. Alanazi, A. A. Albraikan, and F. A. Almalki, "IoT-Based Health Monitoring System Development and Analysis," *Security and Communication Networks*, vol. 2022, 2022. doi: 10.1155/2022/9639195

[18] S. Ahmed, M. Ilyas, and M. Y. A. Raja, "Internet of things: Applications in smart healthcare," *ICSIT 2018 – 9th International Conference on Society and Information Technologies, Proceedings*, pp. 19–24, 2018.

[19] S. Yattinahalli & R. M. Savithramma, "A Personal Healthcare IoT System model using Raspberry Pi", *3rd International Conference on Inventive Communication and Computational Technologies*, 2018.

[20] J. V. Alamelu and A. Mythili, "Design of IoT based generic health care system," *International Conference on Microelectronic Devices, Circuits and Systems (ICMDCS)*, August 2017, doi: 10.1109/icmdcs.2017.8211698

[21] O. Said and A. Tolba, "Design and Evaluation of Large-Scale IoT-Enabled Healthcare Architecture", *Applied Sciences*, 2021. doi:10.3390/app11083623

[22] A. Subasi, M. Radhwan & R. Kurdi, "IoT based Mobile Healthcare System for Human Activity Recognition", *15th Learning and Technology Conference*, 2018.

[23] A.K. Gupta, & R. Johari, "IoT-based Electrical Device Surveillance and Control System", *International Conference on Internet of Things: Smart Innovation and Usages*, 2019.

[24] S.P. Mohanty, E. Kougianos and P. Sundaravadivel, "An Energy Efficient Sensor for Thyroid Monitoring through the IoT", *17th International Conference on Thermal, Mechanical and Multi-Physics Simulation and Experiments in Microelectronics and Microsystem*, pp. 1–4, 2016.

[25] A. Rejeb *et al.*, "The Internet of Things (IoT) in healthcare: Taking stock and moving forward," *Internet of Things (Netherlands)*, vol. 22, 2023. doi:10.1016/j.iot.2023.100721

[26] M. Haghi Kashani, M. Madanipour, M. Nikravan, P. Asghari, and E. Mahdipour, "A systematic review of IoT in healthcare: Applications, techniques, and trends," *Journal of Network and Computer Applications*, vol. 192. 2021. doi: 10.1016/j.jnca.2021.103164

[27] B. Pradhan, S. Bhattacharyya, and K. Pal, "IoT-Based Applications in Healthcare Devices," *Hindawi Journal of Healthcare Engineering* vol. 2021, Article ID 6632599, 2021. doi: 10.1155/2021/6632599

[28] S. Y. Y. Tun, S. Madanian, and F. Mirza, "Internet of things (IoT) applications for elderly care: A reflective review," *Aging Clinical and Experimental Research*, vol. 33, no. 4, pp. 855–867, 2021, doi: 10.1007/s40520-020-01545-9

[29] S. Abdulmalek *et al.*, "IoT-Based Healthcare-Monitoring System towards Improving Quality of Life: A Review," *Healthcare (Switzerland)*, vol. 10, no. 10, 2022. doi: 10.3390/healthcare10101993

[30] M. Javaid and I. H. Khan, "Internet of Things (IoT) enabled healthcare helps to take the challenges of COVID-19 Pandemic," *Journal of Oral Biology and Craniofacial Research*, vol. 11, no. 2, 2021, doi: 10.1016/j.jobcr.2021.01.015

[31] A. Belfiore, C. Cuccurullo, and M. Aria, "IoT in healthcare: A scientometric analysis," *Technological Forecasting and Social Change*, vol. 184, 2022, doi: 10.1016/j.techfore.2022.122001

[32] H. Lin, K. Kaur, X. Wang, G. Kaddoum, J. Hu, and M. M. Hassan, "Privacy-Aware Access Control in IoT-Enabled Healthcare: A Federated Deep Learning Approach," *IEEE Internet of Things Journal*, vol. 10, no. 4, 2023, doi: 10.1109/JIOT.2021.3112686

[33] H. K. Hassan, J. Kaduimabed, and M. A. Waheb, "The IoT for Healthcare Applications," *IOP Conf. Ser. Mater. Sci. Eng.*, vol. 1105, no. 1, p. 012075, 2021, doi: 10.1088/1757-899x/1105/1/012075.

[34] R. A. Rayan, C. Tsagkaris, and R. B. Iryna, *The Internet of Things for Healthcare: Applications, Selected Cases and Challenges*, vol. 933, Springer, 2021. doi: 10.1007/978-981-15-9897-5_1

[35] Z. Alansari, S. Soomro, M. R. Belgaum, and S. Shamshirband, "The rise of Internet of Things (IoT) in big healthcare data: Review and open research issues," *Advances in Intelligent Systems and Computing*, vol. 564, pp. 675–685, 2018, doi: 10.1007/978-981-10-6875-1_66

[36] S. Tyagi, A. Aggarwal, P. Maheswari "A Conceptual Framework for IoT-based Healthcare System using Cloud Computing," In *6th International Conference - Cloud System and Big Data Engineering (Confluence)*, vol. 28, no. 4, pp. 503–507, 2016.

[37] S. Agnihotri and K. R. Ramkumar, "IoT and Healthcare: A Review," *CEUR Workshop Proceedings*, vol. 3058, 2021, pp. 1–52, 2021.

[38] P.J. Lisboa, and Taktak, F.G. "The Use of Artificial Neural Networks in Decision Support in Cancer," *Neural Networks*, vol. 2006, pp. 408–415, 2006.

[39] L. Wang, S. Yang, C. Zhao, G. Tian, Y. Gao, Y. Chen, and Y. Lu, "Automatic Thyroid Nodule Recognition and Diagnosis in Ultrasound Imaging with the YOLOv2 Neural Network," *World Journal of Surgical Oncology*, BMC, pp. 6368–6372, 2019.

[40] S. Reddy, J. Fox, and P.M. Purohit, "Artificial Intelligence-enabled Healthcare Delivery," *The Royal Society of Medicine*, pp. 1–7, 2018.

[41] D. Zhang, G.S. Fu, Y.L. Schwartz, & Q.H. Lin, "Machine Learning for Medical Imaging", *Journal of Healthcare Engineering*, pp. 1–3, 2019.

Chapter 6

Revolutionizing healthcare
Harnessing the power of AIoT for smart wellness

Indu
ABES Engineering College, Ghaziabad, India

6.1 INTRODUCTION

In the 21st century, two prominent technologies, Artificial Intelligence (AI) and the Internet of Things (IoT), have brought significant transformation to the healthcare sector, especially in light of the pandemic. This growing interest is largely due to the emergence of Artificial Intelligence of Things (AIoT), which arises from the convergence of AI and IoT. IoT systems play a pivotal role in facilitating the flow of data to AI algorithms, allowing for data integration, interpretation, autonomous image analysis, and predictive analytics. AI algorithms analyze patient data, including genetics, biomarkers, and therapy response, to create personalized treatment plans, maximizing effectiveness while minimizing side effects. Wearable tech and remote monitoring, powered by AI, enable real-time tracking and intervention, enhancing patient safety and reducing hospital readmissions. The chapter explores AI's impact on medical imaging, where deep learning algorithms boost radiologists' efficiency and accuracy in identifying anomalies, leading to quicker diagnoses and better patient outcomes. Additionally, AI streamlines medical procedures by automating tasks like appointment scheduling and documentation, reducing administrative responsibilities and errors. Intelligent chatbots and virtual assistants enhance patient engagement and satisfaction by providing timely support and symptom triage. The chapter also addresses ethical concerns related to AI in healthcare (Malik and Baghel 2023), emphasizing the importance of patient privacy, data security, and bias mitigation for responsible AI algorithm development. Adherence to ethical standards and legal requirements is crucial to ensuring fair and equitable healthcare practices. Finally, the chapter concludes with a glimpse of AI's potential impact on future healthcare delivery. This chapter offers an extensive examination of AIoT through a literature review, focusing on its benefits, uses, and current state of development. It explores the AIoT concept, encompassing the incorporation of AI techniques (Nazar et al. 2021) and the deployment of smart devices within IoT systems. The growing prevalence of articles related to AIoT in academic literature is highlighted,

DOI: 10.1201/9781003509240-6

supported by a database search. Ultimately, the chapter investigates the hurdles linked to the adoption of AIoT technology in contemporary healthcare.

6.2 THE INTEGRATION OF AI AND IOT IN HEALTHCARE

The convergence of AI and IoT has become a pervasive and influential force across various sectors, encompassing healthcare, industry, and agriculture. This chapter delves into the significance of AIoT within the realm of healthcare. The integration of Artificial Intelligence and the Internet of Things is employed in the healthcare sector for the purpose of monitoring individuals' well-being. The healthcare center seeks advanced technological solutions for the early detection of various diseases, including cancer, COVID, asthma, and infections. This enables prompt initiation of optimal treatment interventions to ensure patient well-being. When a patient is transferred from one hospital to another, it becomes necessary to transfer their medical history to the receiving hospital. This process requires the utilization of technological advancements like cloud computing and network connectivity (Malik et al. 2022). Leveraging IoT technology for seamless and economical patient condition assessment, such as the utilization of a COVID detection kit or the monitoring of blood pressure through wearable devices or intelligent machinery. The potential for IoT to optimize and improve healthcare practices is significant. The realization of intelligent machinery necessitates the integration of Artificial Intelligence (AI) alongside the Internet of Things (IoT). The convergence of AI and the IoT gives rise to a device known as a smart watch, which serves the purpose of monitoring one's health. The inherent constraints of healthcare staffing necessitate the exploration of alternative methods for health monitoring. To address this, the integration of AIoT technology is imperative, benefiting both individuals and medical professionals alike. By utilizing a smart device, one can gauge the oxygen level within the body, thereby obviating the need to contact a medical professional. AIoT facilitates prompt data processing, enabling consultations with medical professionals. For instance, consider the utilization of a smart watch as an IoT device. When employed to transmit real-time messages, it transforms into an AIoT example. In this context, the smart watch diligently monitors the wearer's health. Upon detecting any concerns, it promptly notifies the individual and relays a message to their connected family member.

6.3 UTILIZATION OF AI AND IoT IN HEALTHCARE

AI has become a transformative force, particularly in the healthcare sector. The integration of AI with IoT technology in healthcare has the potential to revolutionize clinical procedures, enhance early-stage diagnostics,

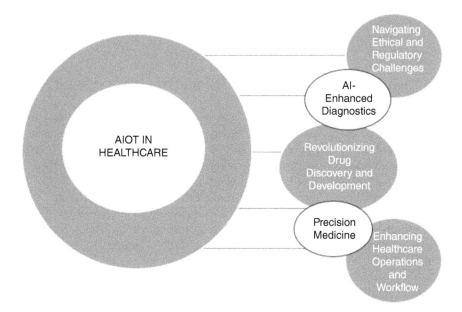

Figure 6.1 AI is applied in healthcare for various purposes, including AI-enhanced diagnostics, precision medicine, the optimization of healthcare operations and workflow, and the transformation of drug discovery and development.

streamline workflows, and improve patient outcomes. AI and IoT devices (Naylor 2018) play a crucial role in ensuring patient safety and early-stage prediction in healthcare (Figure 6.1).

AI-Enhanced Diagnostics: AI has significantly improved disease diagnostics in healthcare compared to manual methods. In the current era, healthcare relies more on smart devices for early-stage prediction. Early disease diagnosis allows for prompt treatment initiation, ensuring patient safety. Healthcare machines have been developed using IoT and AI technology. Deep learning and machine learning are integral components of AI, and they have empowered AI in healthcare. These technologies are employed for tasks like pattern recognition, image identification, and image classification, handling vast amounts of healthcare data (Indu and Baghel 2022). AI, in combination with IoT-based devices, holds the promise of early diagnosis for conditions such as cancer, heart diseases, diabetes, and pregnancy, revolutionizing medical treatment through disease detection at an early stage.

Precision Medicine: Precision medicine, which aims to tailor medical interventions to individual patients based on their specific genetic makeup, lifestyle, and environmental factors, has made significant strides with the help of AI (Akkaş, Sokullu, and Çetin 2020). AI algorithms can identify specific biomarkers, predict susceptibility to diseases, and recommend personalized treatment plans by analyzing extensive genetic data and integrating it with clinical information. This personalized approach has the potential to revolutionize disease management, optimize drug selection, and minimize side effects, ultimately leading to improved patient care and outcomes.

Enhancing Healthcare Operations and Workflow: Healthcare operations and workflow management are undergoing transformations due to the integration of AI technologies. Intelligent automation driven by AI has the capacity to enhance resource allocation, streamline administrative procedures, and enhance operational efficiency (Kumar et al. 2018). AI-based systems can automate functions such as patient triage, appointment scheduling, and the management of electronic health records. This alleviates the administrative burden on healthcare professionals, allowing them to allocate more time to patient care. Furthermore, hospitals and healthcare facilities can enhance resource allocation, optimize bed utilization, and predict patient admissions through AI-powered predictive analytics.

Revolutionizing Drug Discovery and Development: The traditional process of drug discovery and development is known for its time-consuming, challenging, and costly nature. AI has the capability to expedite this process by analyzing a vast amount of biomedical literature, molecular data, and clinical trial information. AI algorithms can identify potential therapeutic targets, predict drug efficacy, and improve drug candidates, thus accelerating the creation of new treatments (Swaroop et al. 2019). AI can also accelerate virtual clinical trials by simulating drug effects and patient reactions, enabling a faster and more cost-effective evaluation of potential treatments.

Navigating Ethical and Regulatory Challenges: The expanding use of AI in healthcare brings about fresh ethical and legal challenges. When applying AI in healthcare, it is vital to consider issues related to privacy, data security, algorithm transparency, and bias mitigation. Clear and comprehensive rules and regulations are necessary to guarantee the ethical and responsible utilization of AI technology, maintain patient trust, and safeguard sensitive medical information. Artificial Intelligence has the potential to revolutionize healthcare by transforming diagnostics, facilitating precision medicine, streamlining healthcare operations, and expediting drug discovery. While AI holds significant promise for enhancing patient care and outcomes, it is imperative to address ethical and regulatory issues diligently. Effective collaboration among healthcare professionals, researchers, policymakers, and technology experts is essential to harness the potential of AI and ensure its responsible adoption. With AI at its core, the future of medicine shines brightly, promising transformative advancements in healthcare delivery and improved quality of life through ongoing innovation and enhancements.

6.4 AI IN MEDICINE: SHAPING THE FUTURE OF HEALTHCARE DELIVERY

Precision medicine is a domain of healthcare delivery experiencing rapid transformation thanks to AI. The use of AI algorithms and machine learning techniques empowers healthcare practitioners to elevate patient outcomes, tailor treatment strategies, and enhance overall patient care. This book chapter delves into the transformative impact of AI in medicine, with a specific focus on its role in precision medicine, the benefits it offers, the challenges it faces, and the promising opportunities it holds for the future.

Personalized Treatment Approaches: AI plays a substantial role in propelling the field of precision medicine forward by tailoring treatment plans to individual patients. AI algorithms excel in identifying specific biomarkers, predicting disease risks, and recommending personalized interventions. This is achieved through the analysis of extensive patient data encompassing genomics, clinical histories, lifestyle factors, and environmental information. This personalized approach enables healthcare providers to administer customized treatments, make more precise drug selections, and mitigate side effects (Gkouskos and Burgos 2017). Consequently, patients benefit from therapies specifically designed to align with their unique characteristics, resulting in improved outcomes and heightened patient contentment.

Timely Disease Detection: Detecting diseases in their early stages is crucial for effective intervention and treatment. AI algorithms have demonstrated exceptional proficiency in this area. AI can identify subtle abnormalities in medical imaging, such as X-rays, MRIs, and CT scans, that human observers might overlook. This capability is particularly valuable for early diagnosis of conditions like cancer, cardiovascular diseases, and neurological disorders. Early detection enables healthcare practitioners to promptly initiate appropriate treatment regimens, potentially leading to improved patient prognosis and survival rates (Indu et al. 2022).

Predictive Analysis: The potential of predictive analytics driven by AI is immense in enhancing healthcare services. AI algorithms can forecast the progression of illnesses, pinpoint individuals at high risk of developing specific conditions, and estimate treatment responses by examining extensive patient data, including electronic health records, physiological metrics, and lifestyle information. By utilizing this data, healthcare (Kishor, Chakraborty, and Jeberson 2021) professionals can personalize treatment plans, undertake preventive measures, and intervene proactively to ensure optimal efficacy. Additionally, predictive analytics can enhance operational efficiency in healthcare institutions by optimizing resource allocation and anticipating patient admissions, among other factors.

Virtual Assistants and Chatbots: AI-driven chatbots and virtual assistants are transforming healthcare delivery by enhancing patient engagement and delivering personalized support. These AI-powered user interfaces can interact with patients, answer their inquiries, share health-related information, and offer self-care guidance. Virtual assistants equipped with natural language processing capabilities can analyze symptoms, provide initial diagnoses, and offer relevant medical advice (Mohapatra, Mohanty, and Mohanty 2019). Healthcare providers can extend their reach, enhance patient access to healthcare services, and offer continuous support by leveraging AI-driven chatbots.

Challenges and Considerations: Despite numerous challenges and considerations, AI holds immense potential for enhancing healthcare delivery. These challenges encompass ensuring data security and privacy, mitigating bias in AI systems, maintaining transparency in decision-making, and addressing ethical dilemmas. Clear regulations are necessary to govern the use of AI in medicine, foster trust between patients and healthcare providers, and ensure responsible and ethical deployment. By enabling personalized treatment plans, facilitating early disease detection, employing predictive analytics, and empowering virtual assistants, AI is reshaping the future of healthcare delivery. The integration of AI into healthcare has the potential to revolutionize patient care, improve outcomes, and enhance overall healthcare system efficiency as it continues to evolve. While the future promises personalized, efficient, and patient-centered care, there are still challenges to overcome. Hence, ongoing collaboration among healthcare providers, researchers, policymakers, and technology experts remains essential. Leveraging AI for Enhanced Diagnostics and Tailored Medicine in Healthcare has substantially improved thanks to the application of AI (Nazir et al. 2019). Healthcare professionals can enhance diagnostic accuracy, optimize treatment regimens, and provide personalized therapies by harnessing AI algorithms, machine learning, and data analytics. This chapter explores how AI is transforming diagnostics and personalized medicine, highlighting its applications, benefits, challenges, and potential.

Enhanced Diagnostic Precision: AI technologies hold the potential to significantly enhance diagnostic accuracy across various medical specialties. By analyzing extensive patient data, including medical images, test results, genetic profiles, and clinical records, AI algorithms can identify patterns, abnormalities, and correlations that may be challenging for human observers to detect. This heightened diagnostic precision can lead to earlier disease detection, reduced instances of missed diagnoses, and improved patient outcomes (Ghazal et al. 2021). Healthcare professionals such as radiologists, pathologists, and others can make quicker and more accurate patient diagnoses with the assistance of AI-driven diagnostic tools, such as computer-aided detection systems.

Advanced Imaging and Radiology: The field of medical imaging and radiology has undergone a significant transformation due to the integration of AI algorithms. Deep learning algorithms enable AI to rapidly and accurately analyze complex medical images, including X-rays, CT scans, and MRIs. Imaging technologies equipped with AI capabilities can identify and emphasize anomalies, assist in tumor diagnosis, monitor disease progression, and even predict treatment responses. This enables radiologists to make quicker and more precise diagnoses while providing better patient management. Additionally, AI can automate image analysis, reducing the workload for radiologists and improving workflow efficiency.

6.5 ENHANCING CHRONIC DISEASE MANAGEMENT WITH AI

AI has the capability to oversee and handle chronic diseases. A risk assessment model is employed to pinpoint patients at a high risk of chronic diseases. Based on the outcomes of this risk assessment, interventions and treatments are initiated for patients. However, these models come with ethical implications linked to potential biases. The accuracy and fairness of these models rely on extensive, unbiased datasets. For instance, if the data source, such as a collection of one million electronic health records, lacks information about Black women with heart disease (Singh et al. 2020), the model might generate inaccurate risk predictions for heart disease in Black female patients.

Health Monitoring Service: Numerous health applications are available for monitoring human health, including devices like smart watches and diabetes monitors. System health monitoring encompasses a wide range of functions, including the tracking of various activities such as monitoring blood pressure (Dwivedi et al. 2019). It involves a set of actions aimed at ensuring a system remains operational. These activities may involve observing the current state of the system, and maintenance and repairs are initiated based on these observations. As shown in Figure 6.2.

Health Monitor Server: A health monitoring server is employed for storing patient data. Storing data on the server enables doctors to easily retrieve patient information. In cases where patients may misplace documents, this data can be readily retrieved from the server. Server data can be accessed at any time and from any location.

Data Center: The Data Center serves as the central repository for all disease-related information in the country. Disease data is collected from various districts, relayed to the provinces, and subsequently archived in the Health Data Center at NIH. NIH bears the responsibility of maintaining and managing historical disease data.

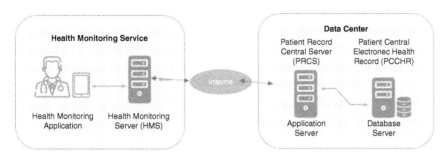

Figure 6.2 A data server is employed in the healthcare sector to store patient records, enabling global access.

Internet: An internet connection is necessary for transmitting data from the local server to the data center. The data center is equipped with servers for data storage, and this data can be accessed globally.

6.6 AI'S INFLUENCE ON HEALTHCARE DELIVERY IN THE FUTURE: A SNEAK PEEK

Artificial Intelligence: Artificial Intelligence (AI) is reshaping healthcare delivery, paving the way for a more patient-centric, efficient, and accessible healthcare ecosystem. With ongoing AI advancements across various healthcare facets, including diagnosis, treatment, monitoring, and patient engagement, the future of healthcare holds immense promise (Ahad, Tahir, and Yau 2019). This chapter explores the potential impacts of AI on healthcare delivery, shedding light on emerging trends, benefits, challenges, and the transformative role AI is poised to play in shaping the future of healthcare.

Enhanced Diagnostic Precision and Decision Support: Medical professionals can utilize AI to analyze diverse patient data, encompassing genomics, medical images, and medical records, in order to detect patterns, identify rare illnesses, and offer more precise diagnoses. AI-driven decision support systems can provide healthcare practitioners with recommendations, treatment guidelines, and personalized treatment plans. The utilization of AI in diagnosis and decision support enables healthcare to be delivered in a more efficient, accurate, and tailored manner to meet each patient's specific needs.

Telemedicine and Remote Care Advancements: In less developed regions and during emergencies, the integration of AI into telemedicine and remote care has the potential to transform healthcare delivery significantly. AI-driven virtual assistants and chatbots can expand access to healthcare services by providing initial triage, symptom assessment, and basic medical guidance. Moreover, AI algorithms can analyze data from wearable devices used for remote monitoring, enabling health-care professionals to remotely track patients' health statuses (Tuli et al. 2020), detect early warning signs, and respond promptly. This facili-tates the delivery of personalized care, reduces unnecessary hospital visits, and enhances patient outcomes.

Enhancing Personalized Medicine and Treatment Optimization: The shift toward personalized medicine, tailoring treatments to the unique charac-teristics and needs of individual patients, is propelled by AI. AI algorithms analyze vast amounts of patient data, including genetic information, lifestyle factors, and treatment results, enabling the creation of custom-ized treatment plans and optimization of medication regimens (Mahdi et al. 2023). These AI-driven algorithms can predict how each patient will respond to different treatments, aiding healthcare professionals in selecting the most appropriate interventions (Esteva et al. 2019). This personalized approach enhances patient satisfaction, reduces side effects, and improves treatment outcomes.

6.7 CONCLUSION

The concept behind smart healthcare devices is to prevent diseases and enable early disease prediction using AI techniques, allowing for prompt treatment by doctors. AI plays a crucial role in detecting diseases like cancer and diabetes. AI and IoT devices make it easy to monitor human health. Ethical considerations, such as patient privacy, data security, and bias miti-gation, must be carefully addressed when implementing AI algorithms in healthcare to ensure fair and equitable healthcare practices in accordance with ethical standards and legal requirements. The abstract concludes by providing a glimpse of AI's potential impact on healthcare delivery in the future, highlighting emerging medical technologies like telemedicine, robot-ics, predictive analytics, and AI-assisted surgery, which hold great promise for transforming the healthcare industry. Collaboration among healthcare professionals, technologists, policymakers, and ethicists is vital to overcome challenges, maximize benefits, and ensure a patient-centered approach in the integration of AI in healthcare.

REFERENCES

Ahad, Abdul, Mohammad Tahir, and Kok-Lim Alvin Yau. 2019. "5G-Based Smart Healthcare Network: Architecture, Taxonomy, Challenges and Future Research Directions." *IEEE Access* 7 (January): 100747–62. https://doi.org/10.1109/access. 2019.2930628

Akkaş, Mustafa Alper, Radosveta Sokullu, and Hüseyin Ertürk Çetin. 2020. "Healthcare and Patient Monitoring Using IoT." *Internet of Things* 11 (September): 100173. https://doi.org/10.1016/j.iot.2020.100173

Dwivedi, Ashutosh Dhar, Gautam Srivastava, Shalini Dhar, and Rajani Singh. 2019. "A Decentralized Privacy-Preserving Healthcare Blockchain for IoT." *Sensors* 19 (2): 326. https://doi.org/10.3390/s19020326

Esteva, Andre, Alexandre Robicquet, Bharath Ramsundar, Volodymyr Kuleshov, Mark A. DePristo, Katherine Chou, Claire Cui, Greg S. Corrado, Sebastian Thrun, and Jeff Dean. 2019. "A Guide to Deep Learning in Healthcare." *Nature Medicine* 25 (1): 24–29. https://doi.org/10.1038/s41591-018-0316-z

Ghazal, Taher M., Mohammad Kamrul Hasan, Muhammad Alshurideh, Haitham M. Alzoubi, Munir Ahmad, Syed Shehryar Akbar, Barween Al Kurdi, and Iman Akour. 2021. "IoT for Smart Cities: Machine Learning Approaches in Smart Healthcare—A Review." *Future Internet* 13 (8): 218. https://doi.org/10.3390/fi13080218

Gkouskos, Dimitrios, and Jonathan R. Burgos. 2017. "I'm in! Towards Participatory Healthcare of Elderly through IOT." *Procedia Computer Science* 113 (January): 647–52. https://doi.org/10.1016/j.procs.2017.08.325

Indu, and Anurag Singh Baghel. 2022. "Evaluate the Growing Demand for and Adverse Effects of Pesticides and Insecticides on Non-Target Organisms Using Machine Learning." *2022 6th International Conference on Computing, Communication, Control and Automation (ICCUBEA*, August. https://doi.org/10.1109/iccubea 54992.2022.10010746

Indu, Anurag Singh Baghel, Arpit Bhardwaj, and Wubshet Ibrahim. 2022. "Optimization of Pesticides Spray on Crops in Agriculture Using Machine Learning." *Computational Intelligence and Neuroscience* 2022 (September): 1–10. https://doi.org/10.1155/2022/9408535

"IOT and AI in Healthcare: A Systematic Literature Review." 2018. *Issues in Information Systems*, January. https://doi.org/10.48009/3_iis_2018_33-41

Kishor, Amit, Chinmay Chakraborty, and Wilson Jeberson. 2021. "Intelligent Healthcare Data Segregation Using Fog Computing with Internet of Things and Machine Learning." *International Journal of Engineering Systems Modelling and Simulation* 12 (2/3): 188. https://doi.org/10.1504/ijesms.2021.115533

Kumar, Priyan Malarvizhi, S. Lokesh, R. Varatharajan, Gokulnath Chandra Babu, and P. Parthasarathy. 2018. "Cloud and IoT Based Disease Prediction and Diagnosis System for Healthcare Using Fuzzy Neural Classifier." *Future Generation Computer Systems* 86 (September): 527–34. https://doi.org/10.1016/j.future.2018.04.036

Mahdi, Syed Sarosh, Gopi Battineni, Mariam Khawaja, Raheel Allana, Maria K Siddiqui, and Daniyal Agha. 2023. "How Does Artificial Intelligence Impact Digital Healthcare Initiatives? A Review of AI Applications in Dental Healthcare." *International Journal of Information Management Data Insights* 3 (1): 100144. https://doi.org/10.1016/j.jjimei.2022.100144

Malik, Indu, and Anurag Singh Baghel. 2023. "Elimination of Herbicides after the Classification of Weeds Using Deep Learning." *International Journal of Sensors, Wireless Communications and Control* 13 (4): 254–69. https://doi.org/10.2174/2 210327913666230816091012

Malik, Indu, Arpit Bhardwaj, Harshit Bhardwaj, and Aditi Sakalle. 2022. "IoT-Enabled Smart Homes." In *Advances in Computational Intelligence and Robotics Book Series*, 160–76. https://doi.org/10.4018/978-1-6684-4991-2.ch008

Mohapatra, Subasish, Suchismita Mohanty, and Subhadarshini Mohanty. 2019. "Smart Healthcare: An Approach for Ubiquitous Healthcare Management Using IoT." In *Elsevier eBooks*, 175–96. https://doi.org/10.1016/b978-0-12-818146-1.00007-6

Naylor, C. David. 2018. "On the Prospects for a (Deep) Learning Health Care System." *JAMA* 320 (11): 1099. https://doi.org/10.1001/jama.2018.11103

Nazar, Mobeen, Muhammad Mansoor Alam, Eiad Yafi, and Mazliham Mohd Su'ud. 2021. "A Systematic Review of Human–Computer Interaction and Explainable Artificial Intelligence in Healthcare with Artificial Intelligence Techniques." *IEEE Access* 9 (January): 153316–48. https://doi.org/10.1109/access.2021.3127881

Nazir, Shah, Yasir Ali, Naeem Ullah, and Iván García-Magariño. 2019. "Internet of Things for Healthcare Using Effects of Mobile Computing: A Systematic Literature Review." *Wireless Communications and Mobile Computing* 2019 (November): 1–20. https://doi.org/10.1155/2019/5931315

Singh, Ravi Pratap, Mohd Javaid, Abid Haleem, and Rajiv Suman. 2020. "Internet of Things (IoT) Applications to Fight against COVID-19 Pandemic." *Diabetes & Metabolic Syndrome: Clinical Research and Reviews* 14 (4): 521–24. https://doi.org/10.1016/j.dsx.2020.04.041

Swaroop, K. Narendra, Kavitha Chandu, Ramesh Gorrepotu, and Subimal Deb. 2019. "A Health Monitoring System for Vital Signs Using IoT." *Internet of Things* 5 (March): 116–29. https://doi.org/10.1016/j.iot.2019.01.004

Tuli, Shreshth, Nipam Basumatary, Sukhpal Singh Gill, Mohsen Kahani, Rajesh Arya, Gurpreet Singh Wander, and Rajkumar Buyya. 2020. "HealthFog: An Ensemble Deep Learning Based Smart Healthcare System for Automatic Diagnosis of Heart Diseases in Integrated IoT and Fog Computing Environments." *Future Generation Computer Systems* 104 (March): 187–200. https://doi.org/10.1016/j.future.2019.10.043

Chapter 7

Futuristic wearable technologies
A fusion of ML and AI capabilities

Monisha Awasthi
USCS, Uttaranchal University, Dehradun, India

Ankur Goel
Meerut Institute of Technology, Meerut, India

Moniya Goel
CAEHS College, Meerut, India

7.1 INTRODUCTION

A wearable electronic gadget is known as wearable technology. It can appear in a variety of forms, such as accessories, jewelry, tools for treating illnesses, garment components, and more. It calls for wearable computing, which describes the item's connectivity and processing capabilities. The technology being used, however, typically determines how sophisticated the wearable is. Google Glass, Artificial Intelligence (AI) hearing aids, Microsoft HoloLens, and many other wearable technology products are among the most complex examples. Disposable skin patches with sensors, however, are a simpler variation of this technology. To a facility control device, they wirelessly communicate patient data. A wearable electronic device is one that is made for users. It can appear in a variety of ways, including as jewelry, accessories, garment components, and more. It calls for wearable computing, which refers to the item's processing and communication capabilities. However, the technology employed typically determines how sophisticated the wearable is.

The most complex examples of wearable technology include Microsoft HoloLens, Google Glass, and hearing aids with AI. However, disposable skin patches with sensors are a less sophisticated variation of this technique. They wirelessly communicate patient data to a facility control device. Fitness trackers, smart watches, and other usabilities fall under the area of wearable technology. Wearable function differently depending on the category they fall under. Fitness, health, and entertainment are some of the well-liked areas. You may sync the data with other gadgets, such as laptops or mobile devices, by using batteries, microprocessors, and internet connectivity. In-built sensors in wearable technologies also monitor your physical motions. Additionally, it has biometric identifications and occasionally aids in location monitoring for the user. The two most popular forms of wearables are

DOI: 10.1201/9781003509240-7

activity trackers and smart watches. They often include a band that fits around the user's wrist to track their daily physical activity and vital signs. The user's mobility and vitals can still be tracked via smart tags, laptops, or smartphones that are portable. Other wearable tracks your speed and movement using intelligent remote sensors. Others employ optical sensors to monitor heart rate or blood sugar levels. The fundamental objective of wearable technology is to track the wearer's data in real-time, which is a common characteristic of the technology.

7.2 HISTORY OF WEARABLE TECHNOLOGY

The first eyeglass was created in the 13th century, marking the beginning of wearable technology. Timepieces were later invented in the 15th century, with some of them being small enough to wear. Modern wearable technology, on the other hand, did not exist until the 1960s. The development of wearable technology is summarized here using several timelines.

7.2.1 The 1960s in the history of wearable technology

Edward Thorpe and Claude Shannon developed the first wearable technology in 1961. It was shaped like a little four-button computer that could be quickly slipped into a shoe or worn around the waist. The goal of this wearable gadget was to help with cheating at roulette in casinos. A timing device that could accurately forecast where the ball would land was also provided by the computer.

7.2.2 The 1970s in the history of wearable technology

The first modern technology was developed by Claude and Edward in the 1960s, but it wasn't until 1970 that it really started to catch on. Pulsar developed the first calculator wristwatch during this decade. After being worn by numerous celebrities, including Sting, the lead vocalist of the band the Police, this new wearable technology quickly became a fashion statement. The concept of wearable electronics wasn't unique to Pulsar; Casio also introduced timepieces in the latter half of the 1970s. For example, Marty McFly was spotted using a Casio calculator in the film, *Back to the Future*, as this quickly acquired popularity.

7.2.3 The 1980s in the history of wearable technology

Sony first made the Walkman available in 1979. The Walkman quickly rose to prominence as the most well-known wearable music player, and it held that title for the entirety of the 1980s. By developing the first digital hearing aids in 1987, the healthcare business entered the wearable technology market as well.

7.2.4 The 1990s in the history of wearable technology

A wearable wireless webcam was developed in 1994 by a researcher from Canada named Steve Mann. Arguably, the future of IoT technologies lies in this webcam technology. The 1990s also saw the emergence of conferences on wearable technology and smart clothing expos. Its popularity in the 1990s dramatically increased as a result.

7.2.5 The 2000s in the history of wearable technology

We can all agree that the wearable technology industry has shown an extensive increase over the past decade. Nike first offered the iPod Sport Kit in the 2000s. Fitbits and Bluetooth headsets both appeared on the scene. In this decade, wearable technology increasingly became a fashion statement.

7.2.6 The 2010s in the history of wearable technology

Wearable technology reached a turning point in this decade. With more technological developments, Google Glass came into existence in 2013. The Oculus Rift Headset debuted in 2016, while Apple Watch also made its debut in 2015. With start-ups springing up all over, there were countless other wearable technology advances this decade.

7.2.7 The 2020s in the history of wearable technology

The start of this decade has been marked by advancements in the gaming sector. New VR and AR headsets are constantly being incorporated into games by developers. In addition, fashion designers are embracing virtual fashion and introducing smart apparel to the general public.

7.3 LITERATURE REVIEW

The communication, network, digital and AI technologies as well as trends have advanced quickly in recent years. The ubiquitous availability of smartphones, multimedia computing, and edge computing devices is another trend. New insights and domains for smart wearable technologies have been produced as a result of various convergent and latest tendencies. The development of AI in wearable technology will be briefly covered in this section, starting with the necessity for wearables, how AI may be applied to wearable and what are the main hurdles in it. More in-depth explanations of the various features will be provided in the next sections of the paper.

The market and public awareness of the advantages of consistent monitoring capabilities for clinical, health, and well-being are expanding. The use of wearables for activity recognition and health monitoring is growing quickly in popularity. The creation of small, complex devices that can integrate several sensors, including temperature sensors, has been made possible by advancements in integrated electronic circuitry and sensing technologies sensors for blood oxygen levels, heart rate, and accelerometers and gyroscopes. Due to the accessibility of these sensors and sensing devices, latest applications for detecting diverse human activities in public and commercial settings have been created. Examples include the use of wearables for tiredness detection [1], fall detection for older individuals [2], sleep monitoring and circadian rhythms [3], and human emotion and stress recognition [4]. Smart wearables can be used to monitor the behaviours and activities of animals and other species. The researchers Nagl et al. [5] created a strategy for using wearable and sensing technology for the management of cattle and animal health. Neethirajan [6] provides an overview of wearable technology use with an emphasis on animal monitoring. Because the wearables' architecture is integrated with ML & AI, these technologies are essential to smart wearables. AI and smart wearables are usually employed in the medical and healthcare industries, as well as in sports, rehabilitation facilities, entertainment, and home security. These wearables support the monitoring of patients' cardiovascular, diabetic, and heart failure conditions. Additionally, it can be used to identify and categorize emotional states, a person's posture, and their stage of sleep. Over the years, numerous ML & AI technologies have been developed. These methods can be divided into traditional deep learning techniques [7] and more contemporary deep learning techniques [8]. Multilayer perceptron (MLP), support vector machines (SVM), decision trees, linear discriminant analysis [9], random forest algorithms [10], Bayesian methods, and hidden Markov models are a few examples of classical machine learning techniques. Convolutional neural networks (CNNs), recurrent neural networks (RNNs), long short-term memory (LSTM) networks, deep reinforcement learning, and stacked auto-encoder architectures are a few examples of deep learning techniques. Our chapter will explore both traditional ML methods and contemporary deep learning methods for smart wearable technology and its use.

The wearable device domain is actively researching ways to increase the comfort level, easily usable, and non-invasiveness of monitoring physiological vital signs and occasionally psychological or emotional state, which can be established by processing data from various sensors. Wearable device development and acceptance have surprisingly reached considerable growth rates in recent years as a result of the massive technological improvements in system on chip (SoC) architecture. Grand View Research's examination of the wearable technology market estimates that the market for wearable devices was worth US$32.63 billion in 2019 and will likely increase significantly over the next several years [11–13].

According to Statista [14], the total number of linked wearable devices is about to hit one billion. Smart watches, armbands, chest straps, shoes, helmets, glasses, lenses, rings, patches, fabrics, and hearing aids are all examples of wearable technology [15, 16]. Despite this amazing progress, much more research in this area is still needed to improve the accuracy of these devices, use diverse biological signals for brand-new application areas, and efficiently handle the complexity of the human body.

7.4 VARIOUS TYPES OF WEARABLE DEVICES

7.4.1 Smartphones

Numerous sensors built into smartphones gather information about user movements. Smartphones are typically carried in pockets, which satisfies the criteria for information collection. Data collecting can be utilized for many different things, such as step tracking, fall detection, elder monitoring, and patient recovery tracking.

7.4.2 Smart wristbands & watches

With numerous built-in sensors that track users' daily sequences, calorie intake, heart rate, and sleep quality, smart wristbands plus watches are widely used and help people get healthy exercise and better sleep.

7.4.3 Smart glasses

The privacy of others may be violated by the smart glasses' recording and filming features. Smart glasses won't compromise privacy, though, as long as their intended use is obvious and the monitoring system is flawless, instead serving as a useful personal assistant and medical device. For instance, Google has previously announced plans to market contact lenses with integrated sensors that can gauge users' blood sugar levels.

7.4.4 Smart clothes and socks

Users' body information is collected by smart clothing through fabric sensors and collection devices, which can be used to track users' energy expenditure and exercise data. Additionally, infants can wear smart baby garments to keep an eye on their physical health.

7.4.5 Smart shoes

Consumers' sports data is mostly collected via smart shoes so that consumers can enhance their exercise regimens. Additionally, some smart sneakers have additional motion sensing features, like Nike's FuelBand SE, which prompts wearers to occasionally get up and exercise.

7.4.6 Smart earphones

New applications for smart headphones, like intelligent voice analysis and processing, make it easier for users to control the devices using voice commands. In coming years, sensors that track movement, body temperature, and heart rate may be included right into in-ear headphones.

7.5 WEARABLE TECHNOLOGY & ITS APPLICATIONS

For many years now, wearable technology has been a significant part of our daily lives and digital transformation. When the first digital hearing aids were introduced in the 1980s, we could not have predicted that they would eventually become a fundamental aspect of our life. With the introduction of AI devices that help you personalize your fitness objectives; the fitness industry is using AI to enable better exercises that don't require gym equipment. Since 2004, which was nicknamed "The year of wearable technology" because of the rapid rise in activity trackers following the release of the Apple Watch, the wearable industry has experienced considerable developments. Wearable gadgets, however, started to lose their appeal at some point between now, when you are reading this chapter, and a few years ago. This was primarily due to the fact that consumers grew tired of keeping track of their steps or receiving call notifications on their smart watch. At this time, rumors of upgrading wearable technology began to spread. In fact, the adoption of cutting-edge IoT applications and product offers for AI is causing a significant shift in the fitness business. (Figure 7.1)

The rise in the adoption of AI assistants, the integration of wireless technology and the development of IoT have driven the market growth of wearable AI. For instance, smart watches have already earned their place in the wearable AI market years back, and the computing power of AI to a tiny watch has truly unlocked a world full of possibilities. In addition, wearables have become increasingly powerful thanks to the rapid use of natural language interfaces; in the future, they may even displace smartphones and PCs.

If you check out the sales of wearable devices, then it is estimated that the smart wearables market will reach a valuation of US$31.95 billion by the year 2026, growing at a CAGR of 11.5%. When compared to all the global regions, North America has 25% of the adult population using wearable devices, followed by the Asia Pacific region (Figure 7.2).

Modern wearable technology falls under a broad spectrum of usability, including fitness trackers like smart watches, VR headsets, AI smart wearable glasses, smart jewellery, and Bluetooth headsets. Each AI wearable device works differently based on the category they belong to, such as fitness, health, or entertainment.

Most of us think that wearable technology is only limited to healthcare and fitness, but has already been incorporated into different types of scenarios. The following are the most popular next in wearable technology applications in various industries.

Number of AI-based wearable device users by region from 2015 to 2022

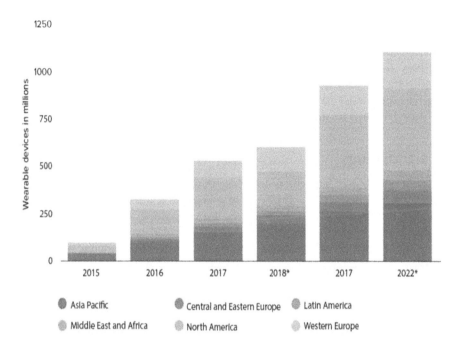

Figure 7.1 Number of AI based wearable devices [17].

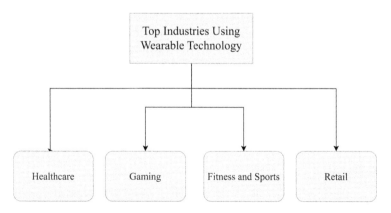

Figure 7.2 Top industries using wearable technology.

7.5.1 Healthcare

Digital transformation has already reshaped the healthcare sector [18] and has led to better and more accurate functionalities with AI analytics in wearable offering stats on patient's health, real-time insights, inference, diagnosis, and reports. The Internet of Things, an AI-driven healthcare IT system, is now connected to medical apps and equipment. Patients can now take preventative healthcare steps at home by keeping track of their health information thanks to AI and wearable technology in healthcare. The Internet of Things (IoT) & AI-based wearable tightly connects all data with real-time health tracking sensors that deliver fast reports and display numerous health variables to assist patients in concluding prompt decisions and taking the required actions to stay healthy.

7.5.2 Gaming

Mobile gaming is a popular industry that will remain in vogue for the next few decades. This could be mainly because it has introduced Artificial Intelligence wearables in its industry. From making AI-enabled real-time audio and visual trackers to AR and VR-enabled games, the industry is moving toward a hedonist user experience. With AI-enhancing wearables, gaming devices have garnered more user engagement. With the release of various VR devices, more and more people have started showing interest in AI-backed gaming. Therefore, wearable devices and gaming are often in a symbiotic linear rate with a common goal of giving the target audience an interrupted AI-driven experience.

7.5.3 Fitness and sports

The fitness and sports industries have recently entered into the tech cosmos. The AI-enabled Bluetooth devices coming in the form of fitness trackers are now featured with biosensors. These biosensors detect elevation, heart rate, proximity, motion, and touch. The application of AI in the sports and fitness industry can also be seen with the introduction of smart headphones that have an AI-based personal trainer which guides the workout process by providing real-time tracking details of cycling, running, and other exercises. Therefore, body-mounted AI wearable devices can successfully provide complete fitness information to their users, simply with voice assistants and real-time insights.

7.5.4 Retail

Artificial Intelligence-wearable monitoring devices have also found their evolution in the retail industry. Consumer retail, especially the clothing sector, is now designing back with the advanced performance of wearable technology. Mobile apps are now synced with AI-driven wearable apparel like hand gloves, jackets, etc., specifically made to ensure the user's or wearer's safety.

7.6 MACHINE LEARNING (ML) & AI FOR WEARABLE DEVICES

Machine learning is the process of instructing wearable technology to react or decide in a given situation without explicit programming. ML is often classified as either supervised, unsupervised, semi-supervised, or reinforced depending on the type of data that is available. To encode prior experience learning, data samples with labels or without labels are employed. The target variable might be categorized or numerical for data with labels. ML is used for a variety of tasks, including clustering for unlabeled data, regression for numerical labels, and classification for categorical target output variables.

While additional works stressed on clustering [19–21] and a limited work on regression problems [22], classification tasks account for the majority of ML research for wearable technology. The use of ML techniques with the body signs described in the previous chapter for health detection, aging care, and fitness control has seen an upsurge in practical research over the past ten years. This part focuses on use cases in the healthcare sector, including activity recognition for tracking fitness or identifying people's daily activities, fall detection, seizure detection, vital sign monitoring and prediction [23], and fall detection. The use of wearable technology in stress detection, heart rate arrhythmia detection, and rehabilitation tasks has also been researched (Table 7.1).

7.7 WHAT HAS CHANGED RECENTLY IN AL AND ML? THE TEN EVOLVING TECHNOLOGIES AT THE MOMENT

In our increasingly digital and data-driven world, Artificial Intelligence has emerged as a driving force behind technological advancement. This is supported by predictions that AI will increase at a rate of 37.3% every year between 2023 and 2030. Making an artificial system that can interact with a constantly shifting environment with a vast number of variables is a problem for AI researchers. We are girded by-products of human intelligence, whether we are discussing culture or consumer items, which is why.

For over a quarter of all workers in developed nations, the nature of employment is changing significantly as a result of technological advancements and the most recent advancements in Artificial Intelligence. As a result, millions of workers must quickly adapt to the new requirements and capabilities in order to keep their employment and income, or else new AI applications will simply replace them.

Table 7.1 Research paradigm related to ML & AI for Healthcare Wearables

S. No.	Research work	AI/ML techniques	Component used
1	Eating Monitoring	Proximity-based active learning [24]	3D accelerometer
		Random forest (89.6% in the laboratory and 72.2% outside the laboratory) [25]	One IMU and a proximity sensor on ear and one IMU on the upper back and a microphone
		DBSCAN clustering [26]	3D accelerometer
		Random forest and DBSCAN clustering algorithm (average precision of 92.3%) [27]	Inertial sensor on the downside of the lower jaw
		Gradient boosted decision tree (80.27% accuracy) [16]	Gyroscope and accelerometer in Apple Watch
2	Fitness Tracking	Logistic regression (0.9356), random forest (0.9203), extremely randomized trees (ERT) (0.9177), and SVM (0.9328)—best accuracy reported in different scenarios [28]	2 accelerometers (hip and ankle)
		L2-SVM [29]	3-Axis accelerometer and 3-axis gyroscope
3	Stress Detection	BN, SVM, KNN, J48, RF and AB learning methods [30]	Zephyr BioHarness for ECG Shimmer 3 GSR for EDA
		Neural network model (92% accuracy for metabolic syndrome patients and 89% for the rest [31]	ECG, GSR, body temperature, SpO2, glucose level, and blood pressure
		LR (87% accuracy) and SVM (93%) [32]	ECG sensor in a chest strap
4	Activity Detection	CNN (UCI-HAR dataset: 95.99%, study set: 93.77%) [33]	Accelerometer and Gyroscope
		Locally linear embedding transfer learning [34]	Accelerometer, magnetometer, gyroscope
		Sequence-to-sequence matching network [18]	Tri-axis accelerometer, tri-axis gyroscopes, magnetometer
		SVM: 90% [35]	sEMG signals of the upper limb by Delsys, accelerometer
		ATRCNN: 97% [36]	Tri-axis accelerometer, triaxis Gyroscope

(Continued)

Table 7.1 (Continued)   Research paradigm related to ML & AI for Healthcare Wearables

S. No.	Research work	AI/ML techniques	Component used
5	Fall Detection	J48 (96.7%), logistic regression (94.9%), MLP (98.2%) [37]	3D accelerometer and gyroscope in smartphone
		KNN (84.1), naive Bayes (61.5%), SVM (68.25%), and ANN (72%) [38]	Accelerometer, gyroscope, and magnetometer
		Temporal signal angle Measurements (93.3%@200 Hz to 91.8%@10 Hz)	Inertial measurement unit (IMU)
		KNN and RF (99.80% KNN and 96.82% for falling activity recognition) [26, 39]	Accelerometer and Gyroscope
		SVM (97% F1 score and 99.7% recall) [40]	Accelerometer and Gyroscope

AI technologies are increasingly popular in marketing, engineering, manufacturing, and healthcare, helping to improve brand mindfulness and reduce costs. AI-powered robots are used for deep earth exploration, space exploration, and complaint control. Advanced AI technologies can also help medical professionals diagnose and treat illnesses, reducing death rates and reducing crime rates in medical practices. The trends in AI that should be aware of will be discussed in more detail now.

7.7.1 Accessories for the meta-universe

- Metaverse: AI technology came generally accepted last time. This year, companies have concentrated on talking about AI's bias to optimize the quality of absorption in the metaverse—made possible by a new type of Internet.
- Panasonic: Possessed Shiftall has released three biases concentrated on the meta-macrocosm:
- Magnex: An ultra-lightweight virtual reality headset.
- Pebble: A mechanism that modifies the physical body's temperature to improve the virtual experience.
- Mutalk [41]: Drug users can interact with people in a virtual environment using a Bluetooth microphone with sound cancellation without disturbing those around them (Figure 7.3).

7.7.2 Smart surveillance

Our homes already have smart security cameras, which are a "must-have" piece of technology, but they also serve additional purposes. Ring, a firm that mostly manufactures doorbells, has revealed a new focus on vehicle security.

Figure 7.3 "Mutalk" is a soundproof Bluetooth microphone.

The Ring automobile Cam has sensors that can determine when your automobile is damaged. The program also functions as a video recorder.

The Bird Buddy feeder is another odd object that has already circulated online. It incorporates Artificial Intelligence, which photographs and catalogs every bird that visits for a snack. By adding several bird species to a companion app, users can make their experience more engaging.

7.7.3 Sleep enhancement

The current trend in artificial intelligence is healthy sleep. It is more crucial than ever, yet the market is flooded with goods that promise higher-quality slumber. The Breeze headphones from LG assess how much time a person spends in each of the three different sleep phases (REM sleep, light sleep, and deep sleep) using sensor data. They can also play sounds to help people fall asleep. (Figure 7.4)

The Pepaminto mattress pad, developed by German startup Variowell Development, can be used to heat or cool different parts of the bed using the Apple Watch. Light and music are used to improve each step of the sleep cycle in this intriguing upgrade to the well-known Hatch Restore 2 alarm clock.

Figure 7.4 Breeze [42].

The updated version adds "morning moments," which let you include motivational quotes or quick exercises.

7.7.4 Smart home devices

It seemed inevitable that healthcare solutions would be included into smart home technology, but some businesses have gone much further. The startup U-Scan, a urine scanner that fits in your toilet, is among the most unexpected. Withings, a medical company, created this cutting-edge AI technology that provides information on reproductive and digestive health.

Samsung has also added an AI-powered oven to its Bespoke Home line. It can function in conjunction with Samsung apps to make recommendations for food items based on exercise data and dietary objectives, in addition to advising the proper cooking temperature for pre-set healthy meals. Another illustration is the Fufuly robotic pillow, which was unveiled by Yukai Engineering (a Honda company), and which aids people in discovering regular breathing patterns.

7.7.5 Wearable devices for wellness

Still a major trend in AI, wellness is becoming increasingly important to many companies. The most recent wearable technology differs from its predecessors in that it incorporates mindfulness-promoting elements and only offers essential information. A Nowatch smart watch is popular because it doesn't display the time but rather the wearer's emotional condition. Based on measurements of heart rate, sweating, physical activity, and sleep habits, this screenless device generates moderate vibrations to elevate mood and lower stress levels. Another recent product is the Citizen CZ Smart. This includes YouQ software, which makes use of NASA research to predict patterns of tiredness phases and increase daily productivity. The use of fashionable wearable AI technology in medical equipment is more common than ever. One of these is the Evie smart ring from Movano Health, which monitors blood oxygen levels and heart rate. It aims to assist women in comprehending sleep and menstrual cycle patterns, among many other things.

7.7.6 Augmented reality

This year, a lot of projects are looking into how to make utilizing modern technology outside more practical. The RayNeo X2 smart glasses were introduced by the high-tech TV manufacturer TCL, a Chinese company. Various valuable information, such as automatic translation and GPS navigation, is superimposed on your field of vision by these augmented reality frames. They can also combine prescription lenses, making them useful for people who wear eyewear. The primary function of Loovic, a GPS-enabled neck band that aids pedestrians in navigating the city without the use of a map, is also navigation.

Another significant AI gadget enables anonymous calls in public settings. A voice-absorbing mask was developed by the French startup Skyted in collaboration with PriestmanGoode, an industrial design firm. They were developed by Airbus for tight or congested areas like buses, vehicles, trains, and airplanes.

7.7.7 Media with light and smell

A few new items can improve the enjoyment of watching movies, listening to music, or playing video games. A video platform developed by the Japanese company Aromajoin combines with the cutting-edge Aroma Shooter technology to produce flavors that enhance whatever is being viewed on screen. There are currently more than 100 different types of scents. A new device from Govee may rival the Philips Hue lighting system. A Matter-certified device that produces vibrant lighting effects to improve the video game experience is the Govee AI Gaming Sync Box Kit.

7.7.8 Artificial Intelligence as a help for parents

The "smart" stroller Ella, which has AI and autonomous driving capabilities, is this year's AI trend. It was released by Glüxkind Technologies, a Canadian firm. The Ella model features an intelligent "Rock-My-Baby" mode, hands-free strolling, and assistance with pushing and braking. (Figure 7.5)

Figure 7.5 AI-powered Ella pram provides an "almost nanny-like experience" [43].

Numerous recent developments in Artificial Intelligence show products made with infants in mind. The brand-new Q-bear baby monitor bills itself as a "baby cry interpreter." It interprets different types of sobbing using a lot of data, making it possible to better understand all emotions. Using Artificial Intelligence to connect light and sound, the device may also assess the cause of pain and discomfort or calm a wailing baby.

7.7.9 Portability and miniaturization

Devices with high performance that were previously stationary are increasingly embracing new formats. That is what the brand-new Brane X portable speaker is. This football-sized speaker offers deep, clean, and powerful bass thanks to cutting-edge new subwoofer innovative technology and substantial built-in processing capability. Amazingly spacious stereo sound is reproduced for an all-in-one speaker.

The Brane X features built-in microphones that enable complete Amazon Alexa functionality with Bluetooth and Apple AirPlay compatibility. Additionally, it has an IP57 rating, making it waterproof and dustproof. According to the manufacturer, a medium volume use of the built-in rechargeable battery would last roughly 12 hours. Because the company's founder has experience with high-precision magnets, he chose to apply his expertise to speakers, which rely on magnets heavily.

7.7.10 Accessibility for all

According to a recent FDA decision, hearing aids for AI can now be purchased in the United States without a prescription, which has created a new market for a technology that is already in demand. The Eargo 7 designer headphones are one of the new Artificial Int products. These hearing AI devices, like earlier models, have noise cancellation and sound processing in addition to being waterproof and fully rechargeable.

Other well-known companies have also introduced goods to aid those with impairments or disabilities. For instance, Sony unveiled Project Leonardo, a PlayStation 5 controller that enables those with limited mobility to play for longer, while L'Oréal unveiled HAPTA, a lipstick applicator designed for those with restricted hand and forearm movement.

7.8 CONCLUSION

The advent of computational technologies like Artificial Intelligence and machine learning enabled a way to transform every walk and dimension of lives of human. One major transition acknowledged in 'Wearable Gadgets' to 'Wearable Technology' as an integral domain of current technological era. Initiated in the 13th century with the invention of the eye glass, wearable technologies are the essential part nowadays whether applied in sports, fitness, healthcare, gaming, education, hospitality, libraries, leisure, tours & travels, retail etc. The smart watches, smart accessories, smart surveillance, smart monitoring & controlling, smart travelling, smart sporting and fitness devices are readily available nowadays which are thoroughly accessible and within the reach of common lives all around the world. There is an immense futuristic capability and possibilities in the field of 'Wearable Technology' as far as new inventions, add-ons and enhancements in the existing devices are concerned.

REFERENCES

[1] Moshawrab, M., M. Adda, A. Bouzouane, H. Ibrahim, and A. Raad. "Smart Wearables for the Detection of Occupational Physical Fatigue: A Literature Review." *Sensors* 22 (2022): 7472.
[2] Pierleoni, P., A. Belli, L. Palma, M. Pellegrini, L. Pernini, and S. Valenti. "A High Reliability Wearable Device for Elderly Fall Detection." *IEEE Sensors Journal* 15 (2015): 4544–4553.
[3] Bianchi, M.T. "Sleep Devices: Wearables and Nearables, Informational and Interventional, Consumer and Clinical." *Metabolism* 84 (2018): 99–108.
[4] Zamkah, A., T. Hui, S. Andrews, N. Dey, F. Shi, and R.S. Sherratt. "Identification of Suitable Biomarkers for Stress and Emotion Detection for Future Personal Affective Wearable Sensors." *Biosensors* 10 (2020): 40.

[5] Nagl, L., R. Schmitz, S. Warren, T.S. Hildreth, H. Erickson, and D. Andresen. "Wearable Sensor System for Wireless State-of-Health Determination in Cattle." In *Proceedings of the 25th Annual International Conference of the IEEE Engineering in Medicine and Biology Society (IEEE Cat. No. 03CH37439)*, Cancun, Mexico, 17–21 September 2003. Volume 4, pp. 3012–3015.

[6] Neethirajan, S. "Recent Advances in Wearable Sensors for Animal Health Management." *Sensors and Bio-Sensors Research* 12 (2017): 15–29.

[7] Goodfellow, Ian; Bengio, Yoshua; Courville, Aaron. *Deep Learning*. Cambridge, MA: MIT Press, 2016.

[8] Michalski, R.S.; Carbonell, J.G.; Mitchell, T.M., eds. *Machine Learning: An Artificial Intelligence Approach*. Berlin/Heidelberg: Springer Science & Business Media, 2013.

[9] Seng, J.K.P.; Ang, K.L.M. "Big Feature Data Analytics: Split and Combine Linear Discriminant Analysis (SC-LDA) for Integration towards Decision Making Analytics." *IEEE Access* 5 (2017): 14056–14065.

[10] Biau, G.; Scornet, E. "A Random Forest Guided Tour." *Test* 25 (2016): 197–227.

[11] "Wearable Technology Market." Grand View Research. Accessed [28/09/2023]. [https://www.grandviewresearch.com/industry-analysis/wearable-technology-market].

[12] Paul, C.; Lefebvre, G.; Duffner, S.; Garcia, C. "Learning Personalized ADL Recognition Models from Few Raw Data." *Artificial Intelligence in Medicine* 107 (2020): Article ID 101916.

[13] Hernandez, V.; Dadkhah, D.; Babakeshizadeh, V.; Kulić, D. "Lower Body Kinematics Estimation from Wearable Sensors for Walking and Running: A Deep Learning Approach." *Gait Posture* 83 (2021): 185–193.

[14] "Global Connected Wearable Devices." Statista. Accessed [28/09/2023]. [https://www.statista.com/statistics/487291/global-connected-wearabledevices/].

[15] Chan, M.; Estève, D.; Fourniols, J.-Y.; Escriba, C.; Campo, E. "Smart Wearable Systems: Current Status and Future Challenges." *Artificial Intelligence in Medicine* 56, no. 3 (2012): 137–156.

[16] Zhang, X.; Kou, W.; Chang, E.I.-C.; Gao, H.; Fan, Y.; Xu, Y. "Sleep Stage Classification Based on Multi-Level Feature Learning and Recurrent Neural Networks via Wearable Device." arXiv (2017): arXiv:1711.00629.

[17] "AI and Wearable Technology." Appinventiv. Accessed [29/09/2023]. [https://appinventiv.com/blog/ai-and-wearable-technology/amp/].

[18] Loncar-Turukalo, Tatjana; Zdravevski, Eftim; Machado da Silva, Jose; Chouvarda, Ioanna; Trajkovik, Vladimir. "Literature on Wearable Technology for Connected Health: Scoping Review of Research Trends, Advances, and Barriers." *Journal of Medical Internet Research* 21, no. 9 (2019): e14017.

[19] Park, S.; Lee, S.W.; Han, S.; Cha, M. "Clustering Insomnia Patterns by Data from Wearable Devices: Algorithm Development and Validation Study." *JMIR mHealth and uHealth* 7, no. 12 (2019).

[20] Abedin, A.; Motlagh, F.; Shi, Q.; Hamid, R.; Ranasinghe, D. "Towards Deep Clustering of Human Activities from Wearables." In *Proceedings of the 2020 International Symposium on Wearable Computers, ISWC '20*, pp. 1–6. ACM, New York, NY, USA, September 2020.

[21] Lee, P.-T.; Chiu, W.-C.; Ho, Y.-H.; Tai, Y.-C.; Lin, C.-C. K.; Lin, C.-L. "Development of Wearable Device and Clustering Based Method for Detecting

Falls in the Elderly." In *Proceedings of the 2021 IEEE 10th Global Conference on Consumer Electronics (GCCE)*, pp. 231–232. Kyoto, Japan, October 2021.

[22] Sabry, F.; Eltaras, T.; Labda, W.; Hamza, F.; Alzoubi, K.; Malluhi, Q. "Towards On-device Dehydration Monitoring Using Machine Learning from Wearable Device's Data." *Sensors* 22, no. 5 (2022): 1887.

[23] Dunn, J.; Kidzinski, L.; Runge, R. "Wearable Sensors Enable Personalized Predictions of Clinical Laboratory Measurements." *Nature Medicine* 27 (2021): 1105–1112.

[24] Torti, E.; Fontanella, A.; Musci, M.; Blago, N.; Pau, D.; Leporati, F.; Piastra, M. "Embedding Recurrent Neural Networks in Wearable Systems for Real-Time Fall Detection." *Microprocessors and Microsystems* 71 (2019): 102895.

[25] Meyer, B.M.; Tulipani, L.J.; Gurchiek, R.D.; Allen, D.A.; Adamowicz, L.; Larie, D.; Solomon, A.J.; Cheney, N.; McGinnis, R.S. "Wearables and Deep Learning Classify Fall Risk From Gait in Multiple Sclerosis." *IEEE Journal of Biomedical and Health Informatics* 15 (2021): 1824–2831.

[26] Chung, S.; Lim, J.; Noh, K.J.; Kim, G.; Jeong, H. "Sensor Data Acquisition and Multimodal Sensor Fusion for Human Activity Recognition Using Deep Learning." *Sensors* 19 (2019): 1716.

[27] Park, K.-B.; Kim, M.; Choi, S.H.; Lee, J.Y. "Deep Learning-Based Smart Task Assistance in Wearable Augmented Reality." *Robotics and Computer-Integrated Manufacturing* 63 (2020): 101887.

[28] Xia, K.; Huang, J.; Wang, H. "LSTM-CNN Architecture for Human Activity Recognition." *IEEE Access* 8 (2020): 56855–56866.

[29] Xia, N.; Yu, W.; Han, X. "Wearable Heart Rate Monitoring Intelligent Sports Bracelet Based on Internet of Things." *Measurement* 164 (2020): 108102.

[30] Moshawrab, M.; Adda, M.; Bouzouane, A.; Ibrahim, H.; Raad, A. "Smart Wearables for the Detection of Occupational Physical Fatigue: A Literature Review." *Sensors* 22 (2022): 7472.

[31] Akbulut, F.P.; Ikitimur, B.; Akan, A. "Wearable Sensor-based Evaluation of Psychosocial Stress in Patients with Metabolic Syndrome." *Artificial Intelligence in Medicine* 104 (2020): Article ID 101824.

[32] Hsu, Y.-L.; Chang, H.-C.; Chiu, Y.-J. "Wearable Sport Activity Classification Based on Deep Convolutional Neural Network." *IEEE* (2019): 7, 170199–170210.

[33] Yen, C.T.; Liao, J.X.; Huang, Y.K. "Human Daily Activity Recognition Performed Using Wearable Inertial Sensors Combined with Deep Learning Algorithms." *IEEE Access* 8 (2020): Article ID 174105.

[34] Ramkumar, P.N.; Haeberle, H.S.; Ramanathan, D.; Cantrell, W.A.; Navarro, S.M.; Mont, M.A.; Bloomfield, M.; Patterson, B.M. "Remote Patient Monitoring Using Mobile Health for Total Knee Arthroplasty: Validation of a Wearable and Machine Learning–Based Surveillance Platform." *The Journal of Arthroplasty*, 34 (2024): 2253–2259. https://doi.org/10.1016/j.arth.2019.05.021

[35] Vos, M.D.; Prince, J.; Buchanan, T.; FitzGerald, J.J.; Antoniades, C.A. "Discriminating Progressive Supranuclear Palsy from Parkinson's Disease Using Wearable Technology and Machine Learning." *Gait Posture* 77 (2020): 257–263.

[36] Rueda, F.M.; Ludtke, S.; Schroder, M.; Yordanova, K.; Kirste, T.; Fink, G.A. "Combining Symbolic Reasoning and Deep Learning for Human Activity Recognition." In *Proceedings of the 2019 IEEE International Conference on Pervasive Computing and Communications Workshops (PerCom Workshops)*, Kyoto, Japan, 11–15 March 2019; pp. 22–27.

[37] Lee, U.; Han, K.; Cho, H.; Chung, K.-M.; Hong, H.; Lee, S.-J.; Carroll, J.M. "Intelligent Positive Computing with Mobile, Wearable, and IoT Devices: Literature Review and Research Directions." *Wireless Ad Hoc Network* 83 (2019): 8–24.

[38] Gao, F.; Wang, L.; Lin, T. "Intelligent Wearable Rehabilitation Robot Control System Based on Mobile Communication Network." *Computer Communications* 153 (2020): 286–293.

[39] Hong, Z.; Hong, M.; Wang, N.; Ma, Y.; Zhou, X.; Wang, W. "A Wearable-based Posture Recognition System with AI-assisted Approach for Healthcare IoT." *Future Generation Computer Systems* 127 (2022): 286–296.

[40] Ali, F.; El-Sappagh, S.; Islam, S.R.; Ali, A.; Attique, M.; Imran, M.; Kwak, K.S. "An Intelligent Healthcare Monitoring Framework using Wearable Sensors and Social Networking Data." *Future Generation Computer Systems* 114 (2021): 23–43.

[41] "MuTalk." Shiftall. Accessed [29/09/2023]. [https://en.shiftall.net/products/mutalk].

[42] "LG Breeze Smart Sleep Care Solution Announced." Gizmochina. Accessed [29/09/2023]. [https://www.gizmochina.com/2023/01/02/lg-breeze-smart-sleep-care-solution-announced/].

[43] "Ella Pram AI by Gluxkind Technologies." Dezeen. Accessed [30/09/2023]. [https://www.dezeen.com/2023/01/12/ella-pram-ai-gluxkind-technologies/].

Chapter 8

Role of IoT in emerging areas

Image processing & data analytics significance in IoT

Salman Khursheed Ahmad

GL Bajaj Institute of Technology and Management, Greater Noida, India

Km Ikra

Mangalmay Institute of Engineering and Technology, Greater Noida, India

8.1 INTRODUCTION TO IMAGE PROCESSING & IoT

IoT: The term Internet of Things (IoT) is related with two terms one is Internet which is network of networks and the other one is Things known as devices. The devices are basically the electronic devices which are capable of sending and receiving the data. In this chapter the intersection of image processing with that of IoT is discussed. So, the data would be in image form from where the useful information is extracted. To technique of image processing is discussed in detail in the next section.

Image processing: This is a method where some actions or operations are being performed on an image, This is done in order to achieve an enhanced image or to help in extracting some useful information from it (Figure 8.1).

IOT KEY BUILDING BLOCK

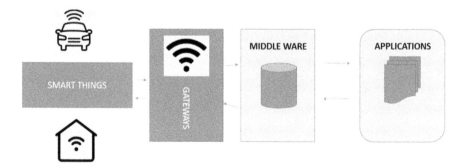

Figure 8.1 IoT key building block.

DOI: 10.1201/9781003509240-8

8.1.1 Importance of image processing in IoT

- The architecture of IoT is based on basically three layers: the layer of sensor, layer of data center, and the layer of service. Each of these individual layers has its self-set of technologies, together with that of unique protocols. Image processing technologies are involved in two of these layers: the sensor layer and the service layer.
- The role of image processing in IoT, various IoT application areas are explored to highlight the participation of image processing in IoT, providing the information about presence of image processing in numerous fields This technique can be applied to solutions in the medical field, to dealing with image processing in agriculture, and to presenting the image processing role in smart cities, smart surveillance systems, smart traffic management system applications and many other areas.

8.2 INSIGHTS OF COMMON APPLICATION AREAS OF IoT AND IMAGE PROCESSING

8.2.1 Application area in medical science

- The major thing which a human body is concerned with is life itself. A human spends a lot of money and dedicates a great deal of effort in order to protect his/her life by many methods. The medical IoT-related applications include the monitoring of patient through remote systems and clinical monitoring. In addition to that, the measures of prevention applications are aspects of healthcare, which are smart in nature.
- As in almost all of the cases some kind of image data is being captured, as in an X-ray. There are many other examples which can be included under this section. These applications need the technology of Image processing which can be integrated to a medical healthcare system (Figure 8.2).

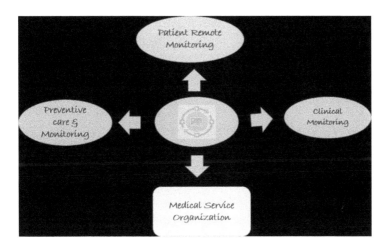

Figure 8.2 Application area in field of medical science.

8.2.2 Application area in agriculture

- The basic need of survival for living beings is food. Thus, it is important to protect food production. In the crowded areas with large populations, there's always a crisis of good food. So, the food need is another large-scale challenge. Applications which are IOT-based helps in providing better food solutions for improved agricultural productivity.
- The good food means that the processing of the food from the initial phase is being monitored and handled carefully. This would be concerned with the checking of the quality of crops and handling the bad condition of the crop as soon as something wrong happens with it. An early preventive measure helps in saving the precious crop. The image-processing system helps in capturing the image of that crop, Identifying the crop diseases etc. (if any) and providing the instant solution for it. IOT-based robots help in taking the real-time images of the crop as early as possible (Figures 8.3 and 8.4).

Figure 8.3 IoT and Image Processing based Crop Health Monitoring.

Figure 8.4 Smart Data Collection.

8.2.3 Application area in traffic management

- One of the most difficult daily problems with which people have to deal are transport systems, and the delays which go with them. Vehicles with a lack of information require an IoT-based automated system. This system will automatically control the traffic light regarding the real-time presence of vehicles.
- The automated system can include the camera. This captures the inputs which could be further handled through techniques of algorithms which are based on image processing.
- In case of emergency, there's an alarm system which can also be developed together with the applications of IoT (Figure 8.5).

8.2.4 Application in wildlife monitoring

- IoT and Image processing technologies has a wide range of applications in the field of wildlife monitoring through tracing the location of the animal to find out the its exact position. This is possible through the means of end –to- end I.O.T Application for wildlife Monitoring.
- It is made possible because of the multi-tier system which is capable of integrating machine language (ML)-based processing of an image which classify animals in an image from a particular remote camera trap (Figure 8.6).

Figure 8.5 IoT and image processing based smart traffic management.

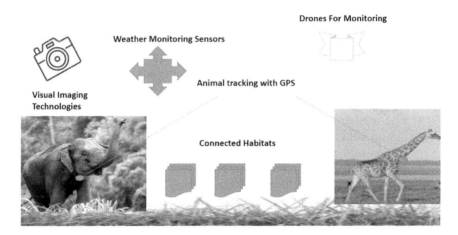

Figure 8.6 Application in wild life monitoring.

8.2.5 Applications in smart homes

- There has been an Increase in the numbers of elderly people living alone.
- The need for smart homes is necessary mainly because of the sudden increase in the number of elderly people who are living alone since their children are either busy with their work or live at some considerable distance from their parents.
- To bridge the medium to resolve this concern, a smart IoT system coupled with image processing can serve the purpose (Figures 8.7 and 8.8).

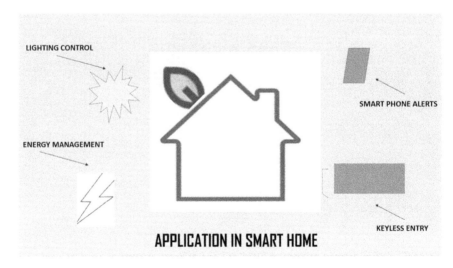

Figure 8.7 Application in smart homes.

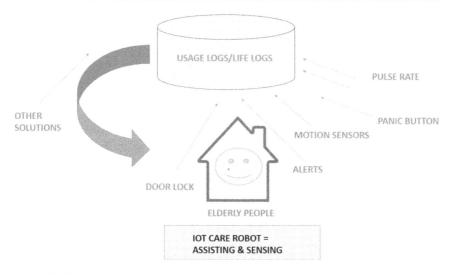

Figure 8.8 Application in smart home for elderly people.

8.2.6 Applications in the biomedical field

- The standalone system either of diagnostic purpose or of a therapeutic purpose cannot yield better results. To cure this, biomedical imaging concentrates on the capture of both diagnostic and therapeutic purposes.
- An image in physiology and physiological purposes can be garnered through the means of advanced sensors and advanced computer technology (Figure 8.9).

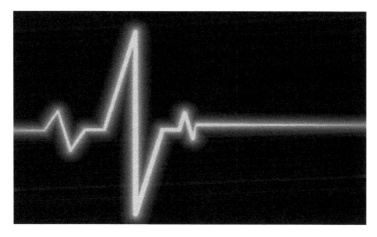

Figure 8.9 Applications in the biomedical field.

8.3 ROLE OF DATA ANALYTICS IN FIELD OF INTERNET OF THINGS

To relate the participation of data analytics in the area of IoT. It is important to see the definition of the Internet of Things with the eye of data analytics.

IoT: This is essentially a platform where devices (also known as things) are connected to the internet; thus, that they can collect and exchange the data with each other at the same time or in real time.

This technology enables the devices to interact, collaborate, and learn from each other's experiences in the same manner as humans.

Data analytics: Data analytics is a broader term which encompasses many different types of analysis of data. An information of any type can be subjected to data analytics techniques. To obtain an insight, the insights can further be used to improve things.

The information gained after this can then be used in optimization of the processes so as to increase the overall efficiency of a business or system.

Role of Data Analytics in IoT

- The data are mostly gained through devices, and these devices have huge volume of data. The organization uses IoT to force the massive amounts of data which are generated by that of the IoT devices, using stacks of analytics.
- IoT analytics combines streams of data which are heterogeneous in nature and then transforms them into consistent and accurate insights. This will provide a clearer view of what the data tells them.
- IoT streams generated insights which help the organizations in improving many of the aspects of their operations. However, this would be unlikely to solve the concern as it is seen as complex to integrate those many types of IoT devices with that of the existing ecosystems and with that of the analytics tools.
- The huge data, also termed big data, can sometimes be characterized by the model of 3 Vs:
  - The 3 Vs are Volume, Variety, and Velocity.
  - Volume is the section which refers to the amount of data.
  - Variety is the section which refers to the number of various types of data and devices.
  - Velocity is the section which refers to the speed of the data processing.

The challenges with which both big data analytics and IoT analytics deal result from that of the simultaneous expansion of all the three properties, rather than just the Volume alone (Figure 8.10).

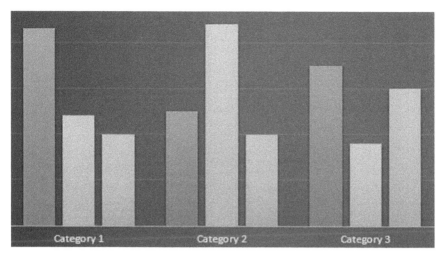

Figure 8.10 Visualization of the analysis of huge volume data collected from sensors.

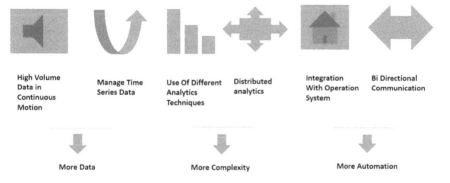

Figure 8.11 Real schema of analysis of huge volume data collected from sensors.

8.3.1 Importance of data analytics in the Internet of Things

8.3.1.1 Analyzing IoT data

The large volume of data is generated by millions of things (or devices) which are connected with the IoT.

Analyzing this kind of data at a larger scale requires the use of Artificial Intelligence (AI). This is made possible with the help of big data analytics in order to know the relations which are contextual and patterns which directly impact the business.

8.3.1.2 Bringing big data analytics and IoT together

IoT helps in demystifying our lives in all best possible ways, including fields like education, smart homes, health-related areas, transportation areas, retail

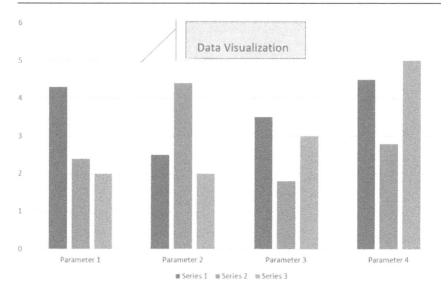

Figure 8.12 Data analysis of huge volume data collected from distinct sensors.

businesses, manufacturing sections, and many more. Here the things (devices) become connected to that of all kind of sensors, apps as software, all kinds of wearables, modern smartphones, smart thermostats, enhanced voice-activated appliances, accurate medical devices, smart lights and smart traffic signals, smart trains and trucks (including cars), and many more, so as to transfer the data in real time without delay to the correct places (Figure 8.12).

The fast-coming data from the devices needs to be collected over some platforms and also to be properly analyzed and visualized. The process helps in the rapid gathering of the data and proper decision-making on the basis of the data collected. There are many IoT analytics platform popular these days; one such platform, which is based on the cloud, is discussed below.

An IoT analytics platform such as Thing Speak is a service which allows us to aggregate the data, to visualize it properly, and to analyze real-time streams of data in the cloud.

The data is transferred to Thing Speak from our devices, creating a visualization of instant live data, and sending the related alerts.

The overall process goes in the following steps as stated below.

Collect and Send: It means whatever data is being collected at the end of sensors are being sent to the cloud in private mode.

Analyze: The analysis and visualization of data using platforms like MATLAB. This will help in making proper decisions based on data received which, in turn, helps in proper action on that very particular data.

Act: Here action is taken based on understanding of the data done in the previous phase where analysis and visualization of the data has taken place (Figure 8.13).

Figure 8.13 Thing speak analysis of huge volume data collected from sensors.

- Smart objects i.e., the objects or devices which are IoT enabled generates *both structured as well as an unstructured data depending on the type of smart objects*.
- Structured data, as the name itself reveals, can be handier as it could be easily managed and processed and also because of its well-defined and an organized schema.
- On the other side, the data which is unstructured, which is basically a combination of say images, audio and video, can be difficult to handle with as it requires a lot of special analytics tools.
- The difference between structured data and the unstructured data is explained in Figure 8.14.

8.3.2 Types of data analytics results

Descriptive Analysis: This type of analysis is used to define the summary of the features in data. With respect to a particular problem, it defines that what is happening by presenting the data in a descriptive way. For e.g. a thermometer placed in the engine of the truck is reporting the value of the temperature of the engine for every second. Here, the descriptive analysis of this event can be represented by providing a summary of the data such as value of average temperature, maximum and minimum temperature etc. (Figure 8.15).

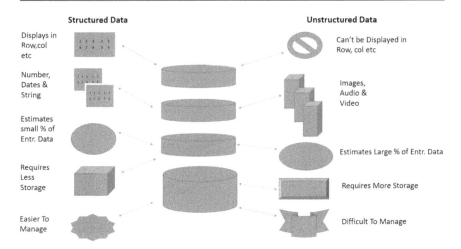

Figure 8.14 Comparison between structured data and unstructured data.

Figure 8.15 Visualization of descriptive and diagnostic analysis of data.

Diagnostic: It is the section, where the word "Why...?" is concerned as diagnostic measure for data analysis, it can help in providing the answer.

Continuing with the same example of truck engine temperature sensor, which we have taken in descriptive analysis, here in this section the instance to diagnostic can be related with the instance where we are interested in finding the cause of the failure

Predictive analysis: This is the section which required as it aims to foretell problems or issues before their occurrence means a priori analysis it is.

For instance, with historical data values of readings of temperatures for the concerned truck engine, predictive analysis provides a rough estimate of the remaining life of certain components of that of the engine, which provides a future-ready solution (Figure 8.16).

Figure 8.16 Visualization of predictive and prescriptive analysis of data.

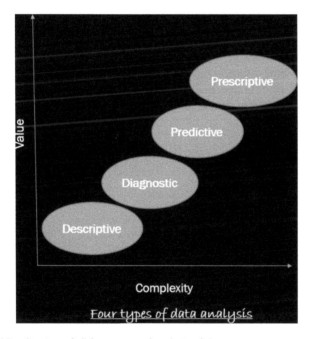

Figure 8.17 Visualization of all four types of analysis of data.

Prescriptive analysis: It goes a step beyond as an extra step or say an add-on step where it suggests possible solutions for the upcoming problems. It provides a cost-effective way to maintain our truck (Figure 8.16).

All of the analysis can be visualized through the following graph between value and complexity, where the descriptive, diagnostic, predictive, and prescriptive analysis are arranged according to their significance

The type of complexity in dealing with different types of analysis is shown in Figure 8.17.

8.3.3 Insights of the Internet of Things (IoT) and data analytics in the field of agriculture

- Unpredictable weather conditions in today's life are a major concern. This creates a huge problem for the farmers as they are unsure how to protect their crop. Thus, making a security for precious food is the major aspect for the most of countries.
- Use of IoT and data analytics also enhances the efficiency and the productivity in the sector of agriculture.
- Seeing the different individual technologies. IoT integrates the several existing technologies, such as wireless sensor networks (WSNs), cloud computing, middleware systems and other user applications to build a better and more robust system (Figure 8.18).

The overall process goes in following steps,

1. Collection of data
2. Sending data using IoT devices
3. Analysis of data and images
4. Visualization and operation management via applications

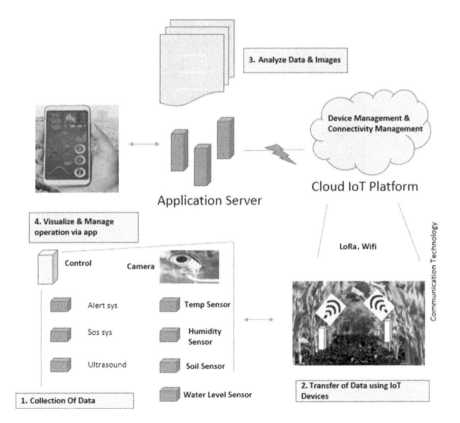

Figure 8.18 Illustration of the Internet of Things-based ecosystem for smart agriculture.

8.3.3.1 Insights of the Internet of Things (IoT) and data analytics in agriculture

Table 8.1 Type of sensors used in agricultural field

Type of sensors	Functions	Examples of application
Optical	Properties of a Soil measured through that of Light	To determine a clay: Photo Diode & Photo Detector, Organic Matter & Content of moisture can also be determined
Mechanical	Mostly measures soil compaction or mechanical resistance	Tensiometers measures the force used by roots in absorption of water
Electrochemical	Electrode measures the specific ions in the soil	ISE & ISEFT for detecting (NPK) in soils
Dielectric soil moisture	Access moisture levels with help of dielectric constant in the soil.	To sense soil water content by FDR or TDR
Airflow	Measures Soil Air Permeability	Moisture & Compaction level of soil can be measured.
Location	Determines the latitude, longitude and altitude by GPS	Provides precise positioning of a corner stone

Table 8.2 Type of sensors with different applications

Type of sensors	Applications
Ultrasonic sensor	It's an electronic device which measures the distance of the object being at a target by electrical signal.
PIR sensor	It is a sensor which allows us to sense the motion.
Rain sensor	The rain sensor is a device which is basically a switching a device connected to automatic irrigation.
LDR sensor	LDR refers to Light Dependent Resistor, which is being sensitive to light that indicates the presence or absence of the light which basically measures the intensity of light.
IR sensor	It detects IR radiation in all of its surrounding environment which can measure the temperature of each individual colour of the light.
Photo diode	Provides an electric current using PN junction diode.

8.3.3.2 A real-time intelligent car parking system

- The initial step here is that all car users can log in into the system in order to find a suitable vacant parking lot.
- The next step is concerned with the authentication purpose. After the authentication and the successful login process, the car users can submit their concerned requests for the parking spaces by using the smartphones they have.
- According to the data regarding the availability of the parking slots, the information to the users will be provided (Figure 8.19).

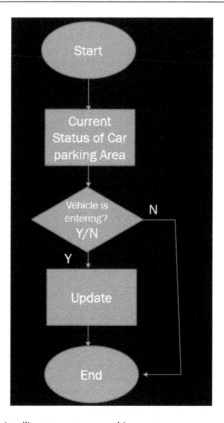

Figure 8.19 Real time intelligent smart car parking system.

8.3.4 Summarizing the contribution of image processing and data analytics in field of Internet of Things (IoT)

To have a better understanding of the role of image processing and data analytics in the field of Internet of Things, A suitable example of smart agriculture through IoT has been considered here.

The overall process goes through the following steps:

1. **Data Collection:** Here, the data is being captured by a robot with an attached camera. Suppose the captured pictures are of the fruits and leaves of the farm. The technology of **image processing** will help in analyzing the disease the leaf or the fruit is going through by clearly processing the captured images.

2. **Data Transmission:** The data being captured by the things (devices, sensor or a robot) is being transmitted by means of the internet. So, the **Internet of Things** comes into the picture.

3. **Data Aggregation:** The data is being aggregated in the cloud (on a platform like ThingSpeak). As huge volume of data is being collected by the sensors. So only a cloud platform can handle it easily.
4. **Data Distribution:** The data aggregated is being distributed on the basis of the need of the receivers.
5. **Data Consumption:** The data being distributed is consumed on the client side so that the data can be properly analyzed and visualized and helps in better decision-making. Thus, **Data Analytics** come into the picture.

The overall process can be cleared through the following figure, which shows the great contribution of the fields of image processing and data analytics in the field of the Internet of Things (Figure 8.20).

The IoT-based smart agriculture involves the following processes:

1. **Crop Yield Analysis:** Here, in order to solve a particular problem forecasting the yielded crop is required where the response of crop to various soil factor is being analyzed. This helps the farmers to know "What to Grow?" together with "When to Grow?"
2. **Auto Spreading:** Here, the fertilizer is being spread out over the land without the involvement of human work, thereby reducing the reliance on manual labor.
3. **Diagnosis of Diseases:** Identification of disease is undergone on the basis of symptoms of the disease like galls, tumors etc. Thus, everything is carried out through visual examinations.
4. **Variable Rate of Fertility:** Here, the number of fertilizers is being varied according to the condition of soil and the needs of the crop.
5. **Water Stress:** This reduces the growth rate of the plant. To form the secondary metabolites, the carbon fixed can be used.

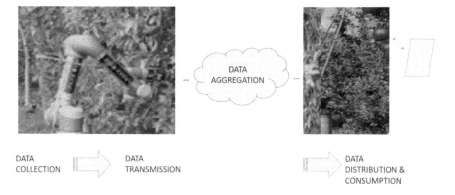

Figure 8.20 Role of image processing and data analytics in Internet of Things based smart agriculture.

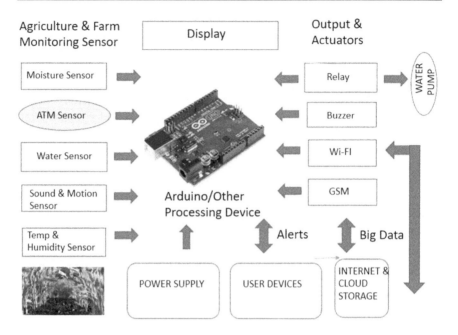

Figure 8.21 IoT based smart agriculture block diagram.

6. **Field Monitoring:** This involves the demonstration of the field using IoT-based sensors, the input to which is being fed by the knowledge base.
7. **Soil Erosion:** This refers to the erosion of topsoil, which is also known as the top layer of dirt. The rate of soil erosion basically depends on many factors, including the vegetation, the intensity of rain etc.
8. **Smart Data:** This helps the farmer to monitor and to measure the deficiencies, if any, in the crop and to provide suitable preventive measures, which, in turn, supports the higher crop yield (Figure 8.21).

It uses recent very latest modern methods and Internet of Things-based technology which manipulates and manages the yields of agriculture. This includes geotracking, sensors, and drones to monitors the fields, crops, and cattle.

8.3.4.1 Benefits of using IoT in agriculture

- Data which are valuable are collected by smart sensors
- Production risks lowered
- Waste reduction and cost management
- Smart production cycle
- Better product quality and larger volumes
- Reduced footprints of on the environment

8.4 CONCLUSION

In order to satisfy the future needs, the development of good image-processing tools is also essential.

In many areas IoT is a vision in the present era and it is expected that in order to make IoT having a more practical dimension with image processing is going to play a good role.

The benefits of the Internet of Things and data analytics has been identified and discussed.

The practical aspects of intersection of both of the fields are separate from the matters which are being discussed here.

8.5 FUTURE WORK/CHALLENGES

- The future work will be mainly concerned with how a good development of image processing and data analytics tools can be made to provide more better solutions in all dimensions.
- The most important aspect is to resolve the issue of real-time data recorded by a variety of sensors in various applications.

REFERENCES

Ahmad, S. K., K. Ikra, & M. Amjad, (2023). "Visitor Friendly Smart Car Parking Management System Using IoT, Web Technology and Deep Learning," *European Chemical Bulletin*, *12* (Special Issue-8 (2023)), 7325–7343. https://doi.org/10.48047/ecb/2023.12.Si8.616

Ahmad, A., M. S. Sayeed, C. Tan, K. Tan, M. A. Bari, & F. Hossain, "A Review on IoT with Big Data Analytics," *2021 9th International Conference on Information and Communication Technology (ICoICT)*, 2021, 160–164. https://doi.org/10.1109/ICoICT52021.2021.9527503

Ahmed, E., I. Yaqoob, I. A. T. Hashem, I. Khan, A. I. A. Ahmed, M. Imran, & A. V. Vasilakos, (2017). "The Role of Big Data Analytics in Internet of Things," *Computer Networks*, 129, 459–471. https://doi.org/10.1016/j.comnet.2017.06.013

Anugraheni, N. A., A. Suhendi, & H. Bethanigtyas, "Image Processing of IoT Based Cherry Tomato Growth Monitoring System", *2019 6th International Conference on Instrumentation Control and Automation (ICA)*, pp. 207–210, 2019.

Bolla, D. R., A. S. Shivashankar, M. L. Bharath, G. B. G. Dharshan, & A. S. Mayur, "Soil Quality Measurement using Image Processing and Internet of Things", *2019 4th International Conference on Recent Trends on Electronics Information Communication & Technology (RTEICT)*, pp. 1119–1122, 2019a.

Bolla, D. R., A. S. Shivashankar, M. L. Bharath, G. B. G. Dharshan, & A. S. Mayur, "Soil Quality Measurement using Image Processing and Internet of Things," *2019 4th International Conference on Recent Trends on Electronics, Information, Communication & Technology (RTEICT)*, 2019b, pp. 1119–1122. https://doi.org/10.1109/RTEICT46194.2019.9016971

Dorothy, A. B., S. B. R. Kumar, & J. J. Sharmila, "IoT Based Home Security through Digital Image Processing Algorithms," *2017 World Congress on Computing and Communication Technologies (WCCCT)*, 2017, pp. 20–23, https://doi.org/10.1109/WCCCT.2016.15

Gonzalez, R. C., & R. E. Woods, *Digital Image Processing using MATLAB*, 3rd edition: Pearson Education, 2005.

Haralick, R., & L. Shapiro, *Computer and Robot Vision*, Addison-Wesley Publishing Company, 1992, Vol. 1, Chap. 7.

Ikra, K., & S. K. Ahmad, (2023). "Analysis of Person Re-Identification Process in Closed World Scenario Through Re-Ranking Method," *Journal of Pharmaceutical Negative Results*, 6972–6981. https://doi.org/10.47750/pnr.2022.13.S07.845

Kumar Kumar, S., A. K. Dahiya, & K. K. Tanwar, "Application of IoT in Agriculture", *9th International Conference on Reliability Infocom Technologies and Optimization (Trends and Future Directions) (ICRITO) 2021*, pp. 1–4, 2021.

Mahato, D. K., S. Yadav, G. J. Saxena, A. Pundir, & R. Mukherjee, "Image Processing and IoT Based Innovative Energy Conservation Technique", *2018 4th International Conference on Computational Intelligence & Communication Technology (CICT)*, pp. 1–5, 2018.

Matsumoto, Y., K. Ogata, I. Kajitani, K. Homma, & Y. Wakita (2019) Development of IoT Robotic Devices for Elderly Care to Measure Daily Activities. In: Duffy, V. (eds) *Digital Human Modeling and Applications in Health, Safety, Ergonomics and Risk Management. Healthcare Applications. HCII 2019*. Lecture Notes in Computer Science, vol. 11582. Springer, Cham. https://doi.org/10.1007/978-3-030-22219-2_19

Pavel, M. I., S. M. Kamruzzaman, S. S. Hasan, & S. R. Sabuj, "An IoT Based Plant Health Monitoring System Implementing Image Processing," *2019 IEEE 4th International Conference on Computer and Communication Systems (ICCCS)*, 2019, pp. 299–303, https://doi.org/10.1109/CCOMS.2019.8821782

Singh, A., & J. Singh. "Image Processing and IOT Based Applications", *International Journal of Innovative Science and Research Technology*, 3(11), 2018. ISSN No:-2456-2165.

Yen, I. L., G. Zhou, W. Zhu, F. Bastani, & S. Y. Hwang, "A Smart Physical World Based on Service Technologies, Big Data, and Game-Based Crowd Sourcing," *2015 IEEE International Conference on Web Services*, 2015, https://doi.org/10.1109/ICWS.2015.111

Chapter 9

AIoT empowerment in agriculture
Enabling smart farming through comprehensive study and implementation

Indu
ABES Engineering College, Ghaziabad, India

9.1 INTRODUCTION

Agriculture is primarily the domain for food production, where farmers employ their best techniques to enhance crop yield. In order to do this, farmers carry out a lot of monitoring. Manual monitoring is very difficult and also potentially inaccurate, requiring a large amount of manpower. However, farmers often face failures because they lack early-stage information about issues such as insects, pests, and crop diseases. This information typically becomes available only after the crop has already suffered, leading farmers to apply protective measures like pesticides when it's often too late. The second major problem in agriculture is water supply, which should be carried out in a timely fashion. The fulfillment of water requirements is crucial for crop health, and irrigation should align with the specific needs of the crop. Manual monitoring of the crop fields is both expensive and challenging. Fortunately, these tasks can now be efficiently accomplished using Artificial Intelligence of Things (AIoT), resulting in improved outcomes and cost-effectiveness. Artificial Intelligence (AI) and the Internet of Things (IoT), two of the most prominent technologies of the 21st century, have significantly transformed the agricultural sector, particularly during the COVID-19 pandemic. The recent surge in interest can be attributed to the emergence of AIoT, which results from the convergence of AI and IoT. IoT systems play a crucial role in facilitating data flow to AI algorithms, enabling data integration, interpretation, autonomous image analysis, and predictive analytics. The traditional agricultural landscape has undergone a profound transformation with the introduction of AIoT technology, effectively addressing various challenges, including pest management and post-harvest management. Despite being a driving force behind smart agriculture, AIoT still faces certain hurdles. This chapter presents a comprehensive review of the literature on AIoT, highlighting its advantages, applications, and current developmental status. It delves into the concept of AIoT, encompassing the adoption of AI methodologies and the utilization of intelligent devices within IoT systems. The increasing trend in article publications related to AIoT topics is showcased based on a database search process. Finally, the

DOI: 10.1201/9781003509240-9

chapter explores the challenges associated with implementing AIoT technology in modern agriculture.

AI, machine learning (ML), and Internet of Things (IoT) sensors providing real-time data for algorithms are significantly contributing to increased agricultural efficiency, improved crop yield, and reduced food production costs. Projections from the United Nations on population growth and hunger indicate a potential increase of 2 billion people worldwide by 2050, necessitating a 60% surge in food productivity to meet their nutritional needs. The U.S. Department of Agriculture's Economic Research Service estimates the value of the food industry in the United States to be approximately $1.7 trillion. Given the expected population growth of a further 2 billion by 2050, AI and ML have already proven their ability to help bridge this food production gap (Indu et al. 2022). In the wake of the COVID-19 pandemic, smart agriculture has emerged as a viable solution to address ongoing challenges in food supply chains and labor availability. While only a few countries, such as the United States and South Korea, have established comprehensive strategies and visions for the implementation of smart agriculture solutions to achieve sustainability objectives, the pandemic has underscored the significance of two highly influential paradigms: AI and the IoT. This integrated system, which represents the most prevalent technology of the 21st century, offers intelligent management, efficient real-time remote monitoring, and data informatization capabilities. The conventional methods of farming have become challenging in today's era, and smart farming has emerged as the optimal approach for achieving improved agricultural outcomes, including increased crop yields and reduced labor requirements. In recent times, smart farming has proven to be a suitable alternative for agricultural practices. Manual monitoring has historically been a cumbersome task, but with the integration of AIoT, it has become considerably more manageable.

9.2 ARTIFICIAL INTELLIGENCE OF THINGS (AIoT)

AIoT, which stands for Artificial Intelligence of Things, represents the integration of Artificial Intelligence and the Internet of Things to create intelligent devices applied across diverse industries and sectors, including manufacturing, agriculture, and healthcare. It combines the data-driven intelligence of AI with the connectivity capabilities of IoT. At its core, this emerging technology is built upon the integration of AI into the infrastructure of the Internet of Things (Stočes et al. 2016). An IoT system usually comprises wireless sensor networks (WSN) strategically positioned across different locations to collect data related to time and location. This system creates a worldwide visualization by connecting an assortment of "things" or objects and devices. These entities are linked via microcontrollers, embedded intelligence, communication channels, sensory capabilities, and actuation functions, all operating on internet protocol (IP). Artificial Intelligence plays a pivotal role in empowering numerous devices and a diverse array of applications within the industrial Internet of Things, including areas like smart grids, urban environments, structures, homes, transportation, and healthcare. In the realm of agriculture, the integration of AIoT primarily revolves around tasks such as managing crop harvesting, automating greenhouse operations, and implementing intelligent fertilization systems that adapt to environmental changes (Szydło and Sendorek 2017). For instance, convolutional neural networks find applications across various scales to predict and identify potential crop diseases based on data collected through IoT sensors. AIoT empowers users to enhance the efficiency, self-sufficiency, and user-friendliness of agricultural operations and management. AIoT serves as a critical driving force behind the advancement of smart agriculture. Nevertheless, several challenges still need to be addressed, including financial considerations and the readiness of technology adoption to reach mainstream status.

9.3 EVOLUTION OF AI & IoT

The rapid evolution of Artificial Intelligence (AI) and the Internet of Things (IoT) has culminated in the convergence known as AIoT, or Artificial Intelligence of Things. While AIoT is still in its early stages, the emerging trends and applications associated with it are reshaping the landscape of substantial business opportunities (Indu and Baghel 2022). In essence, the Internet of Things system enables the seamless flow of data and leverages AI methodologies to enhance integration, conduct analyses, and perform tasks like automatic image analysis and data prediction, among others.

9.4 AIoT IN AGRICULTURE

IoT and AI is used together to improve smart device for agriculture. AIoT devices are smart to process the dataset without an internet connection. To do yield monitoring automatically, AIoT device is the best decision.

- **Greenhouse Automation:** IoT sensors and actuators are employed to monitor greenhouse crop yields, while AIoT devices are utilized for environmental control, including temperature, humidity, and lighting regulation. IoT devices play a crucial role in maintaining optimal conditions, enabling precise cultivation, expediting plant growth, and ultimately enhancing greenhouse productivity.
- **Predictive Analytics for Smart Farming:** Sensors are deployed to gather and analyze data from diverse sources, including weather patterns, soil moisture levels, and water forecasts. IoT is harnessed to

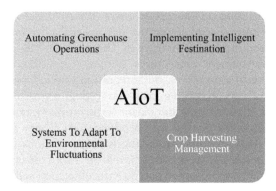

Figure 9.1 The core tasks performed by AIoT include automating greenhouses, implementing intelligent fertigation systems to adapt to environmental fluctuations, and managing crop harvesting.

provide farmers with predictive analytics, enabling them to make well-informed decisions related to irrigation, crop rotation, disease prevention, and resource allocation.

- **Agriculture Drones:** Within IoT, sensors and cameras serve as tools for collecting data related to crop health, irrigation requirements, and plant density. This technology empowers farmers to scrutinize and pinpoint problematic areas, implement preemptive actions, and enhance their farming techniques. Consequently, it results in higher crop yields and decreased resource wastage.

In agriculture, the integration of AIoT primarily centers on tasks like crop harvesting management, automating greenhouse operations, and implementing intelligent festination systems to adapt to environmental fluctuations as shown in Figure 9.1. For instance, applications of convolutional neural networks are applied across various scales to predict and detect potential crop diseases based on the data collected through IoT sensors. AIoT empowers users to enhance the efficiency, independence, and user-friendliness of agricultural operations and management (Malik and Baghel 2023). AIoT stands as a pivotal factor propelling the advancement of smart agriculture. Nonetheless, certain challenges must still be addressed, such as the financial considerations and the readiness of technology adoption to become mainstream.

9.5 INTERNET OF THINGS

IoT, an abbreviation for the Internet of Things, comprises a network of connected devices used for data transmission. Its primary purpose is to collect data from various sources and share it globally via wireless internet connectivity (Nagashree et al. 2023). Wireless networks enable the interconnection of devices in a virtual model across the internet, facilitating seamless data sharing. Every IoT device requires connectivity, falling under the category of device connection. The term "connected devices" refers to the linking of physical devices for information sharing over the Internet. These devices are integrated into technologies encompassing processing chips, software, and hardware. Connected devices represent a fusion of diverse hardware components, including sensors, computers, and mobile phones. They offer the convenience of remote control through smartphones, tablets, or computer systems, allowing users to monitor and manage them remotely using smart devices.

In the past, data collection, transfer, storage, and communication were challenging, but IoT has simplified these processes. The present era relies heavily on technology, where machines are sufficiently intelligent to communicate with each other, without human intervention as shown in Figure 9.2. Technologies can enhance the intelligence of machines, such as Radio Frequency Identification (RFID), which is employed in IoT. RFID is a smart technology which is used to identify individual objects within machines or computer systems. RFID technology can also record metadata, which is data about data. At its core, RFID relies on radio waves to control a target and is capable of collecting real-time data (Sung et al. 2021). IoT leverages RFID technology for object tracking using infrared sensors, GPS, and laser scanner sensor equipment, capturing object movements and locations. IoT plays a pivotal role in data and information exchange, employing smart devices and sensors (Muangprathub et al. 2019). With IoT, the identification of objects, intelligence, location tracking, and monitoring have become effortless. IoT devices are extensively used for data collection across various domains, including environmental monitoring, weather tracking, traffic management,

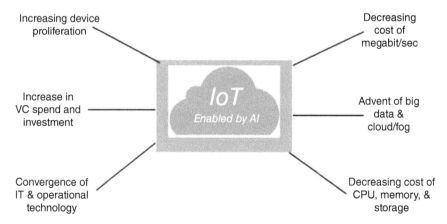

Figure 9.2 AIoT utilizes Internet of Things (IoT) devices to capture and process data, resulting in smart devices capable of pre-analysis.

and more (Malik et al. 2022). The effectiveness of data acquisition hinges on the accuracy of the technology's analytical capabilities. The range of IoT sensors is vast and adaptable to diverse needs. Sensors find application in nearly every sector, encompassing homes, organizations, and agriculture.

9.6 SENSORS IN AGRICULTURE

In agriculture, sensors are invaluable for assessing plant health and optimizing fertilization. Smart farming, an amalgamation of technologies, encompasses sensors, telecommunications, data analytics, and satellites. These technologies contribute to increased crop yields. Agriculture benefits from various sensors for tasks like soil analysis, monitoring water levels, assessing light conditions, detecting crop damage, measuring soil pH, and tracking temperature. Telecommunications technologies encompass networks, GPS, and both hardware and software components. Hardware and software are integral to smart farming, working alongside IoT sensors to enhance crop production. Data analysis stands out as a critical aspect of smart farming, helping in decision-making and forecasting (Mohanraj, Ashokumar, and Naren 2016). Data collection is central to smart farming, as it reflects the yield's quality. Smart agriculture's data collection encompasses meteorological data, fertilizer use, soil conditions, water management, and more. Figure 9.3 illustrates IoT applications with various devices.

Data Collection: Data collection relies on sensors, satellites, and drones, with subsequent data transfer to an AI application for in-depth analysis. This amalgamation of technologies facilitates seamless data exchange

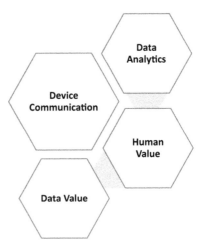

Figure 9.3 AIoT devices serve as applications to assist humans, primarily focusing on tasks like data transfer and precise data analysis.

among machines. The collected data is then stored in a decision support system, offering farmers unprecedented insights into field events at a granular level (Mohanraj, Ashokumar, and Naren 2016). This data is employed with precision to gauge field variability and tailor strategies accordingly. Furthermore, this information plays a crucial role in the precise application of pesticides and fertilizers to crops.

Data Sensing: In the context of data sensing, sensors play a pivotal role as physical devices capable of sensing and capturing data. These electronic components, modules, or subsystems are designed to transmit signals to a server for the purpose of detecting, identifying, and processing events within their vicinity. Sensors are deployed to capture environmental events, a process referred to as data capture or sensor data acquisition.

Device Communication: Device communication serves as a means to transmit data from one node to another across the internet, irrespective of location. In computing, data is transferred using electronic waves. IoT device communication encompasses an infrastructure or system designed for the exchange of data among interconnected devices (Pyingkodi et al. 2022). All devices linked to the system have the capacity to share data with one another. For this system to function, it must be connected to the internet. The data gathered by IoT devices is shared with other connected devices via the internet (Lim et al. 2022). Sensor data can be transmitted for global or local analysis in the cloud. These devices engage in communication with other interconnected devices to acquire information and data.

Data Analytics: Processing a small unit of data is straightforward, but when dealing with large volumes of data, algorithms like machine learning come into play. Data analytics encompasses in-depth data analysis, AI, cognitive computing, and analysis at the edge. Data analysis involves the examination of datasets to identify trends and draw conclusions based on those trends. Its purpose is to extract valuable insights from a dataset (Singh 2021). Specialized hardware and software are employed for the data analysis process.

Data Value: Data value signifies a methodology used for data processing, covering analytical procedures, Application Programming Interfaces (APIs), workflows, and actionable insights. The data employed for inputting records is denoted as data value. Databases encompass a range of data fields (Brewster et al. 2017), encompassing numerical data, names, and contact details. IoT data comes in various forms, including status data and automation data. Status data is organized and transmitted in a linear format, conveying the operational status of interconnected devices. On the other hand, automation data originates from automated systems like sensor-based lighting control systems.

Human Value: Humans engage with smart applications, which do not necessitate human intervention for operation. Technology has seamlessly integrated into human existence, and the advent of IoT has further simplified daily life. Just as human life has evolved alongside technological advancements, IoT continues to expand daily (Adesta, Agusman, and Avicenna 2017). IoT facilitates data exchange and device interaction through communication, enhancing convenience. IoT prioritizes security, and today, humans primarily connect online through IoT devices, facilitating information exchange (Bayih et al. 2022). Technology is now an integral aspect of human life, with continuous technological innovations further streamlining daily existence.

9.7 SMART FARMING

Smart farming represents a contemporary agricultural concept that integrates cutting-edge technologies, including IoT, GPS, sensors, big data, cloud data and machine learning, with the aim of enhancing both the quality and quantity of agricultural production while optimizing manual efforts and costs. This approach, often referred to as "smart farming," leverages information technology to gather data for efficient agricultural management (Đokić, Blašković, and Mandušić 2020). Smart farming introduces advanced technology to automate agricultural management tasks, departing from manual methods. The concept of autonomous farming is a key component of smart farming, empowering farmers with technology-driven tools and techniques to enhance agricultural production's yield and sustainability. Smart agriculture technology has eliminated the need for manual environmental management by farmers (Zhu et al. 2018). The data generated by these systems can be readily accessed and analyzed, providing unprecedented insights into plant health. IoT technology enhances predictive capabilities, assisting farmers in more effectively planning and distributing their produce, and thereby reducing production risks within the agricultural sector. For example, farmers can make informed decisions about harvesting precise crop batches and quantities, resulting in reduced labor and waste. Smart farming harnesses the potential of emerging Fourth Industrial Revolution technologies in agriculture and livestock management to enhance both the quality and the quantity of production while optimizing resource utilization and minimizing environmental repercussions (Yusoff et al. 2023). Furthermore, the integration of technology in agriculture and livestock management holds the promise of enhancing global food security. Smart farming systems also facilitate precise demand forecasting and timely product delivery to markets, thus minimizing wastage (Zhu et al. 2018). Precision agriculture revolves around the efficient management of land resources by tailoring cultivation parameters, such as moisture levels, fertilizer application, and material content, to the specific needs of the in-demand crops. The choice of precision farming systems relies on software for business management. These systems oversee sensor inputs, enabling remote data access for supply management and decision support.

Additionally, they automate machinery and equipment to address emerging challenges and support production effectively.

Smart agriculture is a technology-driven approach primarily focused on modernizing industrial farming. It emphasizes the adoption of smart farming tools by farmers. Smart farming integrates top-notch infrastructure to leverage advanced technologies such as big data, cloud computing, and IoT. Agriculture is increasingly relying on technology to monitor, automate, and analyze farming operations. The foundation of smart farming is laid with the assistance of sensors and software. With the global population continuously growing, smart agriculture continues to advance to meet the escalating demand for crops as shown in Figure 9.4. IoT has had a transformative impact across various industries, including agriculture. In farming, IoT not only addresses challenges but also revolutionizes the farming landscape through cutting-edge technology, resulting in enhanced agricultural production in terms of both quality and quantity (Altalak et al. 2022). Smart farming is a technology-driven approach that relies on real-time information and communication to enhance both the quality and quantity of agricultural production. This innovation has introduced a multitude of intelligent tools and techniques aimed at improving crop yields and the overall sustainability of agricultural practices. Agriculture is integrated with IoT through the use of robots, drones, and sensors equipped with analytical tools for monitoring crop fields. Physical equipment is strategically placed in the fields to capture data. Smart agriculture, which primarily focuses on industrial farming

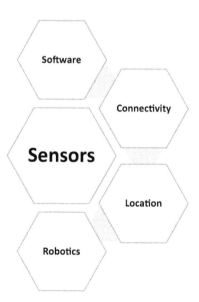

Figure 9.4 Smart farming relies on IoT and AI technologies, where AIoT devices combine sensors, software, and location-based capabilities to process data, even with an internet connection.

practices, necessitates the adoption of advanced agricultural machinery by farmers. Smart farming relies on a robust infrastructure that incorporates cutting-edge technologies like big data, cloud computing, and IoT. Technology plays a pivotal role in agriculture, enabling the tracking, monitoring, automation, and evaluation of farming operations. Smart farming is realized through the synergy of software and sensors.

Sensors: Sensors, although some are non-electronic, are (usually) electronic devices that gather data from the environment and transform it into usable data for further processing. This data can then be processed by either machines or humans. In the context of smart homes, electronic sensors are predominantly employed. These electronic sensors can be classified into two main categories: Analog sensors and digital sensors. Analog sensors are utilized to convert sensor data into analog signals, while digital sensors convert their input data into digital signals. Both analog and digital sensors play a crucial role in creating a smart home environment. Sensors can be integrated with various home appliances, including air conditioners, gas systems, lighting, doorbells, door locks, and environmental monitoring devices (Jagtap et al. 2022). With the aid of sensor data, it is now convenient to remotely monitor and control home functions by humans.

Software: Software consists of a set of instructions that delineate a sequence of steps to perform specific tasks. Computers rely on these instructions to execute various operations. Software is essentially a compilation of these instructions, and it is tailored for distinct purposes. Each software application is designed for a specific function and is not intended to serve multiple, unrelated tasks. Software acts as an intermediary between the hardware and the user, enabling the hardware to function through these software-driven instructions.

Connectivity: Connectivity refers to the means by which systems or applications are linked together. It is the process of establishing connections between various applications or devices. In the context of IoT, connectivity is employed to link IoT devices with servers or the cloud. Data can then be transmitted between devices through these connections. An internet connection serves as a prime example of connectivity. Without a connection, two devices cannot exchange data.

Location: Location denotes the precise spot where an event involving a person or object takes place. Intelligent applications are developed using sensors, with GPS sensors being a prime example for determining precise positions. GPS stands for Global Positioning System and is renowned for its accuracy in providing location data within smart technology.

Robotics: Robotics involves the creation of intelligent machines capable of performing tasks autonomously, providing valuable support to humans. This interdisciplinary field encompasses mechanical engineering, electrical engineering, mechatronics, information engineering, computer engineering, mathematics, software engineering, control engineering, and various other disciplines. Robotics is instrumental in designing machines that can mimic human actions and behaviors, effectively replacing human labor in various applications. Robots find utility in diverse scenarios, including crop inspection, and they are especially useful in hazardous situations such as inspecting radioactive materials, detecting explosives, and identifying bombs.

Sensors: In agriculture, sensors play a crucial role in evaluating plant performance and optimizing fertilization. Smart agricultural technology involves the integration of satellites, satellite communications, sensors, and data analytics. This technology contributes to increased crop yields in smart farming. Various types of sensors are employed in agriculture to collect data, ranging from temperature and pH sensors to those measuring light, crop damage, water levels, and soil conditions. Telecommunications technologies such as networks, GPS, hardware, and software are all indispensable components of smart farming.

Drones: Drones are not the sole robots utilized in smart agriculture; tractors and other agricultural machinery are also equipped with the necessary technologies for autonomous operation. This autonomy has made agriculture less reliant on human labor. The process itself is straightforward, involving the use of AI and location tracking software that relies on map data to program the vehicle's position and speed. In essence, all the essential components, including GPS, control systems, cameras, and sensors, are integrated into the machinery.

Data Analytics: While handling small data units is straightforward, processing extensive datasets requires the application of algorithms such as machine algorithms. Data analytics encompasses in-depth data analysis, Artificial Intelligence, cognitive analysis, and edge analysis. It involves the examination of datasets, identification of trends, and drawing meaningful conclusions from these patterns. Data analytics is employed to extract valuable information stored within a dataset, and specific hardware and software are utilized for this purpose. Post-harvest management involves the handling, storage, and transportation of agricultural commodities following the harvest. In the case of certain products such as coffee and cocoa, post-harvest processes may also encompass drying and fermenting (Sharma et al. 2021). The significance of post-harvest management has been well-established over time, as it bolsters the entire supply chain responsible for producing, transporting, and processing food and related products that sustain the global population. Furthermore, post-harvest management facilitates the strategic allocation of finite resources for sustainable use in the future. In essence, effective post-harvest management enables proactive measures to be taken today, ensuring that the environment remains capable of supporting future generations (Figure 9.5).

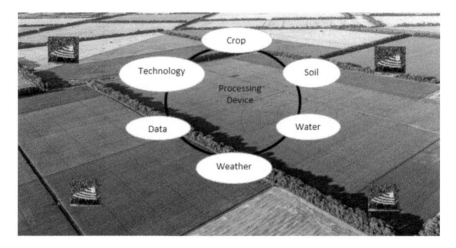

Figure 9.5 AIoT devices in agriculture serve multiple purposes beyond crop management, including weather prediction, soil pH level monitoring, and assessing water requirements. These devices are often referred to as smart or processing devices as they collect real-time data and process it to generate valuable insights.

9.8 PRECISION AGRICULTURE

Precision agriculture (PA) represents an advanced field that concentrates on elevating crop yields and facilitating managerial decisions by employing sophisticated sensor and analysis tools. This scientific approach harmoniously melds technology with agriculture to refine farming practices and optimize productivity (Adesta, Agusman, and Avicenna 2017). By harnessing the capabilities of high-tech instruments, PA aspires to transform the landscape of crop cultivation and decision-making for improved outcomes.

Precision agriculture has emerged as a groundbreaking concept that is gaining global acceptance. Its primary aim is to amplify production, minimize labor demands, and optimize the administration of fertilizers and irrigation techniques. This innovative approach is reshaping the agricultural industry by leveraging state-of-the-art technologies and data-driven methodologies to achieve unprecedented levels of efficiency and sustainability. By implementing PA strategies, farmers can maximize yields, reduce resource wastage, and ultimately contribute to a more productive and environmentally responsible agricultural sector.

The utilization of extensive data and information has become instrumental in elevating the utilization of agricultural resources, optimizing yields, and enhancing overall crop quality. Precision agriculture is a state-of-the-art innovation and refined field-level management approach applied in the realm of agriculture. Its primary objective is to enhance resource productivity within agricultural fields. By harnessing technological advancements and data-driven techniques, PA provides farmers with the capacity to make informed decisions and execute targeted actions to maximize yields while minimizing waste (Malik and Baghel 2023). The essence of precision agriculture lies in its ability to empower farmers with comprehensive insights into crop conditions and health throughout the growing season, necessitating the collection of extensive data at high spatial resolution to ensure precision and reliability. Regardless of the data source used, the ultimate goal of PA is to assist farmers in the effective management of their agricultural operations, often resulting in reduced resource requirements.

9.9 BENEFITS OF AIoT IN AGRICULTURE

- Prior research has indicated that approximately 75 to 80 percent of the population still engages in agricultural activities and resides in rural areas. AIoT technology, which utilizes a range of internet-connected sensors incorporated into satellites, holds the potential to significantly enhance farmers' productivity and crop yields.
- The concept of smart agriculture, also referred to as smart farming, revolves around the utilization of modern technologies for farm management and monitoring with the aim of increasing both the quantity and quality of agricultural outputs.
- Thanks to advancements in sensor technologies, miniaturization, and cost reduction, farmers now have access to tools like navigation systems, soil scanning devices, data management solutions, and pest detection technologies.
- The integration of automation, real-time data collection, and AIoT-enabled devices holds the promise of substantial improvements in the smart agriculture sector.
- In contrast to embedded systems, which facilitate the Internet of Things and leverage AI, smart farming traditionally does not incorporate AI technology.
- Given the inherent advantages of AI and IoT, there is a strong expectation that AIoT has the potential to outperform previous technologies.
- The subsequent subsections delve into the four primary benefits that AIoT is anticipated to bring to the agriculture industry.

9.10 CHALLENGES IN THE AIoT

- Challenges in the Adoption of Technology Artificial Intelligence of Things (AIoT) holds significant potential for ushering in positive transformations across both society and various industries. As numerous businesses have started employing "things" to establish communication, there's a prevailing challenge in many sectors, which involves adopting cutting-edge technologies without prior experience or digital proficiency. The rapid proliferation of internet-connected "things" can potentially introduce several complications for those venturing into new technological realms.

- Complexity stands out as one of the primary issues confronting many businesses. This complexity pertains to the interplay between connected devices and other systems, viewed from the perspective of a cyber-physical system. Financial constraints pose another substantial hurdle for technology adoption, with users often struggling to allocate resources for specific objectives, such as acquiring equipment or providing comprehensive training for the entire system. Additionally, a lack of awareness and expertise has hindered the effective utilization of technology.

- Another challenge lies in the necessity for greater confidence in AIoT technology. The reluctance to embrace new technologies can also stem from a lack of trust in both IoT and AI. In terms of data-handling flexibility, AIoT technology is perceived as dependable, relying heavily on accurate information. Given that farmers may not possess extensive tech knowledge, they may be compelled to rely solely on experts for comprehending and evaluating AIoT systems, making technology adoption potentially daunting for them. Furthermore, the sector faces difficulties in recruiting professionals with digital proficiency to manage and maintain new technology operations, in addition to implementing novel systems.

- Furthermore, concerns regarding security and privacy pose obstacles to the uptake of emerging technologies. The convergence of AI and IoT introduces new security threats, such as data breaches and cyber-attacks. Privacy concerns become increasingly significant as Internet of Things devices collect and transmit vast volumes of data. Consequently, businesses need to stay well-informed about the regulations and standards governing data preservation.

- One of the most challenging aspects of implementing an AIoT model in agriculture is ensuring its consistent performance in various environmental conditions and uncertainties, including factors like temperature, humidity, sunlight, rainfall, and water availability.

- AIoT systems in agriculture require a substantial amount of agricultural data to develop robust AI models. While spatial data can be collected in real time, agricultural data often relies on seasonal patterns. This limitation can make it challenging to achieve the desired accuracy of AI models for specific periods. Inaccurate predictions could lead to unexpected costs, and errors in forecasting and recommendations could result in a year's worth of crop losses, impacting both farmers' livelihoods and global food security. Therefore, strategic planning might involve utilizing a small portion of farmers' land for AI-based data analysis before implementing the AI model across the entire farm.

9.11 DISCUSSION

This chapter delves into comprehensive discussions of intriguing AIoT applications. It draws inspiration from existing, well-tested AI/IoT applications, including infrared cameras, video surveillance systems, and computer vision. The assessment provides recommendations for enhancing AIoT capabilities and applications that are beneficial to users. Additionally, it explores the hurdles associated with the adoption of new technologies. Throughout the post-harvest phase, handlers and producers prioritize the preservation of commodity quality, quantity, and safety. For example, coffee and cocoa producers and traders, in particular, attach great significance to upholding the integrity of the beans, as it has a direct impact on the commodity's market price. This entails ensuring that moisture, contaminants, and pests do not compromise the quality of the commodities. The growth of smart agriculture is driven by the increasing global population, which in turn raises the demand for agricultural products in each nation. IoT has revolutionized various industries, and it has had a profound impact on agriculture as well. It hasn't merely provided solutions to agricultural challenges; it has fundamentally transformed farming practices and enhanced agricultural productivity. IoT sensors have a broad range of applications, adaptable to diverse needs and industries, including agriculture, businesses, and households. Nonetheless, it's important to note that industrial agriculture isn't inherently detrimental. When executed correctly, both industrial agriculture and industrial post-harvest management hold the potential to be transformative forces in addressing challenges like global hunger eradication and ensuring food safety.

9.12 CONCLUSION

The idea behind smart agriculture, often known as smart farming, is centered on the application of contemporary technologies to enhance farm management and monitoring, ultimately leading to improved agricultural output in terms of quantity and quality using AIoT. AIoT represents the fusion of AI and IoT, resulting in smart devices capable of making autonomous decisions without requiring a continuous internet connection. These devices find valuable applications in agriculture, including tasks like assessing water requirements, predicting pest infestations, and measuring soil pH levels. AIoT technology has the potential to boost agricultural production significantly by enabling efficient cultivation and reducing the reliance on manual labor. Recent advancements in sensor technologies, along with miniaturization and cost reduction, have provided farmers with access to various tools such as navigation systems, soil scanning devices, data management solutions, and pest detection technologies. In this chapter, we explore in-depth discussions of compelling AIoT applications, taking inspiration from established AI/IoT applications like infrared cameras, video surveillance systems, and computer vision.

REFERENCES

Adesta, Erry Yulian Triblas, Delvis Agusman, and Avicenna Avicenna. 2017. "Internet of Things (IoT) in Agriculture Industries." *Indonesian Journal of Electrical Engineering and Informatics* 5 (4). https://doi.org/10.52549/ijeei.v5i4.373

Altalak, Maha, Mohammad Ammad Uddin, Amal Alajmi, and Alwaseemah Rizg. 2022. "Smart Agriculture Applications Using Deep Learning Technologies: A Survey." *Applied Sciences* 12 (12): 5919. https://doi.org/10.3390/app12125919

Bayih, Amsale Zelalem, Javier Morales, Yaregal Assabie, and R.A. De By. 2022. "Utilization of Internet of Things and Wireless Sensor Networks for Sustainable Smallholder Agriculture." *Sensors* 22 (9): 3273. https://doi.org/10.3390/s22093273

Brewster, Christopher, Ioanna Roussaki, Nikos Kalatzis, Kevin Doolin, and Keith A. Ellis. 2017. "IoT in Agriculture: Designing a Europe-Wide Large-Scale Pilot." *IEEE Communications Magazine* 55 (9): 26–33. https://doi.org/10.1109/mcom.2017.1600528

Đokić, Kristian, Lucija Blašković, and Dubravka Mandušić. 2020. "From Machine Learning to Deep Learning in Agriculture – the Quantitative Review of Trends." *IOP Conference Series* 614 (1): 012138. https://doi.org/10.1088/1755-1315/614/1/012138

Indu, and Anurag Singh Baghel. 2022. "Evaluate the Growing Demand for and Adverse Effects of Pesticides and Insecticides on Non-Target Organisms Using Machine Learning." *2022 6th International Conference on Computing, Communication, Control and Automation (ICCUBEA*, August. https://doi.org/10.1109/iccubea54992.2022.10010746

Indu, Anurag Singh Baghel, Arpit Bhardwaj, and Wubshet Ibrahim. 2022. "Optimization of Pesticides Spray on Crops in Agriculture Using Machine Learning." *Computational Intelligence and Neuroscience* 2022 (September): 1–10. https://doi.org/10.1155/2022/9408535

Jagtap, Santosh T., Khongdet Phasinam, Thanwamas Kassanuk, Subhesh Saurabh Jha, Tanmay Ghosh, and Chetan M. Thakar. 2022. "Towards Application of Various Machine Learning Techniques in Agriculture." *Materials Today: Proceedings* 51 (January): 793–97. https://doi.org/10.1016/j.matpr.2021.06.236

Lim, Hooi Ren, Kuan Shiong Khoo, Wen Yi Chia, Kit Wayne Chew, and Shih-Hsin Ho. 2022. "Smart Microalgae Farming with Internet-of-Things for Sustainable Agriculture." *Biotechnology Advances* 57 (July): 107931. https://doi.org/10.1016/j.biotechadv.2022.107931

Malik, Indu, and Anurag Singh Baghel. 2023. "Elimination of Herbicides after the Classification of Weeds Using Deep Learning." *International Journal of Sensors, Wireless Communications and Control* 13 (4): 254–69. https://doi.org/10.2174/2210327913666230816091012.

Malik, Indu, Arpit Bhardwaj, Harshit Bhardwaj, and Aditi Sakalle. 2022. "IoT-Enabled Smart Homes." In *Advances in Computational Intelligence and Robotics Book Series*, 160–76. https://doi.org/10.4018/978-1-6684-4991-2.ch008.

Mohanraj, I., Kirthika Ashokumar, and J. Naren. 2016. "Field Monitoring and Automation Using IOT in Agriculture Domain." *Procedia Computer Science* 93 (January): 931–39. https://doi.org/10.1016/j.procs.2016.07.275

Muangprathub, Jirapond, Nathaphon Boonnam, Siriwan Kajornkasirat, Narongsak Lekbangpong, Apirat Wanichsombat, and Pichetwut Nillaor. 2019. "IoT and Agriculture Data Analysis for Smart Farm." *Computers and Electronics in Agriculture* 156 (January): 467–74. https://doi.org/10.1016/j.compag.2018.12.011

Nagashree, N., Shantakumar B. Patıl, K. S. Narayan, N. S. Chethana, N. Chandana, Rakshitha Mansi Ht, and Sparshithraj. 2023. "A Modified Framework for Image Encryption and Decryption Using Modified Chaotic Algorithms towards Medical Image Security." *Zenodo (CERN European Organization for Nuclear Research)* June. https://doi.org/10.5281/zenodo.8069902

Pyingkodi, M., K. Thenmozhi, K. Nanthini, Muthukumarasamy Karthikeyan, Suresh Palarimath, V. Erajavignesh, and G. Bala Ajith Kumar. 2022. "Sensor Based Smart Agriculture with IoT Technologies: A Review." *2022 International Conference on Computer Communication and Informatics (ICCCI)*, January. https://doi.org/10.1109/iccci54379.2022.9741001

Sharma, Abhinav, Arpit Jain, Prateek Gupta, and Vinay Chowdary. 2021. "Machine Learning Applications for Precision Agriculture: A Comprehensive Review." *IEEE Access 9* (January): 4843–73. https://doi.org/10.1109/access.2020.3048415

Singh, Satyanand. 2021. "Environmental Energy Harvesting Techniques to Power Standalone IoT-Equipped Sensor and Its Application in 5G Communication." *Emerging Science Journal 4* (November): 116–26. https://doi.org/10.28991/esj-2021-sp1-08

Stočes, Michal, Jiří Vaněk, Jan Masner, and Ján Pavlík. 2016. "Internet of Things (IoT) in Agriculture - Selected Aspects." *AGRIS On-Line Papers in Economics and Informatics VIII* 1: 83–88. https://doi.org/10.7160/aol.2016.080108

Sung, Tien-Wen, Pei-Wei Tsai, Tarek Gaber, and Chao-Yang Lee. 2021. "Artificial Intelligence of Things (AIOT) Technologies and Applications." *Wireless Communications and Mobile Computing* 2021 (July): 1–2. https://doi.org/10.1155/2021/9781271

Szydło, Tomasz, and Joanna Sendorek. 2017. "Leveraging Virtualization for Scenario Based IoT Application Testing." *Computer Science and Information Systems (FedCSIS)*, 2019 Federated Conference On, September. https://doi.org/10.15439/2017f394

Yusoff, Abdul Hafidz, Muhammad Akmal Remli, Khairul Nizar Syazwan Wan Salihin Wong, Nor Alina Ismail, Alfonso González-Briones, Juan M. Corchado, and Mohd Saberi Mohamad. 2023. "Recent Advancements and Challenges of AIoT Application in Smart Agriculture: A Review." *Sensors* 23 (7): 3752. https://doi.org/10.3390/s23073752

Zhu, Nanyang, Xu Liu, Ziqian Liu, Kai Hu, Wang Yingkuan, Jinglu Tan, Min Huang, et al. 2018. "Deep Learning for Smart Agriculture: Concepts, Tools, Applications, and Opportunities." *International Journal of Agricultural and Biological Engineering* 11 (4): 21–28. https://doi.org/10.25165/j.ijabe.20181104.4475

Chapter 10

Security concerns with IoT
Detecting DDoS attacks in IoT environments

Umar Danjuma Maiwada, Kamaluddeen Usman Danyaro and M. S. Liew
Universiti Teknologi PETRONAS, Seri Iskandar, Malaysia

Abdussalam Ahmed Alashhab
Alasmarya Islamic University, Zliten, Libya

Aliza Bt Sarlan
Universiti Teknologi PETRONAS, Seri Iskandar, Malaysia

10.1 INTRODUCTION

The wireless tethering of internet-connected smart objects or things is known as the Internet of Things (IoT). IoT became known as a promising technical advancement in recent years for connecting a wide variety of heterogeneous devices all around the world. We can access, manage, and control these devices with the help of the IoT to acquire a variety of functions in a variety of application scenarios, such as smart homes, smart hospitals, connected vehicles, smart industry, etc. It may be possible to centralize device management to simplify gadget use, offer a sense of ease to people, and thereby improve their general quality of life. Every area of our lives, including education, our homes, our cars, and healthcare, is being affected by the IoT, which is constantly expanding. IoT technologies face several challenges as the number of devices connected to the internet rises, including disparity, flexibility, quality of service, privacy concerns, and many more [1].

The exponential rise in users who rely on mobile devices like wireless internet access, cellphones, and other smart gadgets has served as a driving force behind earlier studies on the 5G cellular system. A battery, which is a permanent power source, powers these portable devices. A key roadblock to the development of ever-more advanced technologies, such as the highly anticipated "smartphones", is the battery-powered wireless gadgets' constrained power supply. The studies that have lately been published have already focused on research on larger batteries caused by DDoS attack. By contrast, the gradual improvement in battery capacity could be able to keep up with the rapid expansion of the internet and mobile technology. Instead, researchers are actively attempting to increase each network tier's energy

DOI: 10.1201/9781003509240-10

efficiency (EE) [2]. Due to new security challenges that do not exist in older mobile networks, the exponential growth of clients who rely on the website and network, along with an evolution in mobile networks, requires changes to the security architecture. On the other hand, researchers are currently attempting to increase each network tier's EE with 5G systems. One such effort is to develop energy-efficient or "green" computer network topologies [3]. With regards to digitalization and advanced communication, 5G systems are emerging as the base for industrial change. It has pledged to deliver dependable services at incredibly fast speeds with virtually no latency. Mobile broadband services and taxable internet access will both be available anywhere, anytime with 5G. There are a few problems with the previous generation of wireless networks in terms of data throughput, connectivity, and latency. For instance, the 4G LTE-A technology guarantees DL data rates of up to 3 Gb/s and UL traffic rates of up to 1.5 Gb/s with connectivity for about 600 subscribers per cell and a latency of 30 to 50 milliseconds [3].

One sort of cyber-attack, known as a Distributed Denial of Service (DDoS) assault, uses several hacked devices to flood an intended system or website with an overwhelming quantity of traffic, rendering it unavailable to the users who are meant to use it. A DDoS assault's objective is to prevent a network or a website from operating normally; because the attack is spread, it is challenging to counter. DDoS attacks function by saturating a system being attacked with an excessive quantity of traffic originating from numerous sources, causing the system to become overloaded and inaccessible to its intended clients [4]. The IoT devices and network are now protected against cyber-attacks using firewalls and intrusion prevention systems (IPS). However, because most conventional firewalls and IPS filter regular and suspect traffic based on static predefined rules, they are unable to protect against sophisticated DDoS attacks. However, IPS that use Artificial Intelligence (AI) approaches to filter invasive attempts are more dependable and efficient than those that use static predetermined criteria [5].

In the first half of 2019 compared to the same time in 2020, DDoS attacks surged by 200% in frequency and by 85% in volume, according to Neustar's study on cyberthreats and trends. There is an observed increase in DDoS assaults from 2018 to 2023 according to Cisco's annual internet study. By 2023, there would have been twice as many DDoS assaults, or 15.4 million, as there were in 2018. Therefore, it is imperative to have solutions that can quickly identify and destroy DDoS assaults [6]. Security is currently the biggest risk with IoT. The most frequent assaults on IoT networks and devices have reportedly been DDoS attacks. The equivalent of 28.7K DDoS attacks occur each day, and both their frequency and power are steadily rising [7].

The remainder of the chapter is organized as follows: The problem statement is described, to detect DDoS assaults utilizing an ID model more effectively, the proposed approach for improving Energy Efficiency from network traffic in 5G is described. There is a summary of the methodology's results.

10.2 STATEMENT OF PROBLEM

The most frequent attacks in IoT are DDoS attacks. The most sophisticated DDoS attacks are undetectable by the current remedies. The majority of them were taught on 4G networks, leading them to believe that 5G was secure and excluding recent reflected DDoS attacks, including NetBIOS, NTP, SSDP, and UDP Lag. When handover or mobility state detection occurs, network traffic is present. Therefore, data on network traffic needs to consider network pattern recognition to effectively utilize the possibilities of IDS for the identification of DDoS attacks. To manage DDoS, statistical analysis and flow-based network congestion must be examined. Since 5G is literally secured, those aspect are not looked on to leaving the network vulnerable to DDoS attack.

10.3 LITERATURE SURVEY

In literature it has been found that convolution neural networks (CNNs) have gained substantial importance due to their effective performance in the fields of computer vision and image processing [8]. The CNN models have also shown their applicability in identifying network threats. In [8], authors have explored the CNN to identify malicious traffic in NetFlow data. The authors initially utilized feature correlation and then encoded the features before converting the data into images by using a spherical correlation matrix. The models used for deep learning were then fed these created photos. Residual network (ResNet) performed better than the other models in this group.

In [9], the authors suggested a way to transform the network traffic to effectively employ the possible descriptive statistics for detecting network breaches. The authors did this by using the publicly accessible NSL-KDD, applying fast Fourier transformation (FFT) to it, turning it traffic-free, and then feeding it into a cutting-edge CNN model to find network intrusions. In this manner, feature values from the NSL-KDD were converted into binary variables using a binary embedding approach, and subsequently these vectors were changed into flow-based ones. Two deep neural systems received this data and trained on it. The authors concluded that CNN models outperform machine learning techniques.

According to [10], due to their access to the network and the lack of gateways or additional security features, IoT devices play a crucial role in many DDoS assaults as they allow for, and improve, their ability to perform DDoS attacks. Due to their vulnerability to hacking and lack of security features, IoT devices are frequently incorporated into DDoS attacks. Due to this, they become susceptible to hacker control and being included in botnets, which are vast networks of hijacked devices that can conduct coordinated DDoS assaults against targets. (Figure 10.1)

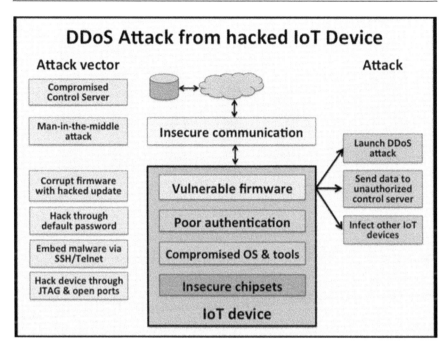

Figure 10.1 DDoS Attack using IoT devices in network.

According to [11], DDoS assaults pose a severe risk to the availability, dependability, and efficacy of the internet in IoT networks. In IoT networks, DDoS assaults can be detected and prevented using a variety of techniques, including machine learning, blockchain, data encryption, etc. These solutions do, however, come with some difficulties and restrictions, such as flexibility, intricacy, expense, etc. DDoS assaults take advantage of IoT devices' constrained resources, like storage space and network capacity, which contributes to this problem in the application that uses IoT devices. The attacks that potentially result in DDoS, which could eventually seriously harm current systems, are thoroughly reviewed in their study.

According to [12], the Internet of Things (IoT) is an internet of networked things that are equipped with software, sensors, and other necessary electronics to collect and exchange data. Due to numerous devices connected to the Internet, it is challenging to ensure consumers' privacy and protection through IoT. When numerous systems attack a single DoS attack system, the result is a DDoS. This happens when many systems exceed the bandwidth or resource limits of the target system, typically at a few servers. This is due to the characteristics of IoT networks that are resource-constrained, which have suffered greatly. Resource-constrained devices won't become targets or succumb to DDoS attacks sooner thanks to early detection. The study focuses on Distributed Denial of Services (DDoS) and other IoT issues. (Figure 10.2)

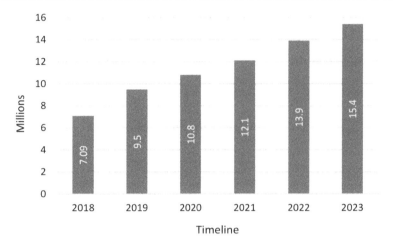

Figure 10.2 2018–2023 Trends in DDoS attack (Annual global report).

10.4 METHODOLOGY

A methodical technique to identify possible threats is used in the methodology for detecting DDoS assaults in 5G systems employing Intrusion Detection System (IDS) in IoT devices. In the context of 5G networks and IoT devices, this technique offers a systematic strategy for creating and implementing an efficient DDoS detection system, with the goal of enhancing network security and reducing the effects of DDoS attacks. The goal of this research is to identify and counteract DDoS assaults on 5G systems using IoT devices. First, relevant data such as IoT device network traffic data and potentially unwanted traffic for the IDS testing is collected. Then, data cleaning and preprocessing steps are performed to address missing values, reducing noise, and harmonizing the data. In next step, extracting or choosing pertinent characteristics of DDoS assaults from network traffic data such as Statistical attributes, flow-based features, and packet-level is done. Furthermore, select or create an IDS system which can function effectively on IoT devices with limited resources. We select from rule-based systems, compact machine learning models, or anomaly detection strategies. We used labeled datasets that comprise both regular traffic and DDoS attack traffic to train the chosen IDS. This aids the IDS in identifying patterns of typical behavior and spotting anomalies connected to DDoS attacks. We embed a qualified IDS on IoT devices to provide continuous real-time network traffic monitoring. We extract pertinent information from the real-time network traffic that IoT devices are producing. We use the IDS to look for anomalies that might point to a DDoS assault in the extracted features. We select from machine learning- or threshold-based anomaly detection methods. We set up the IDS to send out notifications or perform certain tasks whenever a DDoS assault is discovered. Actions could include informing network

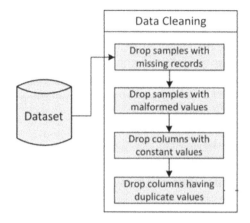

Figure 10.3 Proposed methodology for detecting DDoS in IoT systems.

managers from the simulator, rate restriction, or traffic filtering. We utilize many indicators to assess the IDS's performance, including detection level, false-positive level, and reaction time. We utilize a test dataset that contains examples of known attacks. We continually improve the IDS's detection accuracy and eliminate false positives. We use adaptive learning techniques. We consider the flexibility and resource restrictions of IoT devices when expanding the IDS deployment. In a true IoT context, we keep an eye on its performance. Including the IDS design and efficiency data, record the complete technique. We give a thorough evaluation of the detection system's performance of DDoS (Figure 10.3).

10.5 RESULT AND DISCUSSION

Four generally utilized performance indicators, flow-based, traffic-volume, statistical analysis, and pattern recognition, are used to assess the performance of the suggested methodology.

In the overall setting of Internet of Things (IoT) and Distributed Denial of Service (DDoS) assault detection and mitigation, flow-based monitoring is a basic technique. Flow-based monitoring is a useful method for comprehending, safeguarding, and optimizing network traffic in both IoT and DDoS contexts. It offers perceptions into how the network and devices behave, enabling proactive actions to improve security and performance while averting potential risks.

$$\text{FB} = \frac{NF}{NF + T} \times 10 \tag{10.1}$$

In which NF = Network flow, T = Traffic and FB = Flow-Based

Most Internet of Things (IoT) environments and Distributed Denial of Service (DDoS) assaults depend heavily on traffic volume. We see traffic volume as an important factor in DDoS attacks as well as IoT contexts. Optimizing and controlling traffic volume is crucial for effective network functioning on the IoT. Tracking and minimizing high traffic volumes are essential in the context of DDoS assaults for safeguarding network resources and assuring service availability.

$$\mathbf{TV} = \frac{VN}{VN + W} \times 10 \tag{10.2}$$

In which VN = Volume of network, W = Weight of the network and TV = Traffic volume

In Internet of Things (IoT) systems, statistical analysis is crucial for identifying and thwarting Distributed Denial of Service (DDoS) assaults. Hence, statistical analysis in IoT DDoS detection uses mathematical and analytical methods to find patterns, anomalies, and deviations in network traffic. These techniques are crucial for prompt threat response, effective DDoS attack mitigation, and proactive threat detection in IoT systems.

$$\mathbf{SA} = \frac{NF + VN + SN}{NF + T + VN + W} \times 10 \tag{10.3}$$

In which SN = Statistics of the network and SA = Statistical analysis of the network

In IoT contexts, DDoS attacks must be detected and mitigated with the use of pattern recognition. To identify patterns connected to both legitimate and criminal traffic behavior, pattern recognition in IoT DDoS detection uses mathematical and analytical methodologies. It allows for prompt threat response, efficient DDoS attack mitigation, and proactive threat detection in IoT environments (Figure 10.4),

$$\mathbf{PR} = \frac{FB \times TV}{SA + FB} \times 4 \tag{10.4}$$

In which PR = Pattern recognition of the network.

During the preparation and testing phases, we assessed the suggested approach for recognizing DDoS assaults based on the aforementioned factors for the purpose of detecting and identifying the inbound and outgoing DDoS assaults in IoT networks. For binary classification, the suggested methodology has an 89% success rate in identifying DDoS attacks. When it came to multi-class classification, the suggested methodology had an accuracy rate of 74%. As can be seen, the most accurately detected assaults include Syn (U0), DNS (U3), LDAP (U4), and regular traffic (U11), while UDP Lag attack is mistakenly identified as a NetBIOS attack. However, if we view it from the standpoint of a binary class, then a UDP delayed attack is accurately identified as an assault. (Figure 10.5)

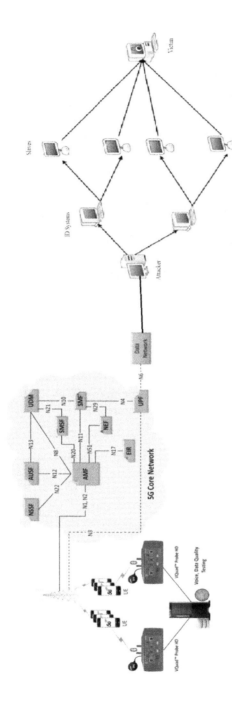

Figure 10.4 DDoS attack on UDP 5G network.

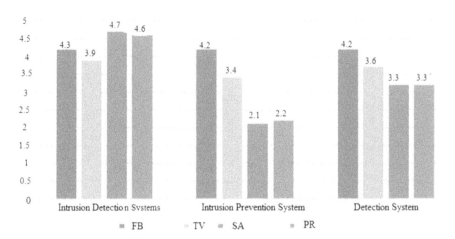

Figure 10.5 Compressive strength of test mortars in detecting DDoS attack.

In general, the proposed methodology for multi-class classification utilizing the IDS model demonstrated accuracy of 78.56% while suffering an error of 0.412 throughout the instruction phase. Testing revealed a 72% accuracy rate. Additionally, we contrasted the outcomes of our suggested methodology with a cutting-edge remedy. The proposed methodology demonstrated 15% greater precision for recognizing DDoS attack patterns than the leading-edge solution. Furthermore, it outperformed the state-of-the-art solution that was put out on the same network by 11% greater recall, or true positive rate, and 14% higher (Figure 10.6).

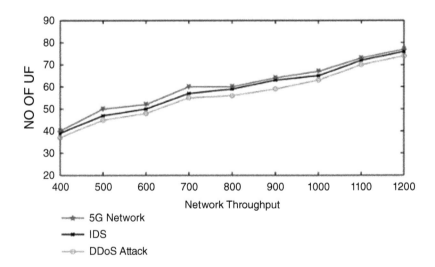

Figure 10.6 Network throughput in detecting DDoS attack with No. of UE's

10.6 CONCLUSION

Using Intrusion Detection System (IDS) in Internet of Things (IoT) devices, this research has examined the critical issue of identifying Distributed Denial of Service (DDoS) attacks in 5G systems. Our study showed that DDoS attacks can be detected and mitigated in IoT devices connected to 5G networks by using IDS. IDS can spot aberrant behaviors suggestive of DDoS attacks by constantly tracking network traffic and examining patterns. We were aware of the issue with IoT devices' resource limitations. Therefore, considering variables like memory utilization and computing power, we examined lightweight IDS models appropriate for IoT. The IDS system's deployment and scalability were also discussed. The IDS system showed encouraging detection precision. However, to minimize false-positives and make sure that genuine traffic is not mistakenly classified as an attack, fine-tuning and ongoing monitoring are crucial. For effective DDoS attack mitigation, the IDS's capacity to deliver real-time alerts and reaction mechanisms is essential. By doing this, the effect on network performance and accessibility is reduced. Even though we've come a long way in tackling DDoS assaults in 5G IoT networks, there are still a few directions we may go in. These include building versatile and self-learning systems, examining methods for detecting zero-day attacks, and investigating sophisticated machine learning models for IDS. In conclusion, integrating IDS into IoT devices is a smart move that will help protect 5G systems against DDoS attacks. Innovations in this field are crucial to ensuring the durability and availability of crucial services as 5G networks and connected devices continue to grow. To keep ahead of evolving cyberthreats and protect the integrity of 5G networks, we encourage further research and collaboration in this area.

REFERENCES

[1] H. F. Atlam and G. B. Wills, "IoT security, privacy, safety and ethics," *Digital Twin Technologies and Smart Cities*, pp. 123–149, 2020. doi:10.1007/978-3-030-18732-3

[2] I. Ahmad, S. Shahabuddin, T. Kumar, J. Okwuibe, A. Gurtov, and M. Ylianttila, "Security for 5G and beyond," *IEEE Communications Surveys & Tutorials*, vol. 21, no. 4, pp. 3682–3722, 2019.

[3] I. P. Chochliouros et al., "Energy efficiency concerns and trends in future 5G network infrastructures," *Energies*, vol. 14, no. 17, p. 5392, 2021.

[4] E. Džaferović, A. Sokol, A. Abd Almisreb, and S. M. Norzeli, "DoS and DDoS vulnerability of IoT: a review," *Sustainable Engineering and Innovation*, vol. 1, no. 1, pp. 43–48, 2019.

[5] M. Gniewkowski, "An overview of DoS and DDoS attack detection techniques," in *Theory and Applications of Dependable Computer Systems: Proceedings of the Fifteenth International Conference on Dependability of Computer Systems DepCoS-RELCOMEX*, June 29–July 3, 2020, Brunów, Poland 15, 2020: Springer, pp. 233–241.

[6] T. E. Ali, Y.-W. Chong, and S. Manickam, "Machine Learning Techniques to Detect a DDoS Attack in SDN: A Systematic Review," *Applied Sciences*, vol. 13, no. 5, p. 3183, 2023.

[7] R. Burton, "Characterizing Certain DNS DDoS Attacks," arXiv preprint arXiv:1905.09958, 2019.

[8] A. R. Shaaban, E. Abd-Elwanis, and M. Hussein, "DDoS attack detection and classification via Convolutional Neural Network (CNN)," in *2019 Ninth International Conference on Intelligent Computing and Information Systems (ICICIS)*, 2019: IEEE, pp. 233–238.

[9] L. Ma, Y. Chai, L. Cui, D. Ma, Y. Fu, and A. Xiao, "A deep learning-based DDoS detection framework for Internet of Things," in *ICC 2020-2020 IEEE International Conference on Communications (ICC)*, 2020: IEEE, pp. 1–6.

[10] I. Cvitić, D. Peraković, M. Periša, and S. Husnjak, "An overview of distributed denial of service traffic detection approaches," *Promet-Traffic & Transportation*, vol. 31, no. 4, pp. 453–464, 2019.

[11] I. Cvitić, D. Peraković, M. Periša, and M. Botica, "Smart home IoT traffic characteristics as a basis for DDoS traffic detection," in *3rd EAI International Conference on Management of Manufacturing Systems*, 2018.

[12] M. Zeeshan et al., "Protocol-based deep intrusion detection for dos and ddos attacks using unsw-nb15 and bot-iot data-sets," *IEEE Access*, vol. 10, pp. 2269–2283, 2021.

Chapter 11

Data privacy and integrity in complex data

An advanced and secure case-based reasoning approach

Shiladitya Bhattacharjee, Tanupriya Choudhury
School of Computer Science, UPES, Dehradun, India

Ahmed M. Abdelmoniem
Queen Mary University of London, United Kingdom

11.1 INTRODUCTION

The reasoning system for any case base or, in other words, case-based reasoning (CBR) is an enhancement of developing idle answers to current problems by examining the known answers to previous problems. As per [1], it provides an alternate option for Artificial Intelligence (AI) [1]. It may be applied based on its effectiveness in problem solving; the CBR can be utilized to construct distinct healthcare systems, financial, legal, and customer assistance for various industries, e-commerce, and so on. A reasoner calls back the previous situations as well as relevant remedies to forecast the new cure for any present issue. Such a system is exactly homogeneous to the thinking and reasoning systems of any individual [1, 2]. Nevertheless, collecting findings or changing a current answer for an unusual situation by paring the enormous case databases is difficult. Simultaneously, the case's intricacy influences the quality of searching for and identifying relevant related solutions [2]. As a result, several sorts of studies have been carried out to identify the most efficient and effective maintenance and searching method for the CBR mechanism. However, the modern CBR system falls short of providing sufficient answers to these unresolved concerns.

Maintaining data privacy and integrity in any CBR-based extensive data management system is equally important. The input of large datasets can be a massive quantity of datasets available in structured, unstructured, or semi-structured forms. Therefore, a secure CBR system should manage the originality of such datasets without compromising their integrity, confidentiality, and robustness during transportation, retrieval, and storage [3].

DOI: 10.1201/9781003509240-11

However, managing extensive data during storage, recovery, and transmission is complex. It can be interrupted due to hardware or software limitations, database limitations, transmission errors, bandwidth problems, excessive data transmission overhead, and numerous security attacks by using different software, viruses, and worms. Especially in extensive data management, controlling data transmission overhead, bandwidth problems, the issues of data loss, and channel congestion are substantial challenges. The current literature suggests several techniques to resolve these issues individually or in an integrated way to handle such situations. However, they still have various limitations which make them inefficient in ensuring data confidentiality, integrity, and robustness against data loss in an integrated way.

Executing a CBR system, ensuring data integrity and privacy of any large complex datasets, needs an efficient parallel processing platform with adequate space efficiency to manage them competently and consequently. Apart from that, managing distinct forms of extensive data, such as structured, unstructured, and semi-structured, requires a dynamic No-SQL database for storage that can handle its query laterally with an economical means. Numerous sorts of studies have been carried out to develop a unified framework capable of managing the storage, retrieval, and security of any substantial data collection using a cost-effective CBR framework [4, 5]. However, no earlier study has addressed the parallel processing method, which may execute numerous jobs concurrently to reduce the time and space complexity of processing any large dataset. Aside from that, previous CBR systems cannot be delivered through the internet or any other communications channel. As a result, they are unable to look for the correct answer to a specific issue in a centralized database containing information from a few different sources. Additionally, due to their localized databases, incapacity to process big datasets using parallel execution, and unable to execute a particular query via the internet, these do not fit the bill for worldwide usage. Each organization must manage and preserve its databases and put superfluous data into its own database. As a result, existing CBR systems are unconcerned with the integrity and privacy of the massive input data set during storage, retrieval, or maintenance [4].

11.1.1 Research scope

The scope of the present research work is limited to developing a CBR system, which will take care of data privacy and integrity with the help of concurrent encryption and data compression for managing large and complex data efficiently. The contemporary mechanism incorporates randomness into the compressed data and enhances encryption quality. Compression and encryption occur so that the outcome can only be decodable with the proposed technique using the same secret key [5, 6]. Another aspect of this projected integrated CBR system is managing any category of large and complex data, whether structured, unstructured, or semi-structured. Therefore, this research aims to incorporate an efficient NoSQL platform that can handle all these categories of data in a parallel processing platform.

11.1.2 Problem statement

Practically managing data security, especially data integrity and confidentiality, in parallel with any efficient CBR system is challenging. The limitation of the user database, security challenges such as channel congestion, channel noise, unlawful interference of illegal third parties, and bandwidth limitations make the administration of extensive complex data more critical [7]. Apart from the current literature fails to suggest any good parallel processing platform for large and complex data processing with any efficient CBR system. Therefore, the various recent confrontation in extensive complex dataset with the existing CBR system is listed as flows.

1. Online storage, retrieval, and updating large and complex datasets over the online platform are challenging [8]. Besides that, searching any data segment from stored large and complex data sets is challenging too. Different researchers have proposed other case-based reasoning systems to resolve these issues. However, the present literature fails to offer a system that can address all these issues combinatorically.
2. Data integrity and privacy are essential aspects of any data management system. Therefore, data integrity and privacy are equally crucial for any case-based reasoning system while updating, storing, retrieving, and transporting data over the online platform [6]. However, the existing CBR systems cannot ensure data privacy and integrity over internet intercourse.
3. Storage space and execution time are the other crucial parameters for managing extensive complex data over any online podium [9, 10]. The current literature suggests numerous combinations of NoSQL and CBR systems to handle such a situation. Nevertheless, these combinations cannot address the data size adequately and offer any parallel processing platform for managing the required time efficiently.

11.1.3 Research objectives

The primary goal is to design an integrated platform incorporating an efficient CBR system for maintaining a huge data collection and providing acceptable privacy and integrity alongside the storage, retrieval, and management of large datasets. Furthermore, it provides a less sophisticated parallel processing platform capable of effectively processing large amounts of data in complex and simple forms, as well as its many formats, such as structured, unstructured, or semi-structured data. Other goals of this research project include:

1. Creating a logical and computationally intelligent system capable of any internet inquiry quickly and retrieving the answer to that challenge with more precision based on the proposed reasoning approach.
2. Maintaining data privacy and integrity while storing, retrieving, and transporting input and output data in parallel over any heterogeneous network.
3. Minimizing the time and space required for storing and transporting any huge and complicated data collection and retrieving entire data using less search efforts and time.

11.1.4 Chapter organization

The remaining part of this chapter is organized as follows: Section 11.2 examines the gap in the current research by inspecting the strengths and weaknesses of previously applied methods; Section 11.3 depicts the design of the proposed incorporated approach; Section 11.4 describes the required test setup to carry out this analysis and specifies the parameters that will be applied to analyze the result to show its efficiencies; Section 11.5 analyses the performance of the projected technique. Section 11.6 finally concludes the entire work, its performances in different aspects and also predicts a future direction for its further improvement.

11.2 BACKGROUND STUDY

The primary goal of this research is to optimize processing performance, efficiently cluster incoming case datasets, improve data security and integrity, and reduce data storage and bandwidth needs. Following a thorough literature review, in a few types of study, separate optimization techniques have been used in distinct CBR applications and eliminated the less essential information through dataset aggregation. Various Artificial Intelligence (AI) approaches are used in various CBR systems during the grouping and elimination of insignificant datasets [11, 12]. Aside from that, conventional CBR systems are incapable of providing an efficient data-searching mechanism that is both time-efficient and operates on an unsecured platform over the internet. In this part, we examined the earlier state of the art based on their effectiveness and drawbacks to determine the present research inequality and what actions would be necessary to address this current

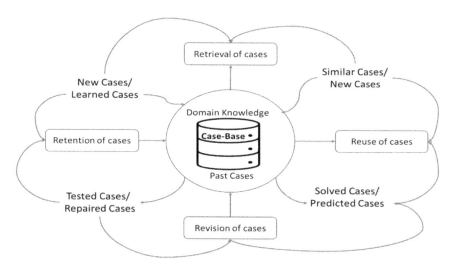

Figure 11.1 Typical structure of CBR system.

discrepancy. A typical structure of the CBR system is shown in the following Figure 11.1.

A neural network and a case-based decision-making system were utilized in the paper [13] to analyze big and complicated medical data. The suggested approach was trained using socio-economic and health-related data from two groups: those who have been afflicted with this ailment and others who have not been diagnosed with their problems. The research that is being conducted in [13] employs a two-tiered approach that combines a black-box machine learning technique in addition to a white-box method to provide anticipated values. Based on this study, the CBR system has been built as a one-of-a-kind integration. To improve the utility of this combination, this combination may search crucial cases and provide rationale with a comparable example found by the CBR system. This research improves data extraction and storage accuracy. A dual system was utilized in this study to assess similar situations and to generate data about separate people. The researcher next tested if the CBR method could be utilized just for data extraction and interpretation. Nevertheless, this system does not provide the necessary precision to justify growth and improvement with a better and more knowledge-rich method. The suggested technique [13] then applies several neural network features to decide the essential and useful variables that it may pick and utilize to show the exactly related occurrences and achieve an adequate level of precision.

According to [14], using the CBR system is quite difficult and necessitates substantial medical data processing. The researchers conducted a thorough literature review to validate the accuracy of detecting a specific ailment. The author went on to say that the accuracy of any CBR system is comparable to the quality of the case bases. The authors of this article have highlighted the issues that many disorders fall into two medical areas. This problem is taken care of in [14] by offering a novel CBR technique that employs a K-nearest neighbor method to discover k unique instances based on Euclidean distance for detecting such complicated disorders. The approach is distinguished by the usage of a self-set tolerance value, which suggests managing a threshold that can be used for sorting out comparable situations. The threshold should be bigger than the topic's given value. Throughout the execution of the suggested approach, a model software tool consisting of a list-driven GUI was created for integrating input instances, evaluating outcomes, and adapting concerns inside the intended technique. The suggested technique's performance in several aspects has been tested in real-world premenstrual syndrome (PMS) instances. Nevertheless, the suggested technique employs localized databases and does not aid in the processing of any point through the internet in conjunction with the distributed database system. As a result, the search approach in this suggested design is inefficient and slow.

The collection, analysis, and presentation of crucial and complicated data with Artificial Intelligence in several areas benefits greatly from the combination of case-based reasoning (CBR) and the Bayesian-oriented network. The enhancement is achieved in any hybrid structure in conjunction with [15], which projects a reconstruction of probability calculation connected to estimated parameters. This study used the Half-Division-Cross approach, which combines the calculation of various parameters for solving it, and Half-Division-Cross (HDC) algorithms. The Probability Change Measurement of Solution Parameters (PCMSP) approach extracts the principal characteristics associated with the main problems based on the implications of results-related characteristics derived from various aspects equivalent to source issues. This PCMSP approach works well with any type of large amount of data, regardless of its complexity or quantity. As a result, the HDC method is used to compute extensive complicated data, thus increasing the efficiencies of offered combinatorial approaches. The HDC algorithms process a large amount of complicated data by segmenting it. At the same time, it delegates each of the extensive data aspects to several sub-processes that run in parallel within the diverse dispersed nodes. It also ensures sufficient efficiency for running huge and complicated data sets in terms of time and space. Nevertheless, neither the HDC nor the PCMSP grants data privacy or integrity throughout data storage, transportation within diverse distributed systems, or data retrieval at the user end. Both strategies are likewise incapable of preventing data loss during storage or transmission of data across an unsecured network [15, 16]. As a result, the suggested paradigm is primarily unsuitable for web-based massive data applications.

Another important aspect in case-based reasoning the data security. Plenty of studies have been conducted to ensure data security for online CBR

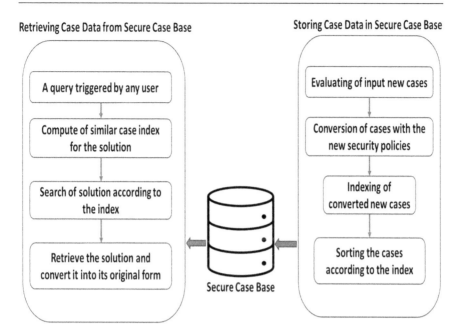

Figure *11.2* A general security structure for CBR systems.

systems. However, various security holes remain in it to date. Therefore, the other aspect of this research is to find out these security breaches and propose a full-proof integrated technique to address them in a combinatorial way. A general security structure of existing CBR systems is depicted in the following Figure 11.2.

Privacy is a critical factor for any large and complex data management system. Any CBR-based extensive data management system must maintain data privacy and integrity simultaneously. Therefore, to preserve privacy, [17] presented a Privacy Advisor software that uses a machine-learning-based technique to support the users in having the correct reconciliation on online privacy. The proposed privacy advisor software uses CBR, which depends on the capability to recognize the identical bearings from the earlier circumstances and apply these to offer suggestions on new latitude. This chapter mainly targets the necessary process for calculating the uniqueness of various privacy-related rules. Consequently, this research provides the solution from a cynosure study group that anticipated the essence. This essay presents the initial framework and construction of a privacy advisor, which aims to offer intelligent systems for helping users with adequate privacy support. The primary objective of constructing such a software application is to recognize and analyze the required privacy policies for a particular application to offer good privacy support. It further incorporates the technique for measuring the uniqueness of existing systems and studies the outcome related to a targeted group to present higher intuition on the method of grasping unique privacy factors [17, 18]. The survey of this target group also shows how the end users apply this privacy technique. Nevertheless, this research needs further improvement and more analyses to rectify similar calculations. Additionally, this research does not focus on data integrity, another essential aspect of any data management system. Especially whenever any method is handling large and complex datasets, it is very much required to ensure data integrity and privacy simultaneously. Therefore, this research needs more expansion to address these aspects.

As a result of our preliminary research, we have discovered that several CBR systems have been built, and diverse security measures have been applied to them to manage case data safely and effectively. However, we discovered that there are still some holes. As a result, a few more current techniques have been examined further regarding their strengths and drawbacks in Table 11.1.

11.2.1 Research gap analysis

We can see from what has already been covered in this section that numerous ways have been offered, and unique research has been undertaken utilizing case-based reasoning to handle the various challenges in the enormous, complicated data processing. According to existing research, none of them focuses on the processing efficiency of huge, complex data sets employing adequate parallel processing capabilities to maximize efficiency, cost, and security. Furthermore, recent CBR-based research for a large data management system focuses on localized storage. In any big and sophisticated data management system, there is no technique available for using the CBR-based distributed storage system while also addressing privacy and integrity concerns. As a result, this present system requires special consideration for storing, preserving, confidentiality, and integrity of huge and complicated case datasets. According to the research, the searching difficulty grows with the amount and complexity of the input case data, causing data loss and compromising data integrity. Simultaneously, effective data compression can minimize input file size; unfortunately, this procedure compromises data privacy [12, 13]. Apart from them, the usage of the internet in such situations is low, even though the internet with adequate speed is easily available. As a result, an improved integrated system is necessary for processing increasingly expensive and complicated data employing a case-based reasoning approach that can handle critical data simply without removing any particulars while also maintaining acceptable privacy of information and integrity [19, 20]. Furthermore, such an integrated system must be time and storage-economical, as well as internet-accessible via a distributed storage environment and along with the parallel processing ability.

Table 11.1 Analysis of various existing CBR systems and their securities

Applied technique	Strengths	Weaknesses
1. Wide-area steady security evaluation and categorization of power systems depending upon synchronized measurements utilizing case-based reasoning classifiers [16]	This research presents a person's intuition-dependent Case-Based Reasoning (CBR) concept for power system Static Security Assessment (SSA). The proposed method was tested on IEEE 14 bus, IEEE 30 bus, and Indian 246 bus networks, and the results were juxtaposed to those gathered with Support Vector Machine (SVM) and Artificial Neural Network (ANN) depending on classifiers to optimize the security system and improve data analysis performance.	It should be noted, however, that the issue of class disparity in input information trends has a significant influence on classifier performance. Apart from them, this proposed case-based reasoning system is unable to handle the network traffic and control the various security attacks on case data or case base.
2. A significantly upgraded paradigm for information system security management across its life cycle [17]	It allows for regular gathering of noticed danger actions via the system's intrusion detection, the filtering and characterization of threats within a time snapshot, and a new assessment of IS protection remedies, with the security supervisor (S-Admin), managers, the intrusion detection system, and the security monitoring system all serving as participants.	This approach should be amended to focus on developing the proposed unified agent-oriented protection control system in order to attain more accurate and seamless compatibility with intrusion detection and remedy systems and to be adaptable to more domains.
3. A vastly safe middlebox architecture for delivering advanced network functions (NFs) on untrustworthy general-purpose servers [18].	The proposed ShieldBox provides an open platform using Click for creating and applying a wide range of NFs by utilizing its unconventional features and C++ expansions. ShieldBox combines an outstanding performance I/O handling toolkit (Intel DPDK) with an Intel SGX-oriented insulated execution (Scone) framework to safely handle data at line rate. It also has several new useful features and optimizations for secure end-to-end network processing.	It is, however, incapable of handling the enormous and complicated case base. At the same time, providing effective security for big and complicated case data sets is inefficient.

(Continued)

Table 11.1 (Continued) Analysis of various existing CBR systems and their securities

Applied technique	Strengths	Weaknesses
4. A reliable content distribution Strategy Based on Blockchain in Vehicular Named Data Systems [19]	This research develops a sharing information system based on a two-layer blockchain. In the NDN paradigm, nodes at the bellow layer advertise their demands for service. The higher-tier nodes convey their demands and supplies to the next adjacent unit to proceed with synchronization. As a matching game, it mimics the demand-supply balance. To encourage nodes to provide favorable services, a reputation management strategy that combines negative and positive transaction records is presented.	This work should be broadened to match with externalities in a one-to-many assignment game, and further examine the data-sharing issue to facilitate content retrieval with a combined matching problem, in addition to taking client demand and server supply into account.
5. An integrated reasoning-dependent approach for predicting disease. Fuzzy set theory, k-nearest neighbor, and case-based reasoning all collaborate to improve forecast results [14].	This work employs FKNN-CBR to create a Privacy-Aware Disease Predictive Support System (PDPSS) to safeguard sensitive patient data from illegal access by others. The authors encrypted vital patient data with the Paillier Homomorphic Cryptosystem to improve security. The efficacy and performance of the proposed FKNN-CBR PDPSS prediction model are empirically validated using Indian Liver Patient data from the UCI database.	It is impossible to predict diseases while ensuring security at low computational and communication costs. A complete privacy-aware model is necessary to address this gap.

11.3 PROPOSED TECHNIQUE

This proposed technique fills a research vacuum by developing a unified mechanism for resolving CBR system difficulties while also ensuring appropriate data privacy and integrity. It employs supervised learning, a novel CBR-based new indexing approach, and a chaotic data compression and encryption technique that operates in the Hadoop system. The usage of Hadoop provides a parallel execution platform and a distributed storage solution for large and complex datasets. At the same time, the integrated chaotic encryption and data compression ensure acceptable data privacy and integrity while minimizing data loss. The distributed storage system and parallel execution may efficiently handle the challenge of managing large amounts of complicated input case data. Simultaneously, the clever scoring (reasoning)-based indexing approach in the Hadoop architecture significantly enhances the performance of searching for and retrieving data. This combinatorial strategy discards no datasets while storing them (forming a case base), improving search quality, and saving any associated solution to any query. The flowchart of the projected integrated technique is shown in the following Figure 11.3.

Figure 11.3 depicts the flow structure of the projected approach. It is divided into three parts: preliminary processing of the input data, system training (reasoning formation), and testing state (operation for searching from case-base and development on initial rationale). During the preprocessing phase, the suggested strategy extracts 80% of case data from the input file. This is used for training the system and 20% for assessing the performance of the planned integrated approach in various areas. As a result, the suggested method employs sophisticated chaotic encryption and compression techniques that encrypt and compress the training and testing data at the same time. Using this chaotic encryption and data compression technique protects data privacy and integrity during the transfer, storage, and recovery of any big and complicated dataset.

During the second phase, the proposed system creates a utility score for each cluster and indexing for all. In this manner, the reasoning originates within Hadoop architecture. It puts the index of each to compressed and encrypted (encoded) clustered data. The predicted system then develops a brief explanation of every cluster and combines the short illustration, index, and matching starting utility score in the third phase of the proposed implementation. At this stage, it inserts the aggregated data within the Hadoop metadata file for all clusters. Using the initial reasoning system, this component of the job assists in the creation of the case basis for the forecasted model. It then rearranges all Hadoop metadata items depending on their beginning useful logic.

Finally, in the fourth phase, it places each cluster into the Hadoop directory depending on its index to generate the final case base. The success rate of the project application is checked using 20% of the supplied case data.

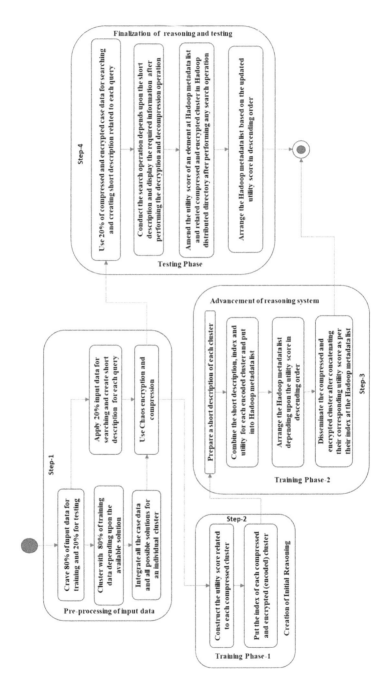

Figure 11.3 Design of proposed integrated technique.

The search procedures are carried out in the performance evaluation section using case data. At the start of this phase, a brief description is created based on the answers to these questions. Similarly, this brief description is compared in the Hadoop metadata list in each search operation to gather the index of the associated cluster in the Hadoop metadata list. The reasoning engine has been upgraded by reordering numerous items in the Hadoop metadata list in descending order depending on updated utility rankings. The sub-sections below provide a full discussion of how to execute each component of the proposed integrated approach.

11.3.1 Preprocessing of input data

We used 80% of the data we provided in preprocessing the input file to complete the first step of training our suggested model. 80% of case datasets and related solutions were collected and grouped based on how they resembled one another in this phase of the suggested approach. Here the Hadoop Map-Reduce functions are used to implement the proposed technique. The operations conducted using the mapper and reducer functions are discussed separately in the following sub-sections.

11.3.2 Operations conducted within the mapper function

In the initial phase, 80% of input data are taken as input in this phase to implement the mapper function. Let the case dataset used to train the proposed model be referred to as the case base and is indicated by C. While the available related solutions are denoted. Let the set of input cases (C) and all the corresponding solutions (S) be set up with the following equations (11.1) and (11.2).

$$C = \{c_0, c_1, c_2, \ldots\ldots\ldots\ldots, c_n\}, \text{where } n \text{ is total input cases} \tag{11.1}$$

$$S = \{s_0, s_1, s_2, \ldots\ldots\ldots\ldots, s_m\}, \text{where } m \text{ is total available solutions and } n \geq m \tag{11.2}$$

Apply the following Chaos encryption and compression for securing the input 80% of data. The suggested method is made up of three main components: An s-Box to implement the chaotic technique, secure and resilient coding with the Huffman technique, and a Keystream Generator with Pseudorandom approach (PRKG). The proposed method includes the Logistic Map (Chaotic) or CLM for introducing necessary restrictions into minimization and uncompressed procedures of secure Huffman Coding (Adaptive) or AHC. The proposed method consists of a chaotic S-Box supported by a Chaotic Sine Map (CSM) for data replacement without affecting the ability to reduce data size. The proposed method implements a pseu-dorandom keystream with suitable masing using PRKG and the Chaotic Logistic Map (CLM) to improve the encryption characteristic.

Inputs and outputs: Synchronous encryption and reduction of data are carried out along with combining the secret keys $K1$, $K2$, and $K3$. CSM includes the applications of these keys in the construction of an S-Box with the chaotic approach. With the aid of CLM, such parts are used to generate the keystreams along with the pseudorandom fashion. Algorithm 11.1 then takes input (I), length (L), and the outcome (C') are employed on this deck.

ALGORITHM 11.1   SIMULTANEOUS DATA ENCRYPTION AND COMPRESSION USING CHAOS

1. Create the initial Huffman Tree using an adaptive approach.
2. Build an S-Box using the chaotic approach along with the private key $K1$.
3. Set the value of the counter (i) as 1 and the outcome (D) as null.
4. Parse the characters from I as inputs.
5. Substitute I_i using the chaotic S-Box and let s_i be the output symbol.
6. Apply encryption to transform s_i, Huffman coding along with Adaptive approach, and the secret key $K2$. Concatenate the output (c_i) along with the D as resultant and $D = D \parallel c_i$.
7. Increase the counter as $i = i + 1$.
8. While $i > L$, reiterate Step 9. Else, reiterate Step 4.
9. Ultimately, $K3$ generates the keystream (KS) in a pseudorandom fashion with the help of a Logistic Map, built with a chaotic approach. It also conceals D fully further. With the conjunction of an XOR operation masking is used, which increases the overall unpredictability of D. This section creates the crucial encrypted text C.
10. End of execution.

After the execution of Algorithm 11.1, create an integer array U of size m for storing the utility score corresponding to each compressed and encrypted cluster. Further, generate a string array C' of size $m \times p$ where p denotes the total number of compressed and encrypted inputs where $0 \leq m \leq n$ and $0 \leq p \leq n$. Initialize both the arrays with the following equations (11.3) and (11.4).

$$\langle C'_i \rangle_{i=1}^{m} = \varnothing \tag{11.3}$$

$$\langle U_i \rangle_{i=1}^{p} = 0 \tag{11.4}$$

After initializing these arrays, these arrays all the clustered case data (Compressed and encrypted) and a total number of cases are sent to the reducer functions for further processing in the next phase of executions.

11.3.3 Operations conducted within the reducer function

After executing the mapper function in the Hadoop parallel processing platform, the reducer function will be executed to calculate the final utility score and create of short description corresponding to the compressed and encrypted cluster. It also places the clustered (compressed and encrypted) case data into the Hadoop distributed database via the Internet according to their corresponding final utility score. The entire compressed and encrypted clusters, number of clusters, and number of total case data are taken as the input in this phase. The various operations of the reducer function with the taken inputs are shown in the following Algorithm 11.2.

ALGORITHM 11.2 POSITIONING THE CLUSTERED CASE DATA IN HADOOP DISTRIBUTED PLATFORM

Input: Compressed and encrypted Clustered case data (C), String array C' for storing the final encoded cluster i.e., compressed and encrypted, and integer array U for storing the final utility score corresponding to each cluster, n number of total case data, and m clusters of compressed and encrypted case data.

Output: Final compressed and encrypted cluster array (C'), and the integer array for storing the final utility score.

1. Cluster the input data depending upon available solutions and their capacities to address the number of input cases.
   for ($int\, p = 0; p < n; p + +$){//Segmentation of input cases to prepare the encoded clusters
       int $l = 0$;
       for ($int\, q = 0; q < m; q + +$){
           $C'_{pq} = C_p$;
           $l = l + l$;
       }
   }
2. Depending upon the length of each cluster, calculate the corresponding utility scores of them.
   for ($int\, p = 0; p < m, p + +$){
       int $k = size\left(C'_p\right)$;
       $U_p = k$;
   }

3. Sort the utility scores from higher to lower order and rearrange the corresponding clusters accordingly.

```
for (int p = 0, p ≤ m; p + +){
    if (U_{p+1} > U_p){
        swap (C'_{p+1}, C'_p);
        swap (U_{p+1}, U_p);
    }
}
```

4. Remove the temporary variables and arrays to free the unnecessary allocated memory.

After generating the final utility score and the encrypted compressed case-based clusters, the relevant utility scores and descriptions are generated. Furthermore, to construct their reference, these brief descriptions are concatenated in the respective cluster. As a result, the modified short description and usefulness score for each cluster are added to the Hadoop metadata list for future reference and to make the search process more efficient.

11.3.4 Retrieval of data from the Hadoop database

When a search query is triggered from any valid user over the internet, the Hadoop mapper function initially creates a short description of the corresponding query. After generating the short description of the particular query, such a short description is searched in the Hadoop metadata list to find the corresponding utility score. After retrieving the corresponding utility score, the reducer program searches the corresponding compressed and encrypted cluster from the Hadoop distributed database depending upon the retrieved utility score. Furthermore, after finding out the corresponding encrypted and compressed cluster, the decompression and decryption operation is performed in the reversal way of encryption and compression to retrieve the corresponding solution. The reducer program then displays the uncompressed and decrypted corresponding solution of any particular case after raising any query by any particular user. Consequently, the corresponding utility score is updated in the Hadoop metadata list and the associated cluster. The metadata list in the Hadoop data base is further updated by shuffling it according to the increasing order of new utility sores. On the other hand, if any query fired, and the corresponding short description, prepared by the Hadoop mapper function is not found in the Hadoop metadata list, then it also informs the particular user that "Solution is not available for that particular query". Thus, the entire data retrieval process is executed over the internet with the help of the Hadoop distributed platform.

11.4 ASSESSMENT PLATFORM

This section provides an investigation basis for building the proposed combinatorial approach and its many components in a diverse scenario. This phase, titled data preparation, incorporates the downloading sources of various mandatory files as inputs, numerous applications, and their proper definition of data generation connected to inputs. Subsequently, this section describes the different performance assessment parameters that may be used to determine the advantage of the proposed combined method and its components over analogous current security solutions. These measurement matrices have been classified and arranged based on their usefulness in achieving the specific goals of this study.

11.4.1 Experimental setup

This section is divided into a pair of subsections: system specifications and data preprocessing. The system required section includes data preparation and both software and hardware configuration for implementing the suggested approach. The data preparation procedure's specifics are detailed in this section's second half. Each part continues to be addressed in the subsections that follow.

11.4.2 System setup

The suggested method and its accompanying components were built using Java (JDK 7.0). Various tests were carried out using the UBUNTU 16.04 LTS operating system. The notion of parallel processing was applied utilizing Java thread programming to speed up the whole process. During the development of the proposed combinatorial technique, the tested Personal Computer was outfitted with 32GB DDR3 RAM and Intel® CoreTM i8 CPUs. During the experiment, all files were transmitted over wireless and wired local area networks.

11.4.3 Data preparation

According to [21, 22], the conventional edition of Calgary Corpuses is usually employed to evaluate the implementation of any data compression technology as the baseline data for inputs to uphold standardization. Therefore, the standard edition of Calgary Corpuses was used as input data in this study effort to investigate the accomplishment of the proposed compression approach and its many properties. Aside from this, text and binary data files ranging in size from 1TB to 1TB were generated throughout the experiment and used as inputs to evaluate the performance of the recommended compressed approach. Since Java can only analyze 64MB of data at a time, a file separator was created to divide the hidden input file into numerous 64MB chunks. The dividing method was performed to quicken up the total process beginning with the point of transmission. In a similar vein at the point of arrival, a file merger was established to combine the incoming little files into a single large file to provide a full output file. Each little file was issued an index address during the separation process. At the receiving end, these index numbers were utilized to combine tiny files into a large file.

11.4.4 Definition of some assessment parameters

The suggested combined strategy was primarily intended to evaluate the suggested compression and encryption performance in many areas. These different important metrics for assessing the efficacy of the suggested integrated method and its many components have been provided and described in the subsequent sub-section based on their ability to meet the stated objectives of this research.

11.4.4.1 Space saving percentage

According to the literary work, compression techniques are applied to any data file to preserve disc space for storage or minimize bandwidth requirements for network transmission by lowering the size of the input file. After conducting any specific compression operation with an input file, space or the bandwidth needs of any reduced file for storing or sending are reduced [5, 6]. It is usually expressed as a percentage. The rate of Space Saving provided by any fixed length or variable length coding compression technique frequently changes depending on the size of the input file. Any compression technique's rate of space savings may be computed as the following equation (11.5).

$$\text{Space Saving} \left(\text{Percentage} \right) = \left(1 - \frac{\text{Reduced File Size}}{\text{Original File Size}} \right) \times 100 \qquad (11.5)$$

11.4.4.2 Latency time

Latency is the time it takes for an input into a process to produce the desired result. This term can be defined differently in different scenarios; therefore, latency concerns varies as well. According to tradition, if a system has a shorter Latency Time, it is deemed to be efficient in data processing, and vice versa [22]. As a result, the suggested combined technique's latency time throughout the construction and execution of the intended reason system must be calculated. In this case, the Latency Time can be shown by the following equation (11.6).

$$\text{Latency Time} = \left(\text{Start time of any process} - \text{End time of its previous process} \right) \qquad (11.6)$$

11.4.4.3 Accuracy Percentage

The Accuracy Percentage measures the number of right answers in relation to the number of questions in a certain situation. The acceptability of the chosen approach in the case base management system is determined by its capacity to deliver higher accuracy [12, 23]. A system is stated to be efficient if it generates a higher Accuracy Percentage or vice versa. Another critical component of our suggested approach is the accuracy of the obtained data. It can be measured by the following equation (11.7).

$$\text{Accuracy Percentage} = \frac{\text{Total correct instances after retrieving}}{\text{total queries}} \times 100$$

(11.7)

11.4.4.4 Entropy Value

The randomness in output file, created by any encryption or security technique, can be verified by the Entropy Values. Furthermore, if any security approach offers higher randomness i.e., higher entropy values, the used security system is considered to be effective to protect the information from various security attacks and offer higher privacy [24]. If in any security approaches, $X(S_i)$ denotes the probability of the input symbol (S_i), the corresponding Entropy Value $E(S)$ for any encryption or any security approach can be measured with the help of following equation (11.8).

$$E(S) = \sum_{i=0}^{2N-1} X(S_i) \log_2 \frac{1}{X(S_i)}$$

(11.8)

11.4.4.5 Throughput

Any work in a computer system is completed within a certain time range. The time required to complete various tasks varies according to the processing speed of the computer system and the nature of the task. Similarly, time is important in the data transmission system since the real data must be delivered within a certain time. Data loss may occur if there is an unfavorable time delay during transfer. As a result, the performance of any data transmission system may be assessed by the amount of time required. According to [11, 23], throughput is the number of tasks completed in each amount of time. Any technique's throughput (TP) may be determined as the following equation (11.9).

$$\text{TP} = \left(\frac{\text{Total Size of Output File}}{\text{Total Execution Time}} \right)$$

(11.9)

11.5 RESULT ANALYSIS

According to the goal of this chapter, the results section has been divided into three parts, the first of which justifies the first objective of this research work, that the proposed technique is capable of effectively placing the user's query and retrieving the accurate answer very quickly. As a result, the second component of this research satisfies the second purpose, namely, it is efficient to protect data privacy and integrity. The final subsection of this section further justifies that the proposed approach is successful in reducing space and time complications in order to meet the research's ultimate goal.

11.5.1 Accuracy of accessing information

One of the goals of this research is to get relevant information from any vast and complicated case base once any end user initiates a query. The suggested approach searches for any given solution based on the utility score connected with it. Furthermore, based on the number of search operations, the corresponding utility score is updated in increasing order in the Hadoop metadata list as well as the Hadoop distributed system. Furthermore, the Hadoop metadata list pieces are ordered in ascending order based on the related utility score. As a result, the search procedure becomes faster and more efficient. The Accuracy Percentage of the obtained information utilizing various reasoning strategies has been determined using equation (11.7) and is displayed in Figure 11.4. The proposed reasoning technique's accuracy is compared

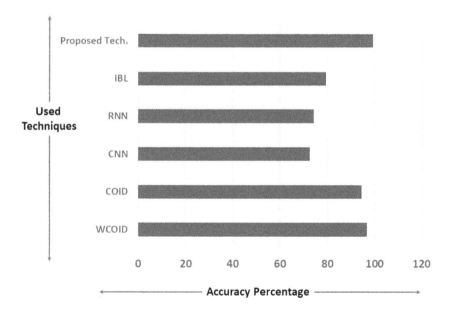

Figure 11.4 Accuracy percentage of accessing information, offered by various reasoning technique.

to a few other existing reasoning techniques, including Weighting as well as Clustering Outliers and Internal cases Detection (WCOID), Clustering as Outliers and Internal Detection (COID), Condensed Nearest Neighbor Rule (CNN), Recurrent Neural Network Technique (RNN), and Instance-Based Learning (IBL) to show its effiiciency.

Figure 11.4 displays that the planned approach offers the highest Accuracy Percentage in compared to other listed reasoning techniques. Consequently, we can claim that the projected technique is more effective than the others in producing accuracy percentage during any search operation which fulfills the first objective of this research work.

11.5.2 Efficiency to offer data privacy

Data privacy is one of the important factors for any online secure data transition system. In this study, we developed 300 binary sequences and L = 1,000,000 bits to measure the cryptic properties of pseudorandom key-streams generated using PRKG problems. The permitted ambit values were chosen at random, with values ranging from 3.6 to 4 for the CLM. Another starting value was randomly chosen from zero to one for the generator pair. The randomness confidence as 99% of pseudorandom sequences of binary strings is created with the aid of PRKG based on CLM [19, 20], the degree of significance was set to 0.01. The various NIST parameters have been tested with the proposed technique and their corresponding passing percentages are plotted in the following Figure 11.5.

Figure 11.5 shows that the proposed technique offers a passing percentage of almost 99% or more than that for all NIST parameters. Therefore, we can claim that the planned chaos approach is effective to produce adequate randomness during any online data dissemination system. Therefore, from the above explanation, we can claim that the planned chaos system is effective to offer adequate data privacy in data retrieval or processing over any online-based distributed platform. Another important parameter for measuring the efficacy of the suggested chaos technique to offer higher privacy is entropy. According to the definition of entropy, if any security technique offers higher entropy value means, the used technique is efficient to produce higher randomness as well as the higher data privacy. Therefore, using equation (11.8), the entropy value produced by the proposed chaos technique and a few more related existing chaos techniques have been calculated and tabulated in Table 11.2.

Figure 11.5 and Table 11.2 display that the projected chaos approach is effective to offers adequate passing percentage with respect to various NIST parameters and higher entropy values than the other existing chaotic security approaches. Therefore, we can claim that the proposed chaotic encryption and compression approach is effective to produce higher randomness during conversion of compressed and cryptic text from the normal case data. Therefore, it justifies that proposed chaos approach is effective to offer higher privacy. At the same time from Figure 11.4, we have seen that the

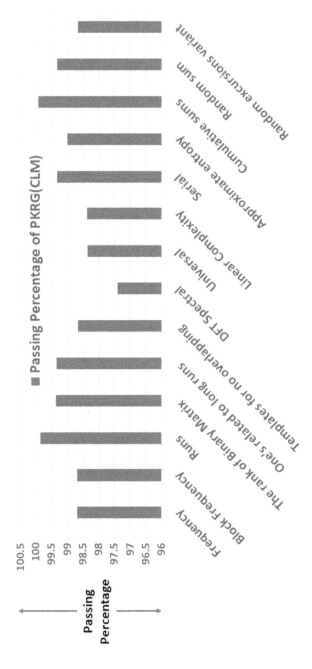

Figure 11.5 Passing percentages of various NIST parameters.

Table 11.2 Entropy values, offered by different chaotic technique

File names	Chaotic Huffman Tree	Chaotic muted adaptive Huffman Tree	Simultaneous arithmetic coding encryption	Proposed technique
		← Entropy Values →		
Text 1 (Bib)	7.93	7.98	7.98	7.99
Text 2 (book 1)	7.93	7.97	7.97	7.98
Text 3 (book 2)	7.95	7.97	7.97	7.99
Text 4 (Geo)	7.97	7.96	7.97	7.99
Text 5 (News)	7.97	7.95	7.94	7.98
Text 6 (obj 1)	7.87	7.91	7.95	7.99
Text 7 (obj 2)	7.96	7.95	7.97	7.98
Text 8 (paper 1)	7.96	7.96	7.96	7.97
Text 9 (paper 2)	7.94	7.96	7.96	7.99
Text 10 (paper 3)	7.95	7.95	7.97	7.99
Text 11 (paper 4)	7.93	7.94	7.96	7.97
Text 12 (paper 5)	7.93	7.93	7.96	7.98
Text 13 (paper 6)	7.94	7.96	7.97	7.99
Text 14 (Pic)	7.91	7.94	7.98	7.99
Text 15 (Progc)	7.95	7.92	7.98	7.98
Text 16 (Progl)	7.92	7.91	7.97	7.99
Text 17 (Progp)	7.90	7.93	7.96	7.99
Text 18 (Trans)	7.95	7.96	7.97	7.98

proposed chaotic technique also offers higher data accuracy during the inserting or accessing data to or from the database. Therefore, we can claim that the proposed technique also offers adequate data integrity in parallel. Thus, it fulfils our second research objective.

11.5.3 Time and space efficiencies

Time and space savings are also essential considerations when dealing with a heavy case base. Because this research is working with a huge case base using the Hadoop distributed platform, its time and space efficiency must also be calculated. As a result, this part investigates the time and space efficiencies provided by the proposed chaos technique as well as other relevant current chaotic techniques. According to the literature, we can check the time efficiency of any security solution that gives faster throughput, reduced latency time, and lower retrieval time. As a result, if the security strategy adopted gives a larger proportion of space savings, it is space-efficient. As a result, using equations (11.6) and (11.9), the time efficiency of the proposed chaotic technique and other comparable chaos techniques to process large and complex case data with distinct distributed data bases is estimated in terms of Latency Time and Throughput. The related findings are provided in Table 11.3 and Figure 11.6.

Table 11.3 Time and processing efficiencies, offered by distinct data bases

	Time Efficiency				Processing Efficiency								
	Throughputs Offered by Different Databases				Latencies for Different Databases (Millisecond) (50% Read and 50% Write)								
					MySQL			Cassandra			Hadoop		
								← I/O Rate (Process/Sec) →					
Used Tech.	MySQL	Cassandra	Hadoop	File Size	5	15	30	5	15	30	5	15	30
WCOID	50.2	52.4	56.7	1.0 (TB)	0.58	0.42	0.24	1.19	0.79	0.38	0.31	0.21	0.12
COID	55.4	58.3	62.5		0.67	0.55	0.32	1.56	0.94	0.64	0.43	0.32	0.21
CNN	48.1	50.2	54.2		0.51	0.43	0.27	1.07	0.72	0.35	0.27	0.18	0.11
RNN	50.1	54.4	57.3		0.49	0.41	0.25	1.03	0.67	0.32	0.21	0.16	0.10
IBL	49.2	53.6	59.2		0.57	0.41	0.23	1.17	0.77	0.37	0.30	0.20	0.12
Proposed Tech.	62.7	69.6	72.6.		0.11	0.09	0.05	0.45	0.23	0.18	0.08	0.05	0.04

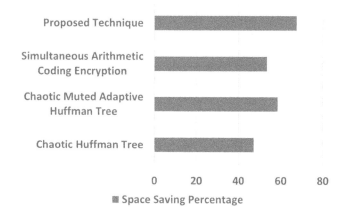

Figure 11.6 Space Saving percentage, offered by various chaotic techniques.

The time efficiencies of the suggested and other current related reasoning approaches to process various queries using diverse databases such as Hadoop, Cassandra, and MySQL are shown in Table 11.3. This comparison is made using a 1 TB large case base as huge input data. The outcome demonstrates that the recommended combination is more time-efficient in terms of delivering better throughput than the other combinations given in Table 11.3. As a result, we can assert that the suggested chaotic combination is more time-efficient than existing correlated chaotic strategies for processing big and complicated queries. Consequently, Table 11.3 compares the offering latency time of the proposed chaotic approach and other current chaotic combinations for the various I/O rates provided by the Hadoop, Cassandra, and MySQL databases. This comparison is also made possible by employing a 1TB huge and complicated case database as input data. The outcome, as shown in Table 11.3, demonstrates that the proposed combination produces shorter latency time in all cases. It denotes that the suggested combination is effective in reducing latency time as well as any number of I/O operations with the distinct database combination to handle any huge and complicated case-base, execute query and retrieval of information in a variety of secure ways.

In large case base handelling, the space efficiency of the used technique is another important aspect. According to the literature, space complexity for nay large and complex case base leads to the channel congestion and information loss during the case insertion, transportation, and retrieval. In consequence, data integrity can be hampered in large case-base processing. Therfore, according to the literature, to manage the large case base, the used data processing technique should be space-efficient. Therefore, to enhance the space efficiency of the proposed combination, a chaotic compression and ecryption technque is added with the proposed combination. The space-saving efficiencies of the proposed combinations and the othr related chaotic combination e.g. Simultaneous Arithmetic Coding Encryption, Chaotic Muted Adaptive Huffman Treee, and Chaotic Huffman Tree are calculated in terms of Space-Saving percentage with the help of equation (11.5) and plotted in Figure 11.6. The Space-Saving percentage of the proposed chaotic technique and other relatecd chaotic combinations are calculated here consideing 1TB of large case as input.

   Figure 11.6 shows that the proposed chaotic combination offered the best Space-Saving percentage among the listed various chaotic combinations. Therefore, the proposed chaotic combination is efficient to offer higher space efficiencies among the rest. At the same time, Table 11.3 shows that the proposed chaotic combination is also very time-efficient to process any large and complex case base. Thus, it can satisfy the third objective of this research work.

11.6 CONCLUSION

Digital leanings are replacing traditional means of treating such big case bases in this sophisticated time of extraordinary accessibility to multiple enormous and intricate medical case bases. The development of new methodologies for dealing with large and complex instances has made addressing some critical concerns for the entire system straightforward. The distribution and control of such a large storage system that can be managed over the internet, as well as improved execution efficiency, are the main issues in such a control system. As a result, several research projects in this sector have been conducted to address these gaps. Aside from that, ensuring data privacy and integrity while administering a huge case database via the internet is a difficult issue. Efforts to ensure data privacy increase data size and induce data loss, or vice versa [20]. As a result, data integrity decreases. The application of any advanced security technique increases the temporal complexity, making the issue more urgent. Similarly, although every efficient data compression decreases data size efficiently, it compromises data privacy and vice versa [23, 24]. However, the present literature fails to address these challenges in a comprehensive manner. As a result, the focus of this study is on developing a chaotic approach capable of resolving both challenges concurrently. It uses chaotic encryption and compression to balance time and space complexity while maintaining data integrity and privacy. As a result, it incorporates a smart indexing method to distribute vast and complicated case bases throughout the distributed database. Finally, it is run within the Hadoop distributed platform, which also provides parallel processing capabilities for doing multiple tasks in parallel. This method improves time efficiency even further. The experiment results also suggest that the proposed strategy is effective in improving data, integrity, and privacy when compared to existing security measures. Furthermore, the results section shows that the suggested strategy is more efficient in terms of time and space than other associated and contemporaneous approaches. However, the proposed method is not completely secure. It must be updated more frequently to improve the data integrity and privacy level gained after utilizing it. With the progress of the suggested chaotic approach, the time and space complexity may be reduced.

REFERENCES

[1] Xie L., S. Wu, Y. Chen, R. Chang, and X. Chen, 2023, A case-based reasoning approach for solving schedule delay problems in prefabricated construction projects, *Automation in Construction*, vol. 154, pp. 105028.

[2] Xiao X., M. Skitmore, W. Yao, and Y. Ali, 2023, Improving robustness of case-based reasoning for early-stage construction cost estimation, *Automation in Construction*, vol. 151, pp. 104777.

[3] Li Z., Z. Deng, Z. Ge, L. Lv, and J. Ge, 2021, A hybrid approach of case-based reasoning and process reasoning to typical parts grinding process intelligent decision, *International Journal of Production Research*, vol. 61, no. 2, pp. 503–519.

[4] Xu W., Y. Huang, S. Song, B. Chen, and X. Qi, 2023, A novel online combustion optimization method for boiler combining dynamic modeling, multi-objective optimization and improved case-based reasoning, *Fuel*, vol. 337, pp. 126854.

[5] Bhattacharjee S., L. B. A. Rahim, J. Watada, and A. Roy, 2020, Unified GPU Technique to Boost Confidentiality, Integrity, and Trim Data Loss in Big Data Transmission, *IEEE Access*, vol. 8, pp. 45477–45495.

[6] Bhattacharjee S., M. Chakkaravarthy, D. M. Chakkaravarthy, 2019, GPU-based integrated security system for minimizing data loss in big data transmission, In *Data Management, Analytics and Innovation: Proceedings of ICDMAI 2018, Springer Singapore*, vol. 2, pp. 421–435.

[7] Kermani F., M. R. Zarkesh, M. Vaziri, and A. Sheikhtaheri, 2023, A case-based reasoning system for neonatal survival and LOS prediction in neonatal intensive care units: a development and validation study, *Scientific Reports*, vol. 13, no. 1.

[8] Wu S. J. and A. Coman, 2023, Altering the past to shape the future: Manipulating information accessibility to influence case-based reasoning, *Journal of Experimental Social Psychology*, vol. 104, pp. 104407.

[9] Cerutti J., I. Abi-Zeid, L. Lamontagne, R. Lavoie, and M. J. Rodriguez-Pinzon, 2023, A case-based reasoning tool to recommend drinking water source protection actions, *Journal of Environmental Management*, vol. 331, pp. 117228.

[10] Xu W., Y. Song, S. Chen, et al., 2023, A new online optimization method for boiler combustion system based on the data-driven technique and the case-based reasoning principle, *Energy*, vol. 263, pp. 125508.

[11] Rahim L. A., K. M. Kudiri, and S. Bhattacharjee, 2019, Framework for parallelisation on big data, *PloS one*, vol. 4(5), pp. e0214044.

[12] Bhattacharjee S., L. B. A. Rahim, and I. A. Aziz, I, 2015, Hiding of compressed bit stream into audio file to enhance the confidentiality and portability of a data transmission system, In *2015 International Symposium on Mathematical Sciences and Computing Research (iSMSC)*, IEEE, pp. 196–201.

[13] Bhattacharjee S., and S. Bansal, 2023, Simultaneous encryption and compression for securing large data transmission over a heterogeneous network, *Applied Intelligence in Human-Computer Interaction*, vol. 1, pp. 129–142.

[14] Guo Y., Y. Sun, K. Wu, and K. Jiang, 2020, New Algorithms of Feature Selection and Big Data Assignment for CBR System Integrated by Bayesian Network, *ACM Transactions on Knowledge Discovery from Data*, vol. 14, no. 2, pp. 1–20.

[15] Bouhana A., A. Fekih, M. Abed, and H. Chabchoub, 2013, An integrated case-based reasoning approach for personalized itinerary search in multi-modal transportation systems, *Transportation Research Part C: Emerging Technologies*, vol. 31, pp. 30–50.

[16] Auconi P., E. Ottaviani, E. Barelli, V. Giuntini, J. A. McNamara, and L. Franchi, 2021, Prognostic approach to Class III malocclusion through case-based reasoning, *Orthodontics & Craniofacial Research*, vol. 24, no. S2, pp. 163–171.

[17] Venkatesh T. and T. Jain, 2018, Synchronized measurements-based wide-area static security assessment and classification of power systems using case-based reasoning classifiers, *Computers & Electrical Engineering*, vol. 68, pp. 513–525.

[18] Solic K., H. Ocevcic, and M. Golub, 2015, The information systems' security level assessment model based on an ontology and evidential reasoning approach, *Computers & Security*, vol. 55, pp. 100–112.

[19] Bhattacharjee S., L. B. A. Rahim, A. W. Ramadhani, M. Chakkaravarthy, & D. M. Chakkravarthy, 2021, A study on seismic big data handling at seismic exploration industry, In *Intelligent Computing and Innovation on Data Science: Proceedings of ICTIDS 2019*, Springer Singapore, pp. 421–429.

[20] Bhattacharjee S., L. B. A. Rahim, I. A. Aziz, 2016, A security scheme to minimize information loss during big data transmission over the internet. In *2016 3rd International Conference on Computer and Information Sciences (ICCOINS)*, IEEE, pp. 215–220.

[21] Lai S., X. Yuan, S. F. Sun et al., 2022, Practical Encrypted Network Traffic Pattern Matching for Secure Middleboxes, *IEEE Transactions on Dependable and Secure Computing*, vol. 19, no. 4, pp. 2609–2621.

[22] Chen, C., C. Wang, T. Qiu, N. Lv, and Q. Pei, 2020, A Secure Content Sharing Scheme Based on Blockchain in Vehicular Named Data Networks, *IEEE Transactions on Industrial Informatics*, vol. 16, no. 5, pp. 3278–3289.

[23] Malathi D., R. Logesh, V. Subramaniyaswamy, V. Vijayakumar and A. K. Sangaiah, 2019, Hybrid Reasoning-based Privacy-Aware Disease Prediction Support System, *Computers & Electrical Engineering*, vol. 73, pp. 114–127.

[24] Li D. and Y. Gong, 2022, The design of power grid data management system based on blockchain technology and construction of system security evaluation model, *Energy Reports*, vol. 8, pp. 466–479.

Chapter 12

EEG-based online finger movement identification

An emerging assistive approach

Alok Kumar Verma

Advanced Remanufacturing and Technology Centre, Agency for Science, Technology and Research (A*STAR), Singapore

Divya Upadhyay

ABES Engineering College, Ghaziabad, India

R. S. Anand and Ambalika Sharma

Indian Institute of Technology Roorkee, Roorkee, India

12.1 INTRODUCTION

Brain–computer interface (BCI) research is used to make a new communication channel that translates brain activities into sequences of control commands for an external device such as a computer application or a neuro-prosthesis system by using noninvasive as well as invasive approaches. In the case of the noninvasive approach, brain signals are recorded by acquiring an electroencephalogram (EEG) from the scalp of patients which attempts to convey their intentions according to some well-defined paradigms, e.g., specific mental tasks or motor imagery. In 1990, Keirn [1] discussed the possibilities for man–machine communications using brain-wave processing. In another work, Gupta and Singh [2] considered the use of preprocessing EEG signals to establish a direct human–system interface. Jonathan et al. [3] described the BCI research and development program, outlining its importance and applications. In other contributions, Mason and Birch [4] proposed a general framework for a brain–computer interface and Gerwin et al. [5] proposed a general-purpose brain–computer interface (BCI) system.

A normally acquired EEG contains several types of artefacts that can disrupt the BCI system. Various approaches for the removal of EEG signal artifacts were used and each of these approaches had varying levels of success, as reported in the past. The caveat with most of the approaches is the low classification accuracy, due to the noisy nature of EEG signals. Major sources of artefacts and noise in the EEG signals are the interferences of other bio-potential sources such as the electromyogram (EMG), the electro-oscillogram (EOG), the electrocardiogram (ECG), and the background activity of the brain itself [6]. Barlow [7] considered the issue of artefact processing in EEG data. Atri et al. [8] proposed a model-based purification of EEG signals to improve the accuracy of the BCI systems. Croft and Barry [9] described ocular artefacts in the EEG and their removal. Fatourechi et al. [10] described EOG and EMG Artifacts in Brain Interface Systems.

It is known that only specific parts of the brain are activated in response to a specific BCI task. This means that active brain regions which are closer to the EEG channels have more useful information with regard to the BCI tasks than all other channels. Therefore, it seems to be very helpful if the purification of the signal of an active channel has been done using the functional relationship between the neighbouring channels. Burke et al. [11] proposed simultaneous filtering and feature extraction techniques for direct brain interfacing. In [12], authors used Spatial Filters for the Classification of Single-Trial EEG in a Finger Movement Task. In [13], authors proposed a single-trial electroencephalogram during the finger movement task and Shoker et al. [14] proposed an EEG-based SVM classifier which distinguished left and right finger movement. This chapter describes a method for the signal purification of the active channels, extracted parameters and classification of EEG signal for finger movement identification. To prove the usefulness of the proposed algorithm, the same methods of purification of the signals of active channel, feature extraction and classification schemes were applied to the EEG data. In this, a support vector machine (SVM) was used to detect the finger movement task.

12.2 EXPERIMENTAL SETUP AND DATA ACQUISITION

The experiment is conducted on the Biopac-EEG100C as shown in Figures 12.1 and 12.2. The entire experimental setup comprises three major subsystems: CAP100C, Biopac-EEG100C, and a computer, as shown in Figures 12.1 and 12.2.

The CAP100C is a fabric cap with recessed tin electrodes attached to Lycra-type fabric. The electrodes are pre-positioned in the International 10–20 montages on the CAP as shown in Figure 12.2. The standard (medium) electrode cap fits most subjects over the age of five; infant, small, and large caps are also available. Leads from the electrode cap terminate in 2 mm pin plugs, which are typically connected to inputs on the EEG100C.

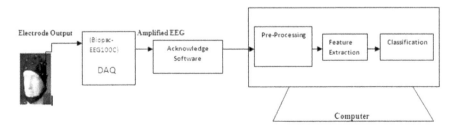

Figure 12.1 Block diagram of EEG machine.

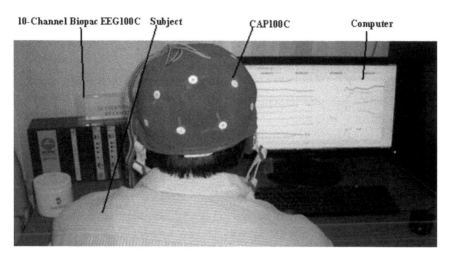

10-Channel Biopac EEG100C   Subject   CAP100C   Computer

Figure 12.2 **EEG signal acquisition.**

Two datasets were considered for the study. Datasets I and II were derived from experiments conducted in our laboratory. In both datasets, EEG signals from six healthy male members with ages ranging between 22 and 30 in a particular session were recorded. The participant sat in a normal chair in a relaxed mood, resting on the chair while their left hand was resting on the knee and their right hand was on the space button of a computer keyboard. In dataset I, the subjects' relaxed forefinger of the right hand was stuck for every 2 sec, whereas in the case of dataset II, the subject relaxed both hands on the knee and no movement was established. Both datasets comprised 29 epochs, each of a minute in length recorded by a sampling rate of 100 Hz for all six patients and divided into 2 sec. The data were recorded from the standard channels of Fp1, Fp2, FZ, F3, F4, F7, F8, CZ, C3, C4, T3, T4, Pz, P3, P4, T5, T6, O1, O2, Gnd, and Reference [15]. In this study, only 10 channels are considered. In this chapter only the 4th channel (C4) is considered for further processing since features of EEG signal for finger movement are extracted on the 4th channel. Further, the dataset was divided into two main classes, with one class comprising EEGs related to the forefinger movement of the right hand and the other class containing EEGs obtained under conditions of no movement. This work aims to extract the features from the EEG signals of the two classes and classify these two signals.

12.3 METHODOLOGY

Background brain activities which are irrelevant to the BCI tasks are artefacts that continuously generate EEG signals which may be recorded anywhere over the scalp in all channels. These artefacts interfere with the EEG signals that are triggered by the BCI tasks and generated by only particular

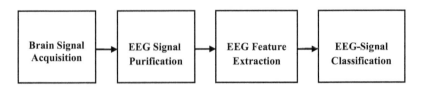

Figure 12.3 BCI common structure.

regions of the scalp. This chapter is divided into a series of sections as shown in Figure 12.3. The first part signal acquisition was already discussed.

12.3.1 EEG signal purification

As mentioned above, in the background of EEG, there are other sources which cause artefacts such as ECG, EOG, EMG, motion artefacts, eye blinking and the 50 Hz frequency from the power line, which usually affects all EEG channels [6–9]. With the exception of the power line, noise is almost similar for all channels. Other noise and artefacts have different effects on different channels depending on the transfer function between the channel and artefact source, hence each channel needs its estimation for the amount of artifact and noise interference. Different noise and artefact sources are not individually isolated, with only the recorded mixture of signals from different sources available. It is believed that the recorded mixture of various signals at different channels can be used for estimating the original artefacts which may be affecting each channel.

In this chapter, the acquired EEG data are first sent to the Biopac-EEG100C Amplifier module, which is set on Normal mode, gain 10000, filtering setting ON and High pass filter set for 0.1 HZ. This module acquires data from the subject's scalp through an electrode cap. This module is an amplifier whose purpose is to amplify the EEG signals and these EEG signals are then fed to a computer for further processing through acknowledged software. In this chapter, MATLAB has been used for filtering the EEG artefacts. In this process, a low pass filter, notch filter and cross-correlation method are used for the removal of artifacts. For two sequences $x(n)$ and $y(n)$, the cross-correlation function, $r(i)$, is defined as

$$r(I) = \Sigma x(n)y(n-1), I = -1, 0, 1, 2, ... \qquad (12.1)$$

or,

$$r(I) = \Sigma x(n+1)y(n), I = -1, 0, 1, 2, ... \qquad (12.2)$$

Where index I is the (time) shift (or lag) parameter.

For the power line artefact, a 50 Hz notch filter is used and for the EMG artefact a low pass filter is used as EMG are high-frequency phenomena.

Similarly, for the ECG and EOG artefacts cross-correlation methods are used because these signals are of definite pattern and can be removed by the cross-correlation method [9, 10].

12.3.2 EEG feature extraction

In this work, the focus is based on the estimation of features from the perturbation-free EEG trials delivered by the preprocessing module. Although the behavior of EEG is non-linear, the conscious level of humans has a direct effect on EEG. To chalk out the conscious level there is a need to calculate EEG parameters [2, 11]. Many EEG parameters show relation, thus evaluating these parameters which can be classified into various categories like time domain and frequency domain. The calculated time domain parameters here are root mean square value and Hjorth parameters (Activity, Mobility and Complexity) and frequency domain parameters are total energy/power, band power (Delta, Theta, Alpha and Beta), δ- Ratio and BA-ratio [16]. The following parameters were calculated for both of the datasets.

(a) *Hjorth Parameter*: Three Hjorth parameters, Activity, Mobility, and Complexity, could convey relevant information about EEG epochs [17]. As per this description, Activity is a measure of the average signal. It could be calculated as the square of the Standard Deviation of the signal or Variance of the signal. Mobility is a measure of average signal frequency. It could be determined as follows:

$$\text{Mobility} = \frac{\text{S.D. of first time derivative of Signal}}{\text{S.D. of Signal}} \tag{12.3}$$

$$\text{Complexity} = \frac{\text{S.D. of second time derivative} \times \text{S.D. of signal}}{\text{S.D. of first time derivative of signal}} \tag{12.4}$$

To find out the Hjorth parameters, calculate the First and Second Derivatives of the signal. Then Standard Deviation (S.D.) of signal, Standard Deviation of First and Second Derivatives of signal were obtained. Accordingly, the Hjorth parameters, Activity, Mobility and Complexity, were evaluated.

(b) *Total Power*: In the frequency domain, this could be expressed as a sum of the squared values of all the Fast Fourier Transform (FFT) magnitudes. Sampled EEG signal data of 4-s duration was taken into the workspace after removing the artefacts. We calculated frequency samples of the signal using formula f = Ratio of product of square of sampling frequency and time sampling instants to the length of signal. Fast Fourier Transform of the signal was calculated. Power spectral density of the signal is obtained by computing the square of modules of FFT divided by the length of the signal. Area under the power spectral density curve using the trapezoidal formula gave information about the total power in the signal.

(c) *Band Power*: The major portion of the EEG spectrum was taken in four bands: Delta, Theta, Alpha, and Beta. We then checked the frequency value at these points starting from first sampling frequency point to one less than the highest sampling point and assigned the index values to all the frequency components between their respective upper and lower limits. The area under the curve for all the respective regions using the trapezoidal formula gave band powers.

(d) *Delta Ratio*: In an effort to improve the stability of band-related changes, the augmented delta quotient or delta ratio was introduced. This is defined as the ratio of power contained in the Delta-band to the Power contained in the combined α and β bands.

$$\delta\text{-Ratio} = \frac{(\alpha\,\text{Power} + \beta\,\text{Power})}{\text{Power contained in } \delta \text{ band}} \tag{12.5}$$

The Delta band extends from 0.5 to 4 Hz, while the α and β band are combined from 8 Hz onwards.

(e) *BA-Ratio*: Beta frequency band of EEG extends from 13.0 Hz onwards and Alpha frequency band extends from 8 Hz to 13.0 Hz. The BA Ratio is defined as the power contained in Beta band divided by power contained in the Beta band divided by power contained in the Alpha band.

12.3.3 EEG signal classifications

The classifications of EEG signal are done by support vector machine (SVM). SVM are basically a set of related supervised learning methods which are generally used for classification. In an N-dimensional space, viewing input data as two sets of an SVM will construct as a separating hyper plane in that space, which is used to maximize the margin between the two datasets. Two parallel hyper planes are constructed to calculate the margin, which is on each side of the separating hyper plane, and which may "pushed up against" both datasets. Therefore, a good separation is achieved by the hyper plane that may have the largest distance to the neighboring data points of both classes. However, the larger the margin the better the generalization error of the classifier [18, 19]. The construction of SVM is based on the idea to create a hyper plane as a decision surface in a way that the margin of separation between positive and negative examples is maximized. The machine achieves this desirable property by following a principal approach of the statistical learning theory. More precisely, SVM is based on the approximate implementation of the structural risk minimization method [19].

We consider the training sample $\{(\mathbf{x}_i, d_i)\}_{i=1}^{N}$ where $\mathbf{x}_i$ is the input pattern for the ith example and d_i is the corresponding desired response (target output). To begin with, it is assumed that the pattern (class) represented by the subset $d_i = +1$ and the pattern represented by the subset $d_i = -1$ are "linearly separable." The equation of a decision surface in the form of a hyper plane that does the separation is

$$\mathbf{w}^T\mathbf{x} + b = 0 \tag{12.6}$$

Where x is an input vector, w is an adjustable weight vector, and b is a bias. Therefore we can write

$$\mathbf{w}^T\mathbf{x}_i + b > 0 \text{ for } d_i = +1 \tag{12.7}$$

$$\mathbf{w}^T\mathbf{x}_i + b < 0 \text{ for } d_i = -1 \tag{12.8}$$

The assumption of linearly separable patterns is made in order to explain the basic idea behind a support vector machine which indicates the goal of a support vector machine is to find the particular hyper plane for which the margin of separation ρ is maximized. Under this condition, the decision surface is referred to as the optimal hyper plane [18].

The discussion so far has focused on linearly separable patterns. To set the stage for a formal treatment of non-separable data points, we introduce a new set of nonnegative scalar variables, $\{\xi_i\}_{i=1}^{N}$.

$$d_i\left(\mathbf{w}^T\mathbf{x}_i + b\right) \geq 1 - \xi_i \text{ for } i = 1, 2, \ldots, N \tag{12.9}$$

With respect to the weight vector w, subject to the constraint described in Equation (12.7) and the constraint on $\|w\|^2$. The function $I(\xi_i)$ is an *indicator function*, defined by

$$I(\xi) = \begin{cases} 0 \text{ if } \xi \leq 0 \\ 1 \text{ if } \xi > 0 \end{cases}$$

To make the optimization problem mathematically tractable, we approximate the functional $\varnothing(\xi)$ by writing

$$\varnothing(\xi) = \sum_{i=1}^{n} \xi_i$$

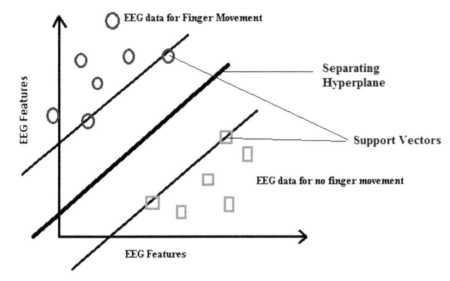

Figure 12.4 SVM for EEG based finger movement and no finger movement classification.

Moreover, we simplify the computation by formulating the functional to be minimized with respect to the weight vector w as follows:

$$\emptyset(w,\xi) = \frac{1}{2}w^T w + C\sum_{i=1}^{n}\xi_i(x)$$

Formulation of the cost function $\emptyset(w,\xi)$ in Equation (12.8) is therefore in perfect accord with the principle of structural risk minimization [20]. Figure 12.4 illustrates the geometric construction of SVM for finger movement detection.

This work deals with the lib-SVM [21] in the MATLAB and the classification result of the work are discussed in the result section.

12.4 RESULTS

Classification rates of finger movement and no finger movement features of the original data are presented in Tables 12.1 and 12.2. As can be seen

Table 12.1 Results of training for "Finger Movement" and "No Movement Data"

Training data	Cost function (C)	Gamma (γ)	Cross validation accuracy	Support vector	Time (s)
90	10000 0000	0.001	90.8%	61	2

Table 12.2 Results of testing for "Finger Movement" and "No Movement Data"

Testing data	Accuracy	Time (S)
178	93.68%	2

in Table 12.2, features of finger movement and no finger movement EEG data provide a better classification rate of up to 93.68%. The data are taken over a minute and for that minute data are divided into 2-second epochs for all the patient numbers 1 to 6 and, finally, a total 29 epochs are taken. The features result of patient 1 out of six patients of their own practical experiments conducted for both the finger movement and no finger movement task are depicted in Figures 12.5 to 12.9. Figure 12.5(a) and (b) show the comparison between calculated activity and mobility parameters between finger movement task and no finger movement task for patient 1. The light lines as shown in Figure 12.5(a) and (b) are for the finger movement task and dark lines are for the no finger movement. Similarly, Figure 12.6(a) and (b) is for RMS value and total power, Figure 12.7(a) and (b) is for delta and theta, Figure 12.8(a) and (b) is for alpha and beta, and Figure 12.9(a) and (b) is for BA-ratio and delta ratio respectively. These figures are used here to analysis the difference between both the tasks.

(a) *Classification Results for "Finger Movement" and "No Finger Movement Task"*: A total of 268 data rows are taken from the above-mentioned features, with 134 from each condition (Finger Movement and No Finger Movement). The dataset is divided into three parts, one for training and two for testing as shown in Tables 12.1 and 12.2. Table 12.1 shows the training of the support vector machine along with the parameter set and Table 12.2 shows the testing results.

(b) *Similarly, for testing*:

The classification between "finger movement" EEG data and "no movement" EEG data has the efficiency of 93.68%. Once the network is trained, it is tested on other data to check its generalization capability. In this case network is tested on 178 instances and the efficiency of classification is shown in Table 12.2. Time gives us the indication about the times taken for the classification. Figures 12.10 to 12.12 shows the graphical user interface (GUI) developed for acquiring and display of the parameters of EEG signal and also the classification of EEG that clearly shows about EEG data are finger movement data or not. This window was used for online finger movement detection with the results of 2 secs epochs for patient 1 of both the task.

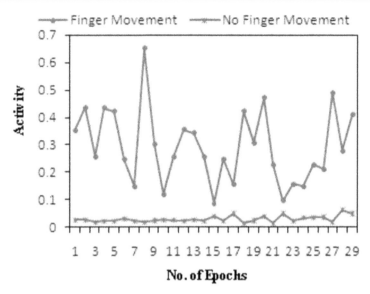

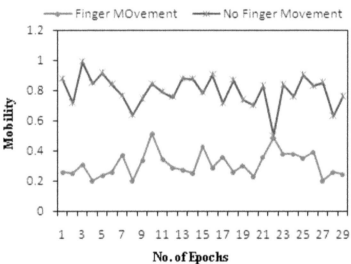

Figure 12.5 (a) Comparison between "Finger Movement" and "No Finger Movement" Task for parameter Activity of Patient 1, (b) Comparison between "Finger Movement" and "No Finger Movement" Task for parameter Mobility of Patient 1.

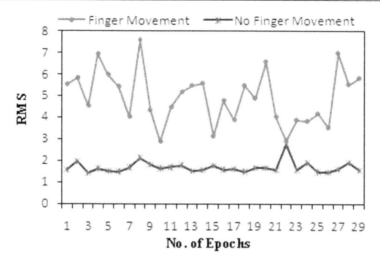

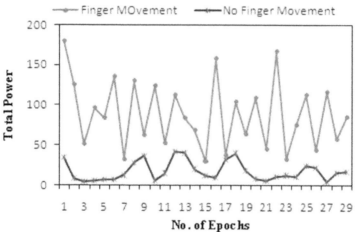

Figure 12.6 (a) Comparison between "Finger Movement" and "No Finger Movement"Task for parameter RMS Value of Patient 1, (b) Comparison between "Finger Movement" and "No Finger Movement" Task for parameter Total Power of Patient 1.

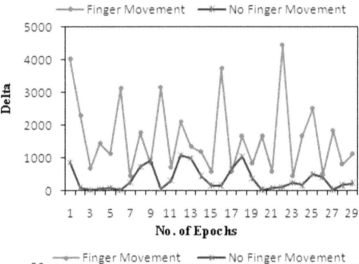

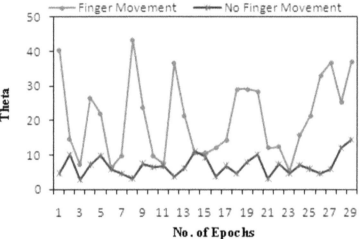

Figure 12.7 (a) Comparison between "Finger Movement" and "No Finger Movement" Task for parameter Delta of Patient 1, (b) Comparison between "Finger Movement" and "No Finger Movement" Task for parameter Theta of Patient 1.

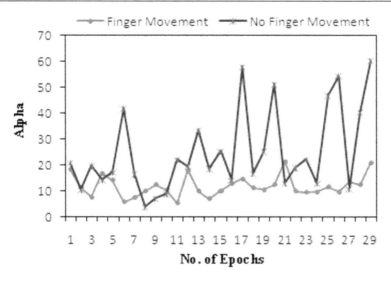

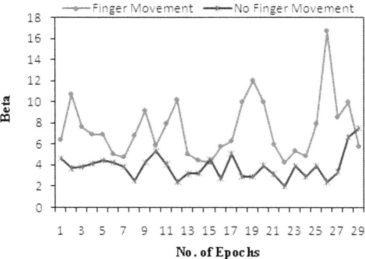

Figure 12.8 (a)   Comparison   between   "Finger   Movement"   and   "No
Finger   Movement"   Task   for   parameter   Alpha   of   Patient   I,
(b):   Comparison   between   "Finger   Movement"   and   "No   Finger
Movement" Task for parameter Beta of Patient I.

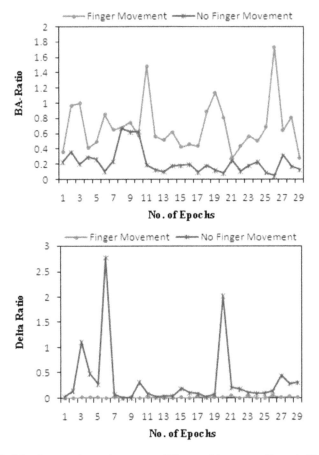

Figure 12.9 (a) Comparison between "Finger Movement" and "No Finger Movement" Task for parameter BA-Ratio of Patient 1, (b) Comparison between "Finger Movement" and "No Finger Movement" Task for parameter Delta Ratio of Patient 1.

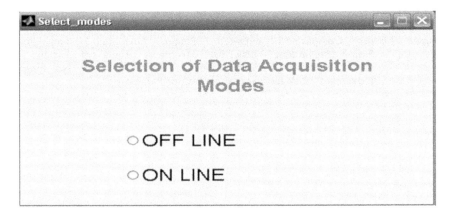

Figure 12.10 Selection of data acquisition modes.

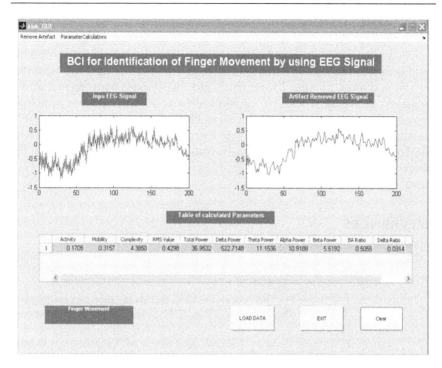

Figure 12.11 GUI for "finger movement task" of patient 1.

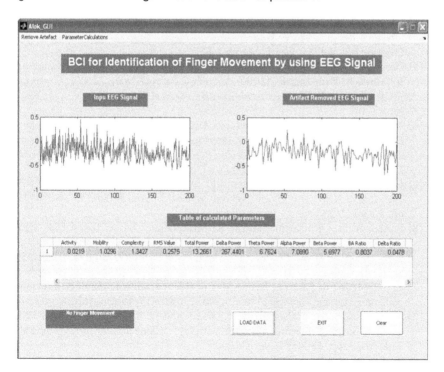

Figure 12.12 GUI for "No finger movement task" of Patient 1.

12.5 CONCLUSION

Achieving an improvement of the accuracy for the classification of EEG signals in BCI research is a major task. In this work, BCI operates with two mental activities, "Finger Movement" and "No Finger Movement," and is displayed in the user-friendly GUI window in which several types of feature extraction methods were considered to characterize the EEG signal. The classification of mental activities from extracted features was done by using SVM-based learning methods. This learning method gives good results. We observe that the signals can improve the classification accuracy of the EEG signals by up to 93.68%.

REFERENCES

[1] Z. A. Keirn, "Man-machine communications through brain-wave processing," *IEEE Engineering in Medicine and Biology Magazine*, Vol. 9, No. 1, pp. 55–57, 1990. doi: 10.1109/51.62907

[2] Gupta, S., and Singh, H., "Preprocessing EEG signals for direct human-system interface", *Intelligence and Systems, 1996, IEEE International Joint Symposia*, 1996, pp. 32–37.

[3] Jonathan R. Wolpaw, Dennis J. McFarland, Theresa M. Vaughan, and Gerwin Schalk, "The Wadsworth Center Brain–Computer interface (BCI) research and development program", *IEEE Transactions on Neural Systems and Rehabilitation Engineering*, Vol. 11, No. 2, June 2003.

[4] S. G. Mason, and G. E. Birch, "A general framework for brain-computer interface design", *IEEE Transactions on Neural Systems and Rehabilitation Engineering*, Vol. 11, No. 1, March 2003.

[5] Gerwin Schalk, Dennis J. Mcfarland, Thilo Hinterberger, Niels Birbaumer and Jonathan R. Wolpaw, "BCI2000- A general purpose brain computer interface (BCI) system", *IEEE Transactions on Biomedical Engineering*, Vol.51, No. 6, June 2004.

[6] Alok Kumar Verma, R. S. Anand and Ambalika Sharma, "Artifact removal of EEG signals for brain computer interface", *National Conference on Recent Advances in Computational Techniques in Electrical Engineering, SLIET Longowal*, pp. 28–30, 19–20 March 2010.

[7] J. S. Barlow, "Artifact processing in EEG data processing", *Handbook of EEG and clinical Neurophysiology* (Revised Series Ed.), Amsterdam: Elsevier, Vol. 2, pp. 15–62, 1986.

[8] F. Atri, A. H. Omidvarnia, and S. K. Setarehdan, "Model based EEG signal purification to improve the accuracy of the BCI systems", *Proceedings of the 13th European Signal Processing Conference EUSIPCO*, Antalya, Turkey, 5–9 September, 2005.

[9] R. J. Croft and R. J. Barry, "Removal of ocular artifact from the EEG: a review", *Neurophysiologie Clinique*, Vol. 30, No. 1, pp. 5–19, February 2000.

[10] M. Fatourechi, A. Bashashati, R. K. Ward, and G. E. Birch, "EOG and EMG artifacts in brain interface systems: a survey", *Clinical Neurophysiology*, Vol. 118, No. 3, pp. 480–494, March 2007.

[11] D. Burke, S. Kelly, P. de Chazal, R. Reilly and Finucane C., "A parametric feature extraction and classification strategy for brain computer interfacing", *IEEE Transactions on Neural Systems and Rehabilitation Engineering*, Vol. 13, No. 3, pp. 7–12, 2005.

[12] X. Liao, D. Yao, D. Wu, and C. Li, "Combining spatial filters for the classification of single-trial EEG in a finger movement task," *IEEE Transactions on Biomedical Engineering*, Vol. 54, No. 5, pp. 821–831, May 2007.

[13] Y. Li, X. R. Gao, H. S. Liu, and S. K. Gao. "Classification of single-trial electroencephalogram during finger movement," *IEEE Transactions on Biomedical Engineering*, Vol. 51, No. 6, pp. 1019–1025, 2004.

[14] Leor Shoker, Saeid Sanei, and Alex Sumich, "Distinguishing Between Left and Right Finger Movement from EEG using SVM", *Proceedings of the 2005 IEEE Engineering in Medicine and Biology 27th Annual Conference*, Shanghai, China, pp. 5420–5430, 1–4 September, 2005.

[15] H. H. Jasper, "The ten-twenty electrode system of the international federation," *Electroencephalogram and Clinical Neurophysiology*, Vol. 10, pp. 371–375, 1958.

[16] J. C. Drummond, C. A. Brann, D. E. Perkins, and D. E. Wolfe, "A comparison of MF, SEF, freq. Band Power ratio, Total and dominance shift in the determination of DoA", *Acta Anaesthesiologica Scandanevica*, Vol. 35, pp. 693–699, 1991.

[17] B. Hjorth, "EEG analysis based on time–domain properties", *Electroencephalography and Clinical Neurophysiology*, Vol. 29, pp 306–310, 1970.

[18] Osuna, E., R. Freund, and F. Girosi, "An improved training algorithm for support vector machine", *Neural Networks for Signal Processing VII. Proceedings of the 1997 IEEE Workshop*, pp. 276–285, Amelia Island, FL, 1997.

[19] A. E. Gavoyiannis, D. G. Vogiatzis, D. P. Georgiadis, and N. D. Hatziargyriou, "Combined support vector classifiers using fuzzy clustering for dynamic security assessment", *Power Engineering Society Summer Meeting*, Vol. 2, pp. 1281–1286, 2001.

[20] C. Cortes, and V. Vapnik, "Support vector networks", *Machine Learning*, Vol. 20, pp. 273–297, 1995.

[21] C. Chang and C. J. Lin, "LIBSVM", *ACM Transactions on Intelligent Systems and Technology*, Vol. 2, No. 3, pp. 1–27, 2001, https://doi.org/10.1145/1961189.1961199

Index

Pages in *italics* refer to figures and pages in **bold** refer to tables

For Product Safety Concerns and Information please contact our EU
representative GPSR@taylorandfrancis.com
Taylor & Francis Verlag GmbH, Kaufingerstraße 24, 80331 München, Germany

www.ingramcontent.com/pod-product-compliance
Ingram Content Group UK Ltd.
Pitfield, Milton Keynes, MK11 3LW, UK
UKHW021120180425
457613UK00005B/164